Pause

with

Purpose

by

Jonathan Edwards

All correspondence to:

J. Edwards

jonandanna24@gmail.com

First published in 2020 ISBN: 978-1-71676-490-5

Introduction

I have always been a keen writer, for the last thirty-five years I have taken notes, written sermons, and kept quotes, that have helped shape my life. Over the years I have gained insight through preachers, teachers, family, friends and even enemies. God uses everything for our good.

Pause with Purpose is a collection of truths, that have helped mature and transform my life, hopefully this book will help transform your life too.

Each reading is a daily investment into your life, we will cover many subjects to gain wisdom, and understanding. You will find each reading encouraging, sometimes challenging, and also applicable to your life. I believe that it is crucially important that the word of God has a practical application through our lives.

I pray that as you read the truths in Pause for Purpose, these will be outworked in your life.
Jesus said, you will know the truth and the truth will set you free.

I would like to dedicate this book to my father, John Edwards, who was promoted to heaven while I was writing this book.

Thank you dad for your dedication to the plan of God, you were an amazing example of a father, and servant of Christ. Thank you for your love, and generosity, and never judging my mistakes, I am eternally indebted to you.
You did not waver, in fulfilling the heavenly vision that you were given.

Thank you to my wife, Anna, who has encouraged and helped in the writing, and proofreading of this book. Without you Anna, I could have never finished this project, your thoughts, and wisdom have helped prepare this book to now be published.

———————-

All scripture that is quoted in this book is from the NKJV version unless otherwise stated.

New Day, New You

Forget the former things;
do not dwell on the past.
See, I am doing a new thing!
Now it springs up; do you not perceive it?
Isaiah 43:18-19 (NIV)

If you are reading this book, then you are entering the start of a new day.

This is the day for starting over, a new beginning, a blank canvas, with unlimited possibilities with God.

You do not have to believe the same lies, hold the same hurts, make the same mistakes, or postpone the God given dream, or vision, for your life. This is the day to shake free of the past, and step into your future.

Do not waste another day.

It is a new day for a new you.

Forgetting those things which are behind and reaching forward to those things which are ahead.
Philippians 3:13

Leave Your Comfort Zone

Have I not commanded you?
Be strong and courageous.
Do not be afraid; do not be discouraged, for the Lord
your God will be with you wherever you go.
Joshua 1:9 NIV

Comfort zones, we all have them even though we might not want to admit it.

When Israel faced difficulties in the wilderness, the Israelites wanted to return to their old life of slavery.

The familiar life in slavery, was less threatening, than the challenges of the unknown in the promised land.

God said to Joshua, "Be strong and courageous, don't be afraid, or discouraged, I am with you wherever you go."

The promise God made to Joshua, is the same guarantee that he makes to us today, so whatever problem, promise, or opportunity we face, we need to factor God into our situations.

With God we can face our fears, conquer our giants, and possess our promised land.

Don't fear failure, fear being in the exact same place next year as you are today.
Anonymous

Choose to Change

*Do not fear nor be afraid of them; for the Lord your God,
He is the One who goes with you
Deuteronomy 31:6*

When you choose to change, move on with God, or embrace your destiny, you and I, will face enemies.

Fear is one of those giants that the devil uses to control, and paralyse our faith. It could be the fear of failure, the fear of failing health, or an uncertain future, which unsettles you today, so let's reprogram our minds with God's word.

Fear is a liar, and you do not have to be bound by it any longer. God constantly declares in his word, fear not for I am with you.

As a Christian, you do not have a spirit of fear, but power, love, and a sound mind.

One of the greatest discoveries a man can make, one of his great surprises is to find he can do what he was afraid he couldn't do.
Henry Ford

His Word in My World

This Book of the Law shall not depart from your mouth, but you shall meditate in it day and night, that you may observe to do according to all that is written in it. For then you will make your way prosperous, and then you will have good success.
Joshua 1:8

At the dawn of a new day, God's instruction to Joshua, was to speak and mediate on his word. God told Joshua, to do this day and night, which would result in success, and prosperity, for his life.

God's word was a priority to Joshua then, as it has to be now for our lives now. To grow spiritually, see victory, and win battles, the word needs to be a constant part, of our daily lives.

Imagine going to the doctor when you are sick, and the doctor giving you a prescription that can make you well, but you only take the medication once, instead of the prescribed daily dose. You can't blame the doctor for not getting well, or say the medicine does not work. When we diligently meditate on the word each day, we are transformed by its truth, and it is that truth, that sets us free.

If you are too busy to spend time with God, you are busier than he intends you to be. Anonymous

Future not Failure

"Let the words of my mouth and the meditation of my heart be acceptable in your sight, O LORD, my strength and my Redeemer."
Psalms 19:14

There is power in our words, what we speak has a creative force, that builds into our present, and future, this can have positive or negative effects.

The bible says that, life and death are in the power of the tongue.

In Genesis One, God spoke, and the universe came into existence, his words created our world as we know it.

The nursery rhyme, sticks and stones, may break my bones, but words will never hurt me, is untrue. Words can harm, they do hurt, and they can destroy peoples lives.

Now is the time, to pay attention to what we speak, and start confessing, faith building, uplifting, positive words, based on scripture, rather than our past, or the circumstances we face right now.

Currently we are in lockdown in Wales, due to Coronavirus. At the beginning of this pandemic, neither myself, or Anna, knew how long we would be unable to work for, but this didn't stop us believing God for our finances.

We chose to make a good confession, even though naturally we had no income, and our savings would not be sufficient, for more than a month or so. God has incredibly blessed us during this time, and we have not lacked anything.

Even the strong and the wealthy grow weak and hungry, but those who passionately pursue the Lord will never lack any good thing.
Psalm 34:10 TPT

Personal reflections

....

....

....

....

....

....

....

....

....

....

....

....

....

....

....

Resurrection

I am the First and the Last.
"I am He who lives, and was dead, and behold, I am alive
forevermore. Amen. And I have the keys of Hades and of
Death.
Revelation 1:17-18

The reality of Easter is something Christians should enjoy every day, because its truths speak to us of resurrection. Everything changed for us when Jesus was raised from the dead, the tomb was empty, and our saviour rose again.

Jesus destroyed the power of sin, and death, and the powers of darkness were stripped of all authority, God raised Christ from the dead, it was impossible for death to hold him. For Christians today the message of Easter, is not about an empty tomb but a risen saviour.

And being found in appearance as a man, He humbled
Himself and became obedient to the point of death, even
the death of the cross.
Therefore God also has highly exalted Him and given
Him the name which is above every name,
that at the name of Jesus every knee should bow, of
those in heaven, and of those on earth, and of those
under the earth,
and that every tongue should confess that Jesus Christ
is Lord, to the glory of God the Father. Philippians 2:8-11

Jesus Christ today is not just a king, he is king of kings, and Lord of Lords, he is God the Son, who was given the name, that is above every other name. God has exalted him, and there is no one higher than Jesus, and no name greater than his name.

Christ has been exalted to the highest place in heaven, and everything is under his feet, demons are under his feet, sickness is under his feet, your problems are under his feet, and every earthly authority is under his feet.

Jesus is the sovereign victor of the universe, therefore we serve not just a risen saviour, but a risen Lord. Whatever is going on in your world or in your life, Jesus rules, and Jesus reigns.

Jesus is the resurrection, and the life, because he conquered, we can conquer, because he rules, we can rule and reign. We can also take authority over the works of darkness, Christ has risen and he is living within you, therefore greater is he, that is within you, than he that is in the world, 1 John 4:4.

Our old history ends with the cross, our new history begins with the resurrection
Watchman Nee

We Reign

When He had disarmed the rulers and authorities [those supernatural forces of evil operating against us], He made a public example of them [exhibiting them as captives in His triumphal procession], having triumphed over them through he cross.
Colossians 2:15 AMP

Through death He might destroy him who had the power of death, that is, the devil,
Hebrews 2:14 KJV

When Jesus died on the cross, the forces of hell were defeated, even though they roam the earth, to steal, kill, and destroy, they have been legally stripped of their power, and authority.

Jesus said, "All authority has been given to me in heaven and on earth," and he is our victorious king.

Sometimes there is a vacuum between what we believe, and what we experience, we read one thing, and live a life at times that seems completely different, but this does not change the truth.

You might feel defeated, but you're not, Satan is the defeated one.

No matter what demonic strategy may come against you this day, or how many demons are assembled together for your destruction, you never have to go down defeated.

Jesus plundered the enemy when He rose from the dead, so when you look into the mirror, you need to learn to see yourself as one who already has the victory. You already possess the authority necessary, to keep Satan under your feet where he belongs, because Jesus reigns, we reigns in life, Romans 5:17.

"...He gallantly strode into Heaven to celebrate His victory and the defeat of Satan and his forces. As part of His triumphal process, He flaunted the spoils seized from the hand of the enemy. Yet the greatest spectacle of all occurred when the enemy himself was openly put on display as bound, disgraced, disabled, defeated, humiliated, and stripped bare...."
Sparkling gems from the Greek Rick Renner.

Personal reflections

....

....

....

....

....

....

....

....

....

....

Think on It

"Finally, brethren, whatever things are true, whatever things are noble, whatever things are just, whatever things are pure, whatever things are lovely, whatever things are of a good report, if there is any virtue and if there is anything praiseworthy—meditate on these things."
Philippians 4:8

When we meditate, we take time to think, and give attention to Gods word, we encounter God through reading the scriptures. In my own personal life, I have found that when I read the bible, I give myself the opportunity to replace wrong thoughts, with the way God thinks about me.

At times, it is easy to fill our minds with worry, anxiety, and negativity, but the key too controlling, and transforming our thought life, is mediating on the word of God.

We mediate on the word by reflecting on what God has said, and allow the truth of his word to go deep into our hearts, this will transform your life.

We draw on Gods wisdom, and begin to know him better by reading, and studying his word.

If we make this a practice in our daily lives, God will prosper and give us success in all we do.

So today, let's prioritise our time, and decide we are not going to allow busyness, or distractions, to get in the way of us meeting with God through his word.

You always have time for what you want to do.
Anna Edwards

But his delight is in the law of the Lord, and in his law he mediates day and night.
Psalm 1:2

Personal reflections

....

....

....

....

....

....

....

....

....

....

....

....

....

....

....

Replace Your Thoughts for God's Thoughts

For the Word that God speaks is alive and full of power [making it active, operative, energising, and effective]; it is sharper than any two-edged sword, penetrating to the dividing line of the breath of life (soul) and [the immortal] spirit, and of joints and marrow [of the deepest parts of our nature], exposing and sifting and analysing and judging the very thoughts and purposes of the heart.
Hebrews 4:12 AMP

We experience overwhelming victory, when we place the word of God, as our final authority in our lives. The word of God will literally change the way we think, and give us the ability to live a powerful and overcoming life.

Start today, focus on God's thoughts about you, and see your life start to transform, and change, before your eyes.

The word is alive, it is full of power, and it is a spiritual weapon, that divides soul, and spirit. Only the word of God can separate us from the internal storms, and emotional battles, we all feel at times.

His word is the dividing line between truth, and error. It has the power to cut like a surgeons knife, and separate every negative emotion, fear, and lie. It reveals the way God sees you.

Remember many books can inform you, but only the Bible can transform you.

Visit many good books, but live in the Bible.
C H Spurgeon

Fill your mind with Gods word, and you will have no room for Satan's lies.
Anonymous

Personal reflections

....
....
....
....
....
....
....
....
....
....
....
....
....
....
....
....
....

Choosing Faith not Fear

For God has not given us a spirit of fear, but of power
and of love and of a sound mind.
2 Timothy 1:7

There are many things in this life, that would seek to cause you to fear, it could be your employment, your heath, your marriage, your children, the future, or a thousand other thoughts that go running through your mind each day. Let's face it, fear prevents us from becoming the best version of ourselves we can be. This leaves us living in less than God's best for our lives.

I remember meeting a lady many years ago, who had a number of her relatives die of cancer. Her life for along time had become consumed, with fear, and worry, she was automatically accepting that these hereditary cancers would affect her life.

I told her that fear was a liar, and all she needed to do was agree, and believe through prayer, that this generational sickness, would be cut off from her family. We prayed the prayer of faith, and believed that the promise of health, and wholeness was yes, and amen, in Christ Jesus. This lady experienced peace and is alive and heathy today.

Someone once said, when fear knocks on the door of your heart, let faith answer.

Face your fears today, with the promises of God, it is your positive guarantee. As you worship, spend time in his presence, saturate your self in scripture, your trust in the Lord will rapidly grow.

Let the forecast for our future, be what God says, not what fear says.

Now this is what Yahweh says,
Listen, Jacob, to the One who created you, Israel, to the One who shaped who you are, do not fear, for I, your Kinsman-Redeemer, will rescue you. I have called you by name, you are mine.
When you pass through the deep, stormy sea, you can count on me to be there with you. When you pass through raging rivers, you will not drown. When you walk through persecution like fiery flames, you will not be burned, the flames will not harm you,
for I am your Saviour, Yahweh, your mighty God, the Holy One of Israel.
Isaiah 43:1 - 3 The Passion Version

Personal reflections

....
....
....
....
....

Don't Deal with the Fruit, go to the Root

For we do not wrestle against flesh and blood, but against principalities, against powers, against the rulers of the darkness of this age, against spiritual hosts of wickedness in the heavenly places.
Ephesians 6:12

I have never been a gardener, but when I was a child, I was asked to help my grandad, on his vegetable patch. He told me to pull out some weeds, which I did, when he came back to examine my work, it was evident that the weeds were not fully removed from the soil. I had pulled out the weeds, but I had not made the effort to dig into the soil, to remove the weeds at the root. I remember his words, "It will never leave until you go to the root."

This principle is also a spiritual one, we have an enemy that would want us to leave the roots in our lives of bitterness, anger and unforgiveness, to grow back time, and time, again.

We do not fight against flesh and blood, it is not those who have hurt you, or persecuted you, that we are fighting against. We are fighting a real enemy that we don't see with our natural eyes, the bible calls him the accuser of the brethren, the thief who comes to steal, kill, and destroy.

My advice to you today is to go to the source, go to the root and change the fruit. As believers, Jesus has given us all authority over the power of the enemy, Luke 10:19.

Get alone with God and pray over those circumstances you are facing right now, because whatever we bind on earth, is bound in heaven, what we loose on earth, is loosed in heaven.

The enemy has no right, to walk all over your life, and do whatever he wants, because greater is he, that is within you, than he that is in the world.

Take a stand on the inside today, declare that enough is enough, and that your circumstances have to change, resist the devil with your prayers of faith and he will flee.

I have God, Jesus and two-thirds of the angels on my side. What do you think I'm going to do? Sit down and cry?
Leonard Ravenhill

Personal reflections

....

....

....

....

....

....

....

First Love

"Nothing binds me to my Lord like a strong belief in His changeless love."
- Charles Spurgeon

The foundation and the future of everything we build our lives upon, has to always be the Agape love of God.

God is love, he is not trying to love, or choosing to love, he is Love, and he is totally eternally in love with you, John 3:16.

Love therefore, is not an option for us, or a theory, but a living, vibrant, day by day, experience that we have with the eternal God.

You shall love the Lord your God with all your heart, with all your soul, and with all your mind.
Matthew 22:37

I remember listening to a preacher years ago say, one night he had a dream, and was taken to heaven and stood before Jesus. The preacher spoke first and said, "Jesus I have served you, and traveled the world preaching the gospel, I gave to the poor, prayed and read your word every day." Then Jesus spoke and said, "But Rob did you love me." Everything in Rob's life came before loving God, but God's love has to be first in our lives.

First love is the key to everything for the church, for without it we have fallen from a great height. Loving God and loving people is what the Christian life is all about.

Let me ask you a question, how is your walk with the Lord? Does your relationship with Christ feel close, intimate, and growing daily, or dry spiritually and more like a chore?

This is the year you and I can change that.

A passionate love for Jesus, is what we need to move forward in our lives.

There is no other substitute for the love of God, nothing else will bring satisfaction to your life.

If we want our best year, we must give our best to God. That starts with love, let's make that choice today.

Personal reflections

....
....
....
....
....
....
....
....
....
....

Time to Let Go of the Past

*Therefore, if any person is [ingrafted] in Christ (the
Messiah) he is a new creation (a new creature
altogether); the old [previous moral and spiritual
condition] has passed away. Behold, the fresh and new
has come!*
2 Corinthians 5:17 AMP

So many people struggle with their past lives, and hurts, in fact people's faults, failings, and fears, so often follow them from month, to month, and year, to year. We can carry the old life into the new, and it becomes like an accuser, that raises its head, to keep us feeling we are no good. The past can also make us feel like we will never achieve anything, ever again, because of circumstances and mistakes that we have previously made.

These things my friend are lies, lies that will keep you contained inside your own prison, until you have dealt with them. It's time now to leave the prison, the prison of broken dreams, broken relationships, bitter regrets, etc.

Someone once said, "The brightest future will always be based on a forgotten past." You can't go forward in life, until you let go of your past failures, and heartaches, the bible is very clear on how we deal with this.

I focus on this one thing: Forgetting the past and looking forward to what lies ahead
Philippines 3:13 NLT

Do not allow the past to rob you of living a life that God intended for you, understand that God has forgiven, and forgotten your past, have faith in the truths found in God's word.
When the devil reminds you of your past, remind him of his future, his future is in the lake of fire for all eternity, while your future is ruling and reigning with Jesus.

Forget about what's happened; don't keep going over old history. Be alert, be present. I'm about to do something brand-new. It's bursting out! Don't you see it?
Isaiah 43:18-19 MSG

Personal reflections

....
....
....
....
....
....
....
....
....
....

The Power of Now

It's now or never
Elvis Presley

Now, is an important word in the bible, the word means, at the present moment of time; or without any further delay.
The Holy Spirit moved the writers and translators of the Bible to use that little word quite often throughout their writings, here are just a few examples.

Now is the day of salvation, 2 Corinthians 6:2.
Now we are children of God, 1 John 3:2.
Now faith is, Hebrews 11:1.
Now the peace of God be with you, Romans 15:33.
Now I will arise says the Lord, Isaiah 33:10.

Now, is a word that is prophetically important for you at this time, I believe it to be one of the keys that defines this season. It is time to experience the God of the now, whether that's, answered prayers, the now salvation of a loved one, launching a ministry, or believing that the dream can happen. Whatever it is, now is your time, and now is your turn, to experience the God of right now.

Therefore, do not project this word into the future, do what God is prompting you to do today, don't delay and don't say, well I will wait until next year.

As you step out, God will step into your situation, and whatever he tells you to do, do it.

Do it now.
Sometimes later becomes never
Anonymous

Personal reflections

....
....
....
....
....
....
....
....
....
....
....
....
....
....
....
....

Come with Praise,
He Comes with Power

I will bless the Lord at All times, His praise will
continually be in my mouth
Psalms 34:1

Whatever time, or season, you find yourself in, now is the right time to give thanks to the Lord. As believers our daily response to God's love and goodness, must be to continually praise him.
Some think that praise and worship is a religious activity, that belongs only in church on a Sunday morning, this is so far from the truth.

From the rising of the sun to it's going down the Lord's
name is to be praised, Psalm 113:3

Psalm 113:3, describes how we should let our first words in the morning, and our last words at night, with everything in-between, be praise to God.
When you praise God it changes your perspective, praise works like a magnifying glass, it causes what you are focusing on to get bigger, and to be magnified.

David said, "Magnify the lord with me, let us exalt his name, together. I sought the Lord, and he heard me, and delivered me from all my fears."

When we magnify God, our problems seem smaller, and our God seems so much bigger.

When we draw near to God, he draws near to us, and he inhabits the praises of his people.

It is a mistake to wait until you have no problems, or fewer problems before you praise the Lord. Praise is one of the great scriptural solutions, to seeing issues resolved and breakthrough released, it redirects our focus from ourselves, and places our focus on God.

I believe that as you release the sound of praise today, heaviness and hopelessness will go, remember God has promised you the garment of praise, for the spirit of heaviness, Isaiah 61:3.

In the happy moments, Praise God, in difficult moments, seek God, in the quiet moments, trust God, in every moment, thank God.

Charles Spurgeon said, "my happiest moments are when I am worshipping God, really adoring the Lord Jesus Christ. In that worship I forget the cares of the church and everything else. To me it is the nearest approach to what it will be in Heaven."

Personal reflections

....

....

....

Hear, See, Do

My sheep hear my voice and they follow me
John 10:27

I remember it well, there I was on the fifth row, the auditorium was packed with thousands of people, the preacher delivered a message, with such power, and eloquence. The title of his message, which he kept referring to again, and again was, what you hear, is what you see, and what you see, is what you do.

This is a truth that God has always reminded me of time, and time, again. If we hear something long enough, we will begin to see it, visualise it, and eventually this will become evident in our lives.

Jesus gave us a warning, he said, "Be careful what you hear." This is because words of life, can build you up, but words of death, and despair, can tear you apart.

It is important that we do not allow the voices of people, the media, doubt, defeat, or the spirit of this age, to become greater, or stronger, than the voice of God. Jesus said, "My sheep hear my voice and they follow me,"

The way we move forward, and get direction, is by hearing his voice.

When his voice becomes stronger than any other voice in our world, we gain vision, and this will create direction for our lives.

If I hear it, I can see it, then I can do it, this spiritual principle has worked in my life, so I know it will work in all areas of your life.

I remember hearing of a man who was paralysed, he was listening to a Sunday service.

The preacher was speaking about how it is God's will to heal today. The man kept listening to that broadcast for months, eventually he said to his wife, "You got to get me to that church."

He knew that when he got to the church he would be healed.

They finally got to the church, as his wife pushed his wheel chair to the door, one of the ushers shook his hand. Immediately, the power of God flowed though him, and as he jumped out of that chair, he was completely healed.

He heard it, he saw it, and God did it.

Faith comes by hearing and hearing by the word of God.
Romans 10:17

Personal reflections

....

....

....

....

God of the Breakthrough

*And David came to Baal-perazim, and he smote them
there, and said, the Lord has broken through my enemies
before me, like the bursting out of great waters. So he
called the name of that place Baal-perazim [Lord of
breaking through].*
2 Samuel 5:20 AMPC

In 2 Samuel 5, we read of a great victory for
David, and Israel, in this passage God is showing
us how his name, reveals characteristics of
himself. The name here that God reveals himself
as, is Lord of the breakthrough, or Lord of
breaking through, that was his covenant name to
his people. It is interesting here that the Hebrew
word is breakthroughs, which is plural, it shows
that just like God, brought victory for David
many times, so he will do it for you time, and
time again.

Our God has always been a breakthrough God,
he parted the red sea, demolished the walls of
Jericho, raised the dead, gave sight to the blind,
fed five thousand, with just a few loaves of bread,
and fishes, with plenty left over. What he did
then, he is ready, and willing, to do again today.

I am glad that the nature of God does not change,
for Jesus is the same yesterday, today, and
forever, Hebrews 13:8.

Whatever you need today, God's word is your guarantee for breakthrough.

If you are sick, he is the Lord who heals you Exodus 15:26.

If you have lost your job, or in a bad place financially, your God is able to meet all your needs, according to his riches, in Christ Jesus Philippians 4:19.

If you feel hopeless, and visionless for tomorrow, God promises you a hope, and a bright future, Jeremiah 29:11.

God, is the God, of many different kinds of breakthroughs, no matter how long you have struggled, it is all about to change.

Personal reflections

....

....

....

....

....

....

....

....

....

....

....

....

True or Truth

"If you abide in My word, you are My disciples indeed. And you shall know the truth, and the truth shall make you free."
John 8:31-32

Whether you realise it or not, there is a difference between what is true, and what is truth. Right now in your life you might be facing uncertainties, sickness, depression or a host of circumstances, that seem intent on shaking you to your very core. These circumstances might be true, but as Christians we know where to find the answers, in the truth of God's word.

God's eternal truth is the medication for the trials you face today.

I remember when my youngest daughter was very ill, and the doctors had done everything they could to aid her recovery, the natural facts, and the advice of these wonderful medical staff, was to expect the worse, but the truth of God's word declared that, I am the Lord your healer.

When you're in a storm, you have to allow the truth to shout louder than your storm, I grounded my faith, and my prayers, on the truth of God's word. I made that choice, and today my daughter has defied all odds, and is healthy, and living life to the full.

Determine today to believe God, and redirect your focus to what is the truth of his word.

Jesus said I am the way, the truth and the life.
John 14:6

Truth sets you free, when you abide in the word. The word abide, means to live, but it also means home. The word is our home, and every time you open the bible, the Holy Spirit says, "Welcome home, welcome back to the place you belong, the place where you see yourself, as I see you." Remember God will not do it all for us, he expects us to pick up the word of truth, read it, and speak it, as we do, things that might have held us back for years, will be broken off our lives, as the truth sets us free.

Remember his word is truth.
John 17:17

Personal reflections

....
....
....
....
....
....
....

God has a Plan, You have a Purpose

You saw me before I was born.
Every day of my life was recorded in your book.
Every moment was laid out
before a single day had passed.
Psalm 139:16 NLT

You are not a mistake, or a mishap, or an accident, even if your parents did not plan you, or want you, God did.

Regardless of your circumstances, God made you for a reason, and a purpose, his intentions towards you were always love. You and I are the focus of his love, and what he says, he means. God does not have a hidden agenda, or ulterior motives, God loves and values you, and he wants you to have the best life.

God was delighted to give us birth by the truth of his infallible Word so that we would fulfil his chosen destiny for us and become the favourite ones out of all his creation!
James 1:18 TPV

It is amazing to think that you're so special to God, you are one of his favourite ones. That your life has a reason, and a meaning, that God is delighted when we fulfil our God given destiny.

You're calling, or destiny, might be a mother, father, a nurse, a cleaner, a teacher or business owner, whatever it is, our commission is to serve the purpose of God, in our generation.

My grandmother Doris Edwards, spent all her life, living in a small town in the South Wales valleys, she worked for the post office, and lived a lifestyle of kindness, and generosity. If someone was in need, and she heard about it, she would buy extra food on her weekly shop, and show through practice, what the love of God was truly like. Many have commented over the years, how Doris cared, and helped people that others over looked.

She contributed to her world, by serving, and fulfilling the purpose of God, like her so must we. Nothing is insignificant when we serve God, every gift, every talent that has been given to us, is to serve others.

When you realise God's purpose for your life, isn't just about you. He will use you in a mighty way.
Tony Evans

Personal reflections

....

....

....

....

....

Hopeful not Hopeless

Now may the God of hope fill you with all joy and peace in believing, that you may abound in hope by the power of the Holy Spirit.
Romans 15:13

Hope, it is one of the foundations of the Christian faith, it is not only a part of our theology, it is also something as believers we can have, and experience in our every day life.

Many people in this world have never encountered this hope. For life without God, is life without hope.

You can survive forty days without food, three days without water, and eight minutes without air, but you cannot last a single second without hope, it is an essential part of life.

When hope is gone, life is over.
Rick Warren

We serve and love a God of hope, who has given us a hope, and a future.

Hope is more than a wish, a dream, or something that may, or may not happen. Hope, is the joyful anticipation of good, it is a future certainty, confident expectation, it is the future according to the word of God that we desire, and that God has promised.

The most universal thing is hope, for hope stays with those who have nothing else.

Hope is our anchor for the soul, it is firm, and secure, it keeps our minds, and emotions fixed on believing, and trusting God for the best outcomes for our lives.

Maybe the forecast for your life does not look good at the moment, maybe you have experienced financial ruin, lost a loved one, or feel you just want to give up on a dream, my encouragement to you is, to begin to hope again.

Problems have expiry dates, but God never puts a time limit on his goodness towards us. When you put your hope in God, you are putting your trust in that which is eternal, not temporal.

And so Lord where do I put my hope? My only hope is in you.
Psalm 39:7 NLT

Personal reflections

....

....

....

....

....

....

....

....

Heaven is My Home

It is a fact, that this world is not your ultimate home, or destination, this life is not the end of the story, it is just the beginning. For every Christian our belief is, to be absent from the body, is to be present with the Lord. When we die we do not leave home, we go home, to spend eternity in the presence of Jesus.

We may speak about a place where there are no tears, no death, no fear, no night, but those are just the benefits of heaven. The beauty of heaven is seeing God.
Max Lucado

One day we will be face, to face with God, we will see Jesus and be fully like him. Today, we must take stock of our lives, and not get attached to those things which are temporary, and passing away.

We have to live in the light of eternity, no one on their deathbed thinks, if only I had spent more time in the office, bought that dream car, or accumulated more wealth, these things become meaningless when faced with the reality that this world is passing away.

Maybe today is the day, to have a long hard look at your life, make change where change is needed, because how we live today will impact our tomorrow. Life is too short to hold on to offence, live with unforgiveness, or love God half heartedly.

Don't live for the here and now, live your life sold out for God, loving him unreservedly, and serving his purpose in your generation.

Then we can confidently declare like the apostle Paul did in 2 Timothy.

I have fought the good fight, I have finished the race, I have kept the faith.
2 Timothy 4:7

Personal reflections

....
....
....
....
....
....
....
....
....
....

No Fear in Death

O death, where is your sting?
O Hades, where is your victory?
The sting of death is sin, and the strength of sin is the
law. But thanks be to God, who gives us the victory
through our Lord Jesus Christ.
1 Corinthians 15:55-57

The end of life is not something that most people want to think about, for most of us it feels like it's way off in the distant future. Yet we must prepare to meet Jesus with faith, and joyful expectancy, not with any fear of facing death.

When God calls his children home, there's no death, no sting. Theres only new life resurrection.
Ted Decker

I remember talking to a man, he was gripped with fear about the thought of dying, he loved Jesus, but was consumed with anxiety, and worry. When I talked with this man, I reminded him that Jesus destroyed the power of sin, and death at the cross, and even though our bodies die, our spirit man, (the real you) is promoted to be with Jesus. For to be absent from the body, is to be present with the Lord.
We prayed and years later, he passed peaceably into eternity.

Jesus said, "The one who believes in me will live, even though they die." We should have a joyful anticipation about heaven, Jesus said that he was going to prepare a place for us, an eternal home, where there will be no sorrow, sickness, sin, or the presence of death.

The beauty of heaven will be Jesus, who we will see face to face.

If you are born again, there is nothing to fear about the future, we have a glorious future, because once we leave this earth, we arrive in the dwelling place of God.

Our natural minds cannot imagine what God has prepared for those who love him, every thought is inadequate, because the reality will be far more than we can ask, think, or imagine.

When we've been there ten thousand years, bright shining as the son, we've no less days to sing Gods praise, than when we first begun.
John Newton
Amazing Grace 1779

Personal reflections

....

....

....

....

....

....

Do Small Things in a Great Way

For who has despised the day of small things.
Zechariah 4:10

Big things have small beginnings, Moses had a staff, David had a sling, Samson had a jawbone, and the widow woman had a tiny coin. These people had something that might have seemed small, and insignificant, but they used it for the glory of God.

God inhabits the tiny seed, empowers the tiny deed, don't discount the smallness of your deeds.
Max Lucado

When you're believing God for big things in your life, they usually start out with a small beginning, do not despise the day of small beginnings.
When you despise something, you regard it lightly, and count it as nothing, God's training ground for greater things, is everything that is before you right now, for if you can't be faithful in little, you will never be faithful in much.
Your life might seem small compared to the promises, and dreams that God has placed within your heart, but faithfulness in doing small things, in a great way will open the door to divine promotion.

If we won't do what God is asking us to do, when it seems like a small assignment, we most likely won't do it when God gives us a big assignment. The everyday mundane things of life are important, and they develop character, and integrity in our lives.

The menial tasks were never above Jesus, he washed feet, helped children, cooked breakfast, nothing was beneath him, when he came to earth he came to serve.

Like Jesus, let us develop a servant's heart, and be ready to do whatever is needed.

Great opportunities often disguise themselves in small tasks. The little things in life determine the big things. Dont look for great tasks to do for God. Just do the not so great stuff, and God will assign you whatever he wants you to do.
Rick Warren

Personal reflections

....

....

....

....

....

....

....

....

The Cross

There is no Christianity without the cross, if the cross is not central to our faith, ours is not the faith of Jesus.
John Stott

On the Fifteenth of April 2019, a devastating fire raged through the Notre Dame Cathedral in Paris, the building was eight hundred and fifty years old, and a national landmark in the city. The inferno destroyed much of the structure, yet one of the few items that was untouched by the blaze was a golden cross, which remained intact even through this devastating fire.

One journalist said, "In the midst of the fire at Notre Dame, the cross still stands." That is beautiful, that is poetic, that is how God shows his majesty to us today.

The cross is the universal symbol of Christianity, at some point in your life you will see one, whether its engraved on a ring, or suspended on a chain, but it's got a far greater meaning for us as Christians.

Through the cross, Jesus bridged the gap between life, and death, the blessing and the curse, heaven and hell, he was the innocent dying for the guilty.

It was the great exchange, the sacrifice that he paid on your behalf, took place at the Cross.

I remember a Pastor telling me of a discussion, that he had with an atheist, in the middle of the conversation the atheist turned to him and said, "If your God is real, why doesn't he come and physically show himself to us?"

He replied, "He did and they nailed him to a cross." The man did not like the answer, but it's true.

The world didn't like the gracious, merciful God, that they got, so they murdered an innocent man, our saviour came to save humanity, and they hung him on a cross.

The cross is the evidence that God loved the world, it is proof that a just and merciful God gave his only begotten Son, to die on behalf of the ungodly.

Love put Jesus there, there was no selfish motive, there was no hidden agenda, the only reason was love.

For God so loved the world, that he gave his only begotten Son, that whoever believes in Him should not perish but have everlasting life
John 3:16

Personal reflections

....

....

....

You Have the Power

But you shall receive power when the Holy Spirit has come upon you; and you shall be witnesses to Me in Jerusalem, and in all Judea and Samaria, and to the end of the earth.
Acts 1:8

Jesus final promise, his guarantee before he went to be with his father in heaven, was that when you receive the Holy Spirit, you will receive power, you are not waiting for power, you have power. This power gives you the ability to rule and reign in life.

We have Holy Spirit power to share the gospel, power to heal the sick, power over sin, power to move mountains, and the power to move strongholds, that are standing in our way.

It is time to go public with the power of God, and make ourselves available for the Holy Spirit to use us, we need to raise our expectation to be used by God. You are not insignificant to God, you are important, and you have been commissioned to show what Jesus is really like. God has enabled you to see things that are impossible, and see them become possible.

Myself, and Anna were recently in a meeting in the USA, and a woman came forward for prayer, she had a number of hernias in her stomach and was due for surgery the following week. We prayed for her, and the power of God flowed through her body, at the end of the meeting, she said the presence of the Holy Spirit was like fire flowing through her, and she literally felt the hernias melt like butter and disappear under her hands.

It is so fulfilling to be used by God, I want to encourage, and remind you that, God wants to use you too. We all have to be available to step out to share the gospel, lay hands on the sick, or pray for somebody in need, when we do God's power is released.

Personal reflections

....

....

....

....

....

....

....

....

....

....

....

....

....

It is Finished

Jesus not only paid the price, but he also completed his work at the cross, the final words he cried were, "It is finished." This was not a cry of defeat, but a cry of victory, he was your substitute, and he took your place.

Christ has redeemed us from the curse of the law, having become a curse for us. For it is written, "Cursed is everyone who hangs on a tree."
Galatians 3:13

Jesus, the sinless son of God, took upon himself the sins of the world, so we could be declared not guilty. Our part is simply to believe in our hearts, and confess with our mouths, that Jesus is Lord, and we shall be saved, Romans 10:8-10.
Jesus was the sacrifice, he became the curse, all the judgement of God was placed upon Christ. Jesus took every sin, every disease, all cancer, depression, mental illness, and sickness, whether that is past, present or future, so that you and I could enjoy and live in total freedom.
The reality of the cross, is that you're no longer condemned, your accepted and forgiven, you do not have to live a life of worry, but you can live with God's peace. Sin is forgiven and forgotten, healing and wholeness is your divine inheritance.

If you're struggling, or in pain today, believe and apply the truth of God's word to your life, and declare, that by his finished work, you are healed, and you are whole.

Who Himself bore our sins in His own body on the tree, that we, having died to sins, might live for righteousness —by whose stripes you were healed.
1 Peter 2:24

Satan cannot legally lay on us, what God laid on Jesus, Christ became sick with our disease, that we might be healed, he knew no sickness until he became sick for us. The object of Christ's sin bearing was to make righteous all those who would believe in him as their sin bearer.
The object of his disease bearing was to make well all those who would believe in him as their disease bearer.
Healing the sick TL Osborn

Personal reflections

....
....
....
....
....
....
....

The Secret to Truly Living is Dying to Self

John the Baptist said it like this, "he has to increase, and I have to decrease." The cross is not ancient history, but a present day reality, its message means I die to self, and I live for Christ.

I have been crucified with Christ; it is no longer I who live, but Christ lives in me; and the life which I now live in the flesh I live by faith in the Son of God, who loved me and gave Himself for me.
Galatians 2:20

We hopefully will never be placed on a cross like Jesus, but we have to live the crucified life. God loves you just the way you are, but he refuses to leave you that way. His desire is to make you more like Christ in your character, actions, and daily life. Part of the way that this happens, is by dying to self, and living for Christ.

Anger, bitterness, lust, selfishness, jealousy, pride, greed, foul speech, negative attitudes and many more issues have to be dealt with through the power of the Holy Spirit. We need to get fresh revelation from the word of God. Paul said, "I die daily," meaning, the only way to deal with the flesh is to kill it.

Today, is the day for change, and it's a process, that process starts by you deciding, that you do not have to stay the way you are. You can change the things you don't like about yourself, or your situations. You can make the decision to put off the old self, and put on the new self, which is created to be like God.

I knew a person who struggled with his self image, every time he went to work, he use to say to himself, "I hate my life," eventually he became depressed and very angry. This man use to internally beat himself up. One day he said it again, "I hate my life" and immediately God said to him, "Why do you hate what I love."

That became a turning point for him, it was like a light bulb moment, that shone the love of God into his heart. Over the coming months he started killing those negative thoughts, and started believing what God said to him, and today he's a different man.

God does not want you stuck in a rut any longer, allow him to strip you of all the bad stuff, that holds you back from serving him fully.

Decide to remove the blockages, and the hindrances, let's be honest we all know what they are, then you will experience a newness of life and freedom you have never known before.

Victim or Victor

But God, who is rich in mercy, because of His great love with which He loved us, even when we were dead in trespasses, made us alive together with Christ (by grace you have been saved), and raised us up together, and made us sit together in the heavenly places in Christ Jesus.
Ephesians 2:4

Don't allow mistakes, or your past to define you, this can give you a victim mentality. Many of us at some point, have struggled with rejection, hurt, or worry and depression, whatever name tag it carries, it makes you feel like a victim, but that's not what the Bible says you are.

We have to identify with who God says we are, which is more than conquerors, Romans 8:37.

We are seated with Christ in heavenly places, which is far above all principalities and powers of darkness. Our seating, and reigning with Jesus, is a position of authority, honour, and triumph, not failure, depression, and defeat.

This is part of our inheritance now, we can see things from God's perspective, and realise we face no battle on our own, our fight is from the throne and from a place of victory. This is where we are spiritually placed, because when Jesus was seated in triumph, we were seated with Him, we rule and reign with Jesus now, as we exercise our rightful authority.

That might not be what your circumstances are saying to you right now, but that's subject to change, when you get a revelation of who you are in Christ, these truths will transform your life.

Change your mindset, read Ephesians and Colossians again and again, and your outlook on life will start to change, according to what the word says, because you are not a victim you are a victor.

Personal reflections

....

....

....

....

....

....

....

....

....

....

....

....

....

....

Prayer Releases Power

Worry is a conversation you have with yourself about things you cannot change. Prayer is a conversation you have with God about things he can change.
Anonymous

I have always believed in the power of prayer, over the years I have seen many answers to prayer in my life, and the lives of others. Prayer to me has never been an option, but rather a lifestyle of communication to God, I have sought to practice prayer every day.

We are encouraged to;
Pray always, Luke 18:1.
In everything, Philippians 4:6.
When suffering, James 5:13.
For our enemies, Matthew 5:44.
For the saints, Ephesians 1:16.
For the government, 1 Timothy 2:1-3.
For labourers to be sent into the harvest, Matthew 9:38.

Our father in heaven hears, answers, and rewards prayer, it is like a heavenly invitation to engage with him, because the prayers of righteous people like you, and me, are powerful and effective, James 5:16.

To pray affectively you don't have to beg, or plead, or come with false humility before the Lord. I have found that the prayers he answers and hears, are prayers of faith.

Someone once said to me, pray in faith as if it's already done for you, don't pray as if you're standing outside of the promise, pray like its already yours.

My wife is a woman of faith, and she has proved God through prayer many times. I remember on one occasion she had incredible pains in her back, and nothing was removing the intense agony she was in. Anna had a revelation that Jesus was her healer, and that the issue in her back had no place in her body, so she prayed and stood in faith, within a few weeks she was completely healed, and the issue has never returned, it was gone once and for all.

Do not be anxious about anything, but in every situation, by prayer and petition, with thanksgiving, present your requests to God.
Philippians 4:6

When we pray and give thanks for what God has promised he will do, miracles will happen, prayer is the request, thanksgiving is the action of faith.

Do not grumble or complain today, pray, you will be amazed at what a simple prayer can do.

*The greatest tragedy in life, is not unanswered prayer,
but not offered prayer.   F. B. Myer*

Personal reflections

....
....
....
....
....
....
....
....
....
....
....
....
....
....
....
....
....
....
....
....
....

A Celebration Meal

This cup is the new covenant in my blood; do this, whenever you drink it, in remembrance of me. For whenever you eat this bread and drink this cup, you proclaim the Lord's death until he comes.
1 Corinthians 11:25-26

Communion was never instigated by Jesus to be a religious ceremony, the Lords supper is a gift to us, it is an opportunity for us to leave the problems, and pressures of this life behind, and fellowship with Jesus. The bread represents his body, that was broken and sacrificed in our place, the cup represents his blood, which declares the reality today, that our sins have been forgiven and forgotten.

Whether we are gathering together as the church, or in our homes, we can take part in this covenant meal, and celebrate the victory that Jesus has accomplished at the cross.

Taking of the bread and wine is a proclamation of his death, that we are told to do until he returns.

Next time you take communion, don't just see it as a ritual, but an opportunity to thank, and worship Jesus, for the work that he finished at the cross.

We Pray God Provides

"The size of prayers depends on the size of our God. And if God knows no limits, then neither should our prayers. God exists outside of the four space-time dimensions He created. We should pray that way!"
Mark Batterson, The Circle Maker

As believers we have power, and authority when we pray, as the church we are called to bind the powers of darkness, and loose the promises of God, whether we are praying individually, or as a corporate body. When believers come into agreement with God's word, and one another, Jesus said it would be done for us by our father in heaven.

What a promise, God pays attention to our cry, Jesus is in our midst by the Holy Spirit, and when we ask, his answer is yes.

I am writing this book, in the midst of one of the worst pandemics the world has seen in my lifetime, Covid 19. Todays count of people who have sadly lost their lives to this disease, is well over Forty-Three thousand in the UK alone, as a result we are all in lockdown, churches, shops and restaurants are closed, and this is the same across the world.

I might not be able to leave the house, but I can pray, there is an urgency and a necessity to intercede, stand in the gap, and decree that this disease must end.

Our fight is not against flesh, and blood, but powers, and principalities, in the heavenly places, God has given us power through prayer to change things.

In 1940, at the start of World War Two, King George called for a national day of prayer. The King attended Westminster Abbey, whilst millions of his subjects in all parts of the Commonwealth, flocked to the churches to join in prayer. Nazi Germany had advanced through France, and pushed the troops to the beaches of Dunkirk, where thousands were potentially going to be killed.

Miraculously, Hitler decided to stop his advance, and there was a great calm on the English channel, this calm managed to get all the armed forces home, without any loss of life. God was the answer then, and God is the answer now, when we pray God provides.

Assuredly, I say to you, whatever you bind on earth will be bound in heaven, and whatever you loose on earth will be loosed in heaven.
"Again I say to you that if two of you agree on earth concerning anything that they ask, it will be done for them by My Father in heaven. For where two or three are gathered together in My name, I am there in the midst of them." Matthew 18:18-20

Vision

Where there is no vision, the people perish.
Proverbs 29:18 KJV

Vision, is a foundational quality within our lives, that we need to fulfil our destiny, it is an indispensable quality we cannot live without.

Vision primarily has to do with seeing. The root Hebrew word means, to gaze, to look, to see, to perceive what God wants, and how he is going to do it.

In other words, it's a clear picture in your heart, and in your mind, of all that God wants to do through your life, and your calling, to build his kingdom.

It is seeing with God's eyes, it is knowing what God wants you to do, and knowing how to do it, that's vision.

If you look at the history books, you will find that the men and women, who have turned the world upside down, the churches who have affected their city and nation, have all carried vision. The apostle Paul said it like this, "I was not disobedient to the heavenly vision," I hope we can say the same for what God has entrusted to our lives.

I believe God wants to revive fresh vision, and purpose within you today, he wants to blow the dust off your dreams, and cause you to consider what you are building with your life.
Is what you are building temporal, or eternal?

Don't allow anything, or anyone, to kill the vision that is attached to your destiny.

Do not quit, or become disillusioned, make a fresh commitment today, to the plan God has entrusted to your life.

Personal reflections

....
....
....
....
....
....
....
....
....
....
....
....
....
....

Make Vision a Reality

Brethren, I do not count myself to have apprehended, but one thing I do, forgetting those things which are behind and reaching forward to those things which are ahead. I press toward the goal for the prize of the upward call in Christ Jesus.
Philippians 3:13-14

God does not want us to live a visionless life, he wants us to dream big, have purpose, and direction, and to focus on our divine goals, our vision creates our future.

What you see, is usually what you become, the apostle Paul, had a crystal clear picture of what God, was going to do through his life.

One thing I do, I place my priority on forgetting what is behind me, and I focus on the call, which I have received through Jesus Christ. This means I do not quit, I do not compromise, I shake off disillusionment, and I give myself to what God has called me to do.

I read a story once of a man visiting a construction site, and he went to where the stonemasons were working, the man asked the first stonemason, "What are you doing?"

The stonemason said, "I am chipping away at a stone." The man walked over to the second

stonemason and asked, "What are you doing?" He answered, "I am building a wall."
Finally the man walked over to the third stonemason and asked, "What are you doing?"
The mason replied, "I am building a cathedral."
All three were doing the same job, but what a difference vision makes.

Vision enables us to build something big for the future. Whether you are a house wife, a doctor, a teacher or a retired person, through us, Christ is building his church and extending his kingdom, we are all involved in that, however big or small that part might seem.

Myself, and Anna learnt many years ago, that vision needs to be made practical, Habakkuk 2:2 says write down the vision and make it plain.

I remember one year, that we wrote down all the goals we had and wanted to achieve within that year, we were in unity and worked towards them, we prayed and by the end of the year, we had fulfilled everything in that vision.

I want to encourage you today, to make practical the vision God has given for your life, write it down, commit to it, partner with God and it will be fulfilled.

Personal reflections

....

....

Holy Spirit My Best Friend

*Do you not know that you are the temple of God
and that the spirit of God dwells in you?
1 Corinthians 3:16*

What a thought, what a reality, God, the Holy Spirit lives within me, he is not an it, or a thing, or a cloud, or a vapour, the Holy Spirit is a person, and he has been sent by Jesus to make God real to us. God the father, and God the Son are in heaven, but the Holy Spirit is here and he wants to fill you with his presence.

As Christians it is vital that we are baptised, and filled with the Holy Spirit, it will transform your life, and give you power.

When you study the book of Acts, you find that believers were filled with the Spirit, and also spoke in tongues. In fact the first time that the Holy Spirit came in Acts two, he filled them and gave them the gift of tongues.

When the Day of Pentecost had fully come, they were all with one accord in one place. And suddenly there came a sound from heaven, as of a rushing mighty wind, and it filled the whole house where they were sitting. Then there appeared to them divided tongues, as of fire, and *one* sat upon each of them. And they were all filled with the Holy Spirit and began to speak with other tongues, as the Spirit gave them utterance. Acts 2:1-4

Now if this had happened just once, you could maybe contest whether Spirit baptism, and tongues are for today, but as you find it numerous times in the book of Acts, I believe, it is for today also; Acts 8:12-17, Acts 9:17-18, Acts 10:44-46.

When I got baptised in the Holy Spirit, it totally revolutionised my Christian life, God became personal, I felt alive, and passionate for Jesus.

I had a boldness I had never known before, I shared my faith, and prayed for the sick without fear, or intimidation. I could hear God's voice, and sense his direction, and over the years I have realised that I cannot live without him.

What he has done for me, he wants to do for you, just ask and you shall receive.

Personal reflections

....

....

....

....

....

....

....

....

....

....

Help is at Hand

And I will pray the Father, and He will give you another Helper, that He may abide with you forever— the Spirit of truth, whom the world cannot receive, because it neither sees Him nor knows Him; but you know Him, for He dwells with you and will be in you. I will not leave you orphans; I will come to you.
John 14:16-18

I am so glad that we are not alone in this world, God said, "I will never leave you, or forsake you," Hebrews 13:5.
We have a helper and representative here on earth, the Holy Spirit, he does not want a distant relationship, he wants you to know and depend on him, and call on him for help.

If we realised that God lived within us, we would realise that there is nothing impossible for us. Why, because we as human beings are the containers for God.
Anonymous

Don't ignore the Holy Spirit, fellowship with him, and talk to him, he is here to give you answers to the problems you face right now.
The amplified version, gives us a glimpse of what Jesus was saying.

And I will ask the Father, and He will give you another Helper (Comforter, Advocate, Intercessor—Counselor, Strengthener, Standby), to be with you forever.
John 14:16

The Holy Spirit is called along side us, he is here to assist us to live a victorious life in Christ.

All things are possible, because we have God with us and in us. He will help and comfort, strengthen, and intercede, and standby you, when everyone else walks out the door, you can always rely, and depend on the Helper.

If you have more questions than answers today, or you feel gripped with uncertainly, do not stand alone, ask the Holy Spirit for help.

Personal reflections

....
....
....
....
....
....
....
....
....
....
....
....

Without Measure

For the one whom God has sent speaks the words of God, for God gives the Spirit without limit.
John 3:34 NIV

We were never called to live an empty life, like Jesus we are called to live our daily lives full of God. Christ received the Holy Spirit without measure, and so must we, it's called being filled with the Spirit. I have met Christians who have told me sentimental stories from years ago, about how they were baptised in the Holy Spirit and the difference it made, but that's no good for today, you need to get a fresh filling of the power of the Holy Spirit now.

Before Jesus entered into his ministry, preached, taught, healed the sick, performed the miraculous, he was first baptised, and filled with the Holy Spirit, because, it's not by might, nor by power, but by my Spirit says the Lord.

It is the will of God for you to be filled with the Spirit today, all you have to do is ask.

You and I do not have to live with a stale or barren faith, the remedy for you, and me, is to experience God's presence afresh daily.

What was a necessity for Jesus is also needful for us today.

And do not be drunk with wine, in which is dissipation;
but be filled with the Spirit.
Ephesians 5:18

Drink the Spirit of God, huge draughts of him.
Ephesians 5:18 Message Translation

The Greek meaning to this verse, is being filled, and staying full all of the time, it is not a one-off experience. The solution to being transformed, and knowing God more deeply, is to allow the Holy Spirit to be poured out into your life today.

You and I will be able to do more in one year, than in the
previous fifty, when we have been truly filled and
empowered with the Holy Spirit.
Smith Wigglesworth.

Personal reflections

....
....
....
....
....
....
....
....
....
....

Your Heavenly Language

For he who speaks in a tongue does not speak to men but to God, for no one understands him; however, in the spirit he speaks mysteries.
1 Corinthians 14:2

When we speak and pray in tongues, we communicate with God, and it is so important to recognise that it is not a pointless exercise. We speak in a heavenly language, that our mind does not comprehend, but our father in heaven does. When you speak in tongues, you edify yourself, one of the Greek words for edify, is charge.

The word "charge" could be used in connection with charging a battery. There has been times when I have had a car, or van, and the battery was flat, when I put the charger on it, it puts power in the battery, and that battery starts to work again. When you speak in tongues, you charge your spirit, you build yourself up in your inner man, and faith comes, you're energised, that is why Paul said, "I speak in tongues more than you all."

Speaking in tongues is one of the ways we gain access to God, your mind might be unfruitful, but your spirit pray's to God through your heavenly language.

Our prayers might be amiss at times when we pray in English, but when we pray in tongues we pray the perfect will of God.

I have been amazed over the years, how I have heard the voice of God, received insight, wisdom, and clarity on situations, when I have prayed in the Spirit. Naturally it makes no sense, but supernaturally we are communicating with God, spirit to spirit, and answers come.

When we pray in tongues, we do not just help ourselves, we intercede for others.

Likewise the Spirit also helps in our weaknesses. For we do not know what we should pray for as we ought, but the Spirit Himself makes intercession for us with groaning's which cannot be uttered. Now He who searches the hearts knows what the mind of the Spirit is, because He makes intercession for the saints according to the will of God.
Romans 8:26-27

Praying in tongues keeps selfishness out of our prayers, because the Holy Spirit prays through us, and enables us to pray the perfect will of God, not just for ourselves but also for others.

When we pray in the Spirit we stand in the gap, and pray for those in need around the world.

Start developing the habit of speaking in tongues today, it will make a significant difference to not just your life, but people around the world.

For if I pray in a tongue, my spirit pray's, but my understanding is unfruitful.
1 Corinthians 14:14

Personal reflections

....
....
....
....
....
....
....
....
....
....
....
....
....
....
....
....
....
....
....
....
....
....

Renew or Repeat

Consider how precious a soul must be, when both God and the devil are after it.
Charles Spurgeon

We were born again into a battle, a spiritual war zone, and there is a constant clash between the kingdom of God, and the kingdom of darkness. Our faith is in the finished work of Christ, and this gives us the victory, we are born of God so we can overcome everything that we face in this life. We must therefore renew our minds, or we are prone to repeat the same issues again, and again, or go through the same problems time, and time again.

And do not be conformed to this world, but be transformed by the renewing of your mind, that you may prove what is that good and acceptable and perfect will of God.
Romans 12:2

The will of God is not that we conform, but be transformed, by the renewing of our minds.
The J.B. Phillips version puts it like this, don't allow the world to squeeze you into its mould.
Our minds and our soul are not to conform, or be squeezed into worldly and carnal thinking.

We do not have to accept the lies, the lust, and the doubt, that the enemy would seek to put into our minds, we can rule over them, and certainly stop them from producing bad fruit.

The word transformed here is the Greek word metamorphisi, it is the root word from where we get our word metamorphosis. Metamorphosis is the process a caterpillar goes through, when its changing from its original state into a butterfly. The term metamorphosis by definition means, a complete change of physical form or substance. It is a process that represents complete transformation, when a caterpillar is transformed, it becomes a butterfly and thus becomes unrecognisable. Instead of ugly it's beautiful, it looks different, instead of crawling around on the floor, it is released to fly into the air, and become all that it was destined to be.

Just like the dramatic process a caterpillar undergoes to become a butterfly, so we are called to undergo a complete renovation, and renewal under the supervision of the Holy Spirit. This renovation will create a new state of being, emotionally, mentally and spiritually in our lives.

Since, then, you have been raised with Christ, set your hearts on things above, where Christ is, seated at the right hand of God. Set your minds on things above, not on earthly things.
Colossians 3:1-2 NIV

Personal reflections

....
....
....
....
....
....
....
....
....
....
....
....
....
....
....
....
....
....
....
....
....
....
....
....
....
....

Meditate

Blessed is the man
Who walks not in the counsel of the ungodly,
Nor stands in the path of sinners,
Nor sits in the seat of the scornful;
But his delight is in the law of the Lord,
And in His law, he meditates day and night.
He shall be like a tree
Planted by the rivers of water,
That brings forth its fruit in its season,
Whose leaf also shall not wither;
And whatever he does shall prosper.
Psalm 1:1-3

There was a time when I use to rush through reading my bible, and do my spiritual exercise of trying to read through the word in a year. To be honest, all I got was information, hear me right, I am not against reading through the bible in a year, but we often need more time to absorb the truths in the word. What changes us is not information, but revelation, and I have found that this occurs when we meditate on the word.

The word meditate, is the same word that is used for when a cow chews the cud, for when it chews the cud it takes grass, swallows it, then regurgitates it, and then the cow swallows it and goes through the same process again, and again, until as much of the nutrients have been taken out of that piece of grass.

In the same way we have to daily meditate on the truth's of the word, and get them into our thought process, so God's word is no longer information, but revelation.

When it becomes revelation, it will be life-changing, you will be a different person in twelve months, because what you read won't be just words on a page, but the truth in which you live by.

The bible revives and transforms the soul, which results in a new you.

One of the ways you can practically meditate on the word, is by writing notes on what God is highlighting to you, then you can go back and think about what he has said. You can also take a word, or phrase, and do a word study through the bible on that word, this can be life changing.

For example, if you are struggling with anxiety, look at what God has said about it in the scriptures, and the solution he gives. Studying the bible like this will cause you to know the truth, and the truth will set you free.

This Book of the Law shall not depart from your mouth, but you shall meditate on it day and night, that you may observe to do according to all that is written in it. For then you will make your way prosperous, and then you will have good success. Joshua 1:8

Angels on Assignment

*The angel of the Lord encamps all around those who fear
Him,*
And delivers them.
Psalm 34:7

Just like Kings, Queens, or heads of state are surrounded by security guards, so we have angels assigned to aid us, and protect us.
There is angelic activity on our behalf, Psalm ninety-one makes that very clear, as we dwell in the secret place of the most high, we benefit from angels being dispatched on our behalf.

*God will put his angels in charge of you, to protect you
wherever you go.*
Psalm 91:11 GNT

I remember reading a true story about Dr James McConnell, founder of Whitewell Metropolitan Tabernacle, in Belfast, Northern Ireland.
One Sunday, he was preaching during the troubles, and a paramilitary with a gun came into the church to kill him. The man took only a few steps up the aisle when he stopped dead in his tracks, turned and ran out of the church. The man with the gun later became a Christian, and he testified that he had seen two big angels

standing on either side of Pastor McConnell, so he was unable to shoot him, as he had intended to do, when he walked into the building that day.

Angels are on assignment, and they are watching over you right now as you read this book.

"If you are a believer, expect powerful angels to accompany you in your life experience."
Billy Graham

Personal reflections

....

....

....

....

....

....

....

....

....

....

....

....

....

....

....

....

....

They are Many and They are Mighty

Are they not all ministering spirits sent forth to minister for those who will inherit salvation?
Hebrews 1:14

There are over three hundred scriptural references to Angels in the bible, they do various tasks, I have listed some here for you;

They bring messages from God, Judges 6, Luke 1 and Luke 2.
They protect God's people, Daniel 6:22 and 2 Kings 6:17.
They take special care of children, Matthew 18:10.
God sends Angels at specific times to comfort, and strengthen, believers, 1 Kings 19:7-8 and Matthew 4:11.
They are also used to bring God's judgement, Revelation 12:7-9.
They continuously worship God, Revelation 5:11-12.

Angels are numerous and mighty, they are marked with incredible strength, and obey the voice of God. We have angels assigned to us, to assist us in our times of need.

Over the years a school of thinking has crept in, where people have thought that they can pray to angels, or speak to their angels, and they will obey their commands. As far as I can see, there are no examples of this anywhere in the bible, so I cannot see any biblical basis for such claims. We pray in faith to the father, based on the promises in his word, and God will send his angels when needed to assist.

I remember my dad traveling to Portugal, while he was living there as a missionary. The car he was driving was full, and overweight with items he was bringing home, suddenly, he had a puncture in his tire. Unfortunately, he was in the middle of the countryside, and there was no town, or house, for miles.

The car had too much weight to remove the tyre without unloading all of the contents, and the spare wheel was underneath the car. My dad was on his own, and it would have taken him hours to unload the car, so he started praying, and thanking God for divine helpers. After he prayed for a few minutes, the side of the car where the tire was a flat, started to raise up.

My dad knew angels were helping him, and had been sent to assist, so he could change the wheel. This is a true story where a miracle really happened, angels are active on the earth today, so expect them to help you too.

Praise the Lord, you his angels,
you mighty ones who do his bidding,
who obey his word.
Psalm 103:20 NIV

Personal reflections

....
....
....
....
....
....
....
....
....
....
....
....
....
....
....
....
....
....
....
....
....

Restoration

*Restore us, O God, cause your face to shine and we
shall be saved*
Psalm 80:3

I have found that when you feel your life is in ruins, or experience brokenness, God promises a plan of restoration. One of the meanings of restoration in the English dictionary, is to restore or repair, an item to its original condition.

The restoration God promises is far greater than anything we can think of, he can to do more than you can ask, think, or imagine. When you read about restoration in the bible, it always results in a greater return than what was lost.

This is the nature of God, and what God has done for others, he can do for you. You might have made some mistakes, or feel forgotten, do not give up, God will never leave you or forsake you. It is time to believe again, and expect God to restore everything, that you have lost from your life. I can honestly say that God has shown me great mercy, even when I have made mistakes. His restoration in my life has left me speechless. So today, do not write yourself off, or see yourself as a failure, you are a child of God, and his grace is more than sufficient, for anything you face in your life today.

Revive Me

Turn away my eyes from looking at worthless things, And revive me in Your way
Psalm 119:37

Many times in the book of Psalms, David is shown to have a cry for revival. David uses the words revive me, a number of times in Psalm 119:88, and Psalm 138:7. David's longing and plea was for personal revival, and what David desired here, we should also desire today.
If you need reviving today, God is willing and able, we just have to be honest with God, and allow him to burn up the dross in our lives, and restore the joy of our salvation.

The only reason we don't have revival is because we are willing to live without it.
Leonard Ravenhill

Don't live without God, draw close to him, we never need to live empty lives, or have a lifestyle of lukewarm christianity, that is certainly not God's best for you. Be honest with yourself and with God today, allow the Holy Spirit to revive in you a first love for Jesus.

Give God your worries, fears, selfishness or pride, they always melt away, when he fills you with his presence.
Our God is a consuming fire, a jealous God, and he wants us consumed with him, and him alone.
Let David's prayer, be our prayer today.

Let revival start, and let it start in me.

Personal reflections

....

....

....

....

....

....

....

....

....

....

....

....

....

....

....

....

....

The Perfect Miracle

Jesus answered and said to him, "Most assuredly, I say to you, unless one is born again, he cannot see the kingdom of God."
John 3:3

It is easy at times to forget, that the greatest miracle we will ever experience, is the new birth, for without being born again, we will not enter into the kingdom of God.

The new birth changes everything in our lives;
It transfers you from death, to life, John 10:10 and Ephesians 2:1.
From a sinner, to a child of God, Romans 3:23 and Romans 8:19.
From a life of darkness, to living in the light, 1 Peter 2:9.
From knowing God's wrath, to experiencing God's forgiveness, 1 John 1:7.
From your eternal destination being hell, to now being heaven, John 3:36.

Jesus said you must be born again, that is not a choice, it is a commandment. We can start over in our lives, and experience our past being completely forgiven, and everything becoming new.

The moment we ask God to forgive us for our sinful lives, and believe in our heart, and confess with our mouth that Jesus is Lord, we are saved.

Bart Millard is the lead singer of Mercy me, he was raised in a home with an abusive father, his dad use to beat him so hard, that he was unable to sleep at night because of the pain, this continued through his childhood. Bart's father in later years, had terminal cancer, then gave his life to Jesus, this brought healing, and the power of forgiveness to their relationship.

Bart said, "My dad was a monster and I saw God transform him, only the gospel can do that."

The gospel is still the power of God for salvation, it is the miracle that has the power to remove hate, and anger, lust, and shame, and every other evil that has bound us before we had a revelation of Jesus.

Take a moment and thank God for your salvation today.

Personal reflections

....

....

....

....

....

....

....

Your World is Waiting

And He said to them, "Go into all the world and preach the gospel to every creature. He who believes and is baptised will be saved; but he who does not believe will be condemned."
Mark 16:15-16

Jesus did not tell us to stay, he told us to go into the world, and preach the gospel, sharing the good news of the gospel, is our commission, and Christ declares it, not as a suggestion but a commandment.

Whether you are a pastor, teacher, wife or business leader, whatever your calling in life is, you, and I, have the amazing opportunity of sharing our faith. You can become active in helping others discover the good news about Jesus, who has transformed your life, and my life, there is nothing more rewarding.

Paul became all things to all men, he used whatever methods he could, to win people to Christ, and so must we.

Our personal testimony is powerful, you can use it to share how God has changed your life, I have also used a tract called Bridge to Life, which is a simple step, by step explanation of the gospel message.

Bridge to Life is a great tool for explaining the love of God, and the mission of Jesus.

You may want to pray, and ask God, for divine appointments too, you will be amazed at the people he leads you to.

There was a survey recently in the USA, that stated there were thirty-four million people, who wanted to know more about God, and would go to church if someone invited them. This challenges me, the fact that there are more people ready for an invitation, than we are ready to invite.

Let's start to change that, let's be committed to change our world, one person at a time, you don't need to be a preacher, or a missionary to be used by God, you just got to be prepared to say, here I am Lord send me.

Personal reflections

....

....

....

....

....

....

....

....

....

....

Flesh Verses Spirit

The cravings of the self-life are obvious: Sexual immorality, lustful thoughts, pornography, chasing after things instead of God, manipulating others, hatred of those who get in your way, senseless arguments, resentment when others are favoured, temper tantrums, angry quarrels, only thinking of yourself, being in love with your own opinions, being envious of the blessings of others, murder, uncontrolled addictions, wild parties, and all other similar behaviour.
Galatians 5:19-21 The Passion Version

Let's be honest, while we live on this earth there will always be an ongoing battle between the flesh, and the spirit. This battle is fought in our emotions and minds. The cravings of the flesh are selfish desires, lustful feelings and prideful thoughts, it is human nature corrupted by sin, but there is an answer.

The key to conquering the flesh, is to walk in the Spirit, to live in daily obedience to the Holy Spirit. Walking in the Spirit is simply having a life controlled by the Spirit. Some of the things that help us walk in the Spirit, are prayer, worship, reading, meditating in the word, and praying in tongues.

Maybe there is a prevailing problem stalking your life today, explosive temper, secret addition, rotten attitude, the remedy is a daily dependency on the power of the Holy Spirit, to conquer the flesh.

Let's take off the mask today, and be honest with God, he knows all our failings anyway.

Someone once said, "That you cannot stop birds flying over your head, but you can certainly stop a bird from building a nest on your head."

In the same way, you cannot stop temptations, sinful thoughts and desires from passing through your head, but you can certainly stop yourself from acting on those thoughts, and desires.

God's divine power has given us everything that pertains to life, and godliness, 2 Peter 1:3.

We can reject fleshly carnal desires, and overwhelmingly conquer through Christ Jesus.

I say then: Walk in the Spirit, and you shall not fulfil the lust of the flesh.
Galatians 5:16

Personal reflections

....

....

....

....

....

....

....

....

The Price is Paid

Much more then, because we have now been declared righteous by his blood, we will be saved through him from God's wrath.
Romans 5:9 NET

On the cross Jesus became, sin, so that we could become what he is, which is righteous.

Without Jesus's death, our sins would have separated us from God forever, but Christ became the sacrifice, who in turn paid the price for the wrath of God. The innocent one died for the guilty, but God demonstrates his own love for us, in that while we were still sinners, Christ died for us.

In him we have redemption through his blood, the forgiveness of our trespasses, according to the riches of his grace.
Ephesians 1:7

Many years ago, there was a film that was released called Schindlers list, the film followed the life of a man called Oscar Schindler, who was a businessman in Nazi Germany, during the second world war. Oscar employed Jews in his factory, and had a compassion for their people, when the Nazis came to his factory, they sentenced the Jewish people who worked for him to the concentration camps, and the gas chambers. Even though Oscar was German, he had a deep conviction that killing Jews was wrong, so he started to make payments to the German guards, or officers, to save the lives of the Jews, from the gas chambers.

During World War Two, Oscar Schindlers focus was not on how much money he could make, but how many lives he could save.

Towards the end of the war, Oscar, had used all his wealth to purchase the lives of over One thousand two hundred Jewish people.

When he was interviewed later he said, "I felt that the Jews were being destroyed, and I felt an overwhelming sense of compassion for them, I had to use everything within my power to help them, there was no choice."

What Oscar Schindler did out of compassion, Jesus has done so much more spiritually.

God felt an overwhelming sense of compassion for you, and did everything within his power to help you, and save you.

God brings peace to your past, purpose to your present, and hope to your future at the cross.

Personal reflections

....

....

....

Fruit not Fruits

But the fruit of the Spirit is love, joy, peace, long suffering, kindness, goodness, faithfulness, gentleness, self-control. Against such there is no law.
Galatians 5:22-23

The Holy Spirit is one person, has one nature and one fruit, please notice, that it's not fruits here, but the fruit of the Spirit, with nine characteristics or qualities.

The characteristics of the Holy Spirit are love, joy, peace, patience, kindness, goodness, faithfulness, gentleness and self control.

God wants our character defined by the fruit of the Spirit, character development is God's goal for our life on earth. God does not want us to lose our personality, or become a mindless clone, but he does wants us to become more Christlike in our character, attitude, and actions.

If we are living full of the Holy Spirit, there should be evidence of spiritual fruit in our lives. Ephesians 2:10 says, we are God's masterpiece, which means we are God's, greatest piece of work.

You are lovingly valued by your creator, and he is committed to helping you reflect, the nature and character of Jesus. Just like it takes time for natural fruit to grow and mature, so it takes time and patience, to see a manifestation of all the fruit of the Spirit in our lives.

Do not give up, be committed to change, let God work on your weaknesses, and make you stronger, and more like Him.

Personal reflections

....
....
....
....
....
....
....
....
....
....
....
....
....
....
....
....
....
....
....
....

I Choose Love

"Let me give you a new command: Love one another. In the same way I loved you, you love one another. This is how everyone will recognize that you are my disciples — when they see the love you have for each other."
John 13:34-35

One of the characteristics of the fruit of the Spirit is love, Galatians 5:22. Love is the first quality mentioned in this passage, when you encounter God, you will encounter his divine love.

The God kind of love is unconditional and sacrificial, it is less of a feeling, and more of an action. It is God's deliberate, and intentional choice, to do something without a logical cause. There was no logical reason, why God would ever love us, there was no attraction, and nothing for God to gain in choosing you, yet he showed us unconditional love.

God wasn't attracted to you and didn't choose you because you were big and important — the fact is, there was almost nothing to you. He did it out of sheer love Deuteronomy 7:7 The Message Translation

Human love can be selfish and sometimes say, I will love you as long as you meet my expectations, agree with my points of view, attend my church, or fit into my social circle.

God's love is not like that, because he did not wait for you, to become worthy to make the first move. God showed his great love, by sending Christ to die for us.

Romans 5:8 says, "God demonstrated his own love, for us while we were yet sinners."

The love of God we have now received, is the love we should now show to others.

Bill Hybels once said, "When I set out the task of loving, I usually end up giving, instead of receiving. Love inevitably costs me the three commodities most precious to me, my time, my energy, and my money."

Walking in love means that we not only love God first, but secondly we love our neighbour as we love ourselves, that at times seems impossible, but through God's grace it is possible.

Loving like Jesus loves is more than words, it is action, and it costs us something, whether this is our time, money, or other valuable commodity.

Helping the helpless, forgiving those who annoy us, praying for our enemies, going out of our way for someone in need, or being a listening ear, when we could be doing something more important for ourselves, all of these are qualities of the love of God operating in our lives.

We love others best when we love God most
Kyle Idleman

"Love suffers long and is kind; love does not envy; love does not parade itself, is not puffed up; does not behave rudely, does not seek its own, is not provoked, thinks no evil; does not rejoice in iniquity, but rejoices in the truth; bears all things, believes all things, hopes all things, endures all things. Love never fails."
1 Corinthians 13:4-8

Personal reflections

....
....
....
....
....
....
....
....
....
....
....
....
....
....
....
....
....
....

I Choose Joy

These things I have spoken to you, that my joy may remain in you, and that your joy may be full.
John 15:11

Joy is a quality of the fruit of the Spirit within you, Jesus said that his joy, would become our joy, and we could stay full of joy in our lives.

Joy means happiness, delight, and a true feeling of gladness in your soul, produced by the Holy Spirit. It is not based on favourable circumstances, or whether life treats you well or not, the joy of the Lord will strengthen you whatever you face today.

Joy gives you the ability to weather the most difficult storms, Paul commended the churches in Macedonia for this characteristic.

For even during a season of severe difficulty and tremendous suffering, they became even more filled with joy.
2 Corinthians 8:2 TPT

Just like these believers knew gladness, and joy in very difficult trials and tribulations, so can we. Do not allow anything, or anyone to steal your joy today, it is your strength. Decide to get full of the Holy Spirit, for in his presence is fullness of joy, Psalm 16:11.

Personal reflections

....
....
....
....
....
....
....
....
....
....
....
....
....
....
....
....
....
....
....
....
....

I Choose Peace

And the peace of God, which surpasses all understanding, will guard your hearts and minds through Christ Jesus
Philippians 4:7

Pain, suffering, war, and heartache, are what we find within the world in which we live.

Wikipedia, the online encyclopaedia, defines world peace, or peace on earth, "As a concept of an ideal state of happiness, freedom, and peace within and among all people, and nations on planet earth." Unfortunately a lasting solution to world peace has not be found through human rights, diplomacy, medication, or education. Peace cannot be earned, it can only be found through a person, called Jesus.

When we have the Holy Spirit living within us, we can draw on the power, and presence of his peace. This peace guards your heart, calms your head, and as one writer once said, "Peace is an inside job."

The Hebrew word for peace, is the word, Shalom, it means welfare, wholeness, health, prosperity, and peace. It is medicine for your soul, tranquility for your mind, a state of restful calm internally, without anxiety, and stress.

Jesus has already made peace with God, Romans 5:1, therefore we have open access to his peace, its rightfully and legally a blessing from our heavenly father, to enjoy and receive.

Peace I leave with you, My perfect peace I give to you, not as the world gives do I give to you.
Do not let your heart be troubled, nor let it be afraid. Let my perfect peace calm you in every circumstance, and give you courage and strength for every challenge.
John 14:26 AMP

You have peace with God, now have peace with yourself, stop believing lies, and condemning yourself, and worrying about what might never happen.
Tell the negative committee in your head to be quiet, stop talking about the problem, and start drawing on the peace of God, that passes all understanding.
Choose his perfect peace today.

When peace like a river, attendeth my way,
When sorrows like sea billows roll
Whatever my lot, thou hast taught me to say
It is well, it is well, with my soul
Peace like a river
Horatio Gates Spafford (1873)

Peace is not the absence of trouble but the presence of Christ
Sheila Walsh

I Choose Patience

I waited patiently for the Lord
Psalm 40:1

Patience is the fourth quality mentioned of the fruit of the Spirit, and it has been described as the capacity to accept, and tolerate delay, trouble, or suffering, without getting angry, upset, or impatient.

God is patient with us, he shows us this in, Romans 2:4 and 2 Peter 3:9.

He expects us to wait for him to act on our behalf without complaining. Our world is full of instant gratification, from the drive thru, to the information we require online, if you want it, you can have it now.

God is in charge but he is not in a hurry.
Dr Bill Pritchard.

Let patience be an attitude you choose, to embrace in your life today. Maybe a person at work is irritating you, or you are going through a trial, or you have prayed for an unsaved loved one for many years, and there seems to be no change. God uses all these things to develop, and perfect our character. If God can be patient with us, we can be patient with others.

If you need more patience today, it is yours, just ask the Holy Spirit to help you right now.

But let patience have its perfect work, that you may be perfect and complete, lacking nothing.
James 1:4

Personal reflections

....
....
....
....
....
....
....
....
....
....
....
....
....
....
....
....
....
....
....

I Choose Kindness

And be kind to one another, tender-hearted, forgiving one another, even as God in Christ forgave you.
Ephesians 4:32

Every day we have opportunities to show kindness to others, whether it is at home, at church, in the workplace, kindness is love in action.

Kindness is the opposite of selfishness, and stinginess, it is having a caring compassion, not just for nice people, but all people. It is not easy to be kind to those who have hurt you, or offended you, or someone who has no relevance in your life, but so often these are the types of people the Holy Spirit prompts us to reach.

We have to practice being kind, it is a daily choice we make.

Colossians 3:12 says, put on kindness, in other words you have to intentionally do it, because sometimes being kind is the last thing on our minds.

God wants to cultivate an attitude of kindness in us all, which shows a genuine interest in the welfare of others. I am sure we can all improve on how we treat others, and how we show kindness to those in our world, so let's make a commitment today, to be kind.

Kindness makes us a better person, I remember the first time myself, and my wife, went to Canada, we met a lady who knew our family for many years, as we left our meeting, she said, "Next time you come to Canada, please come and stay at our house." That was four years ago, and since then both her, and her daughter, have provided a home for us to stay in, for the time we spend in Canada. The family have shown great kindness, and exceptional generosity, beyond what we could ask, think, or imagine.

Maybe today you can be a listening ear, buy someone a coffee, or take a food parcel to somebody in need, whatever God prompts you to do, be kind, it is challenging but totally fulfilling.

You can't love God without being kind to those he loves
Bob Gass

Personal reflections

....
....
....
....
....
....
....
....
....

I Choose Goodness

Taste and see that the Lord is good
Psalm 34:8

*Oh how great is your goodness, which you have laid up
for those who fear you, which you have prepared for
those who trust in you*
Psalm 31:19

God is good all the time, and all the time, God is good, this is a saying I have declared for many years, and it is definitely true. God, is a good God, and he only does, what is good.

Goodness is one of the attributes of God, it is his nature, and character, and it is what he specialises in.

In the beginning when God created the heavens, and the earth, he declared everything he created was good, Genesis 1:4-18.

Realise today that you are special, and eternally valuable to your father in heaven, be expectant to see good things happen in your life today.

For the Lord God is a sun and shield, the Lord will give grace and glory, no good thing will he withhold, from those who walk uprightly
Psalm 84:11

If we are living right before God, we need to stop expecting bad things to happen all the time, we are to believe like David did, that goodness, and mercy, will follow me all the days, of my life, Psalm 23:6.

We are recipients of his goodness, because the Holy Spirit is living within us, Jesus went about doing good, and healing all who were oppressed by the devil.

The fruit of goodness is doing what is good, beneficial, and right, towards others, not manipulating people, or using them for our own personal gain.

Today, choose goodness.

Be good, do good, feel good
anonymous

Personal reflections

....

....

....

....

....

....

....

....

....

I Choose Faithfulness

To the saints who are in Ephesus and faithful in Christ Jesus
Ephesians 1:1

God is faithful, we cannot deny it, it is a part of his unchanging character, when we are faithless, he is faithful. When everyone walked out of your world, God was still there, he said, "He will never leave you, or forsake you." From the breaking of dawn, to the moment you lay your head to rest, God, is a faithful God.

Times, and seasons of life, may come, and go, but our faithful God is always exactly the same.

The popular hymn declares, great is thy faithfulness, o God my father, there is no shadow of turning with thee.

As God is faithful, we also must be faithful, and if we can become faithful, and trustworthy in the little, he will entrust us with much.

King David started out as a shepherd, Elisha a farmer and Peter a fisherman, these people were all called to do great things for God, but they were as faithful in serving God when they were unknown, as they were, when they were famous.

When it comes to serving God, and others, set your heart on being faithful, and not prominent. Psalm 75:6-7 says, promotion comes from the

Lord, so do not try to promote yourself, let God do that, just concentrate on being faithful, and trustworthy, with whatever he has placed in your life to do now.

Myself, and my wife, Anna, for many years had a catering business, which was successful, but hard work, we would start early, and finish late, and for that appointed season of our lives, it was what God had called, and anointed us to do. Our dream was to be in full-time ministry, but we kept running the business until God released us into ministry. The day came when we sold the business, and entered into full-time ministry, not just because it was our calling, but also because we were faithful, with the business he had instructed us to manage.

The same principle is true for you, be faithful, do not quit, keep on serving, God rewards faithful service.

He who is faithful in what is least is faithful also in much
Luke 16:10

Personal reflections

....
....
....
....
....

I Choose Gentleness

Be peaceable, gentle, showing all humility to all men
Titus 3:2

Take My yoke upon you and learn from Me, for I am
gentle and lowly in heart, and you will find rest for your
souls.
Matthew 11:29

Gentleness, it is something that Jesus said we could learn from him, it also should be a fruit of our Christian living. Being gentle means having a temperament that is kind, mild-mannered, polite, and having a humility in our dealings with people.

One of the meanings of the word gentleness, is meekness, and meekness should never be interpreted as weakness. Moses, was the meekest man on the face of the earth, yet he boldly stood before Pharaoh.

Jesus said, "I am gentle, and lowly of heart, he was meek, but he was certainly not weak.

One day he took a whip, and went through the temple, to remove everyone who was practicing wickedness in the Lord's house, he was not weak, he was meek.

Gentleness, or meekness, can be interpreted as power under control, it is the opposite of being proud, arrogant, blunt, or having an explosive temper.

Psalm 37:11 says, "The meek shall inherit the earth." Meekness is a character trait that God loves.

I remember years ago, a man coming to my dad's house, and accusing him of something he had not done. The man was shouting, and pointing his finger at my father, and once the man had finished speaking, dad said, "Clearly you are very angry about this issue, but that was not me."

My father did not raise his voice, and he did not carry any offence. A few weeks later, the man returned to our house, to apologise to dad, and said that he was completely in the wrong.

A gentle answer turns away wrath, but a harsh word stirs up answer.
Proverbs 15:1

Maybe you struggle with anger issues, or when you talk to others, your like a bull in a china shop, ask the Holy Spirit to help you change today, choose gentleness.

"I choose gentleness... Nothing is won by force. I choose to be gentle. If I raise my voice may it be only in praise. If I clench my fist, may it be only in prayer. If I make a demand, may it be only of myself."
Max Lucado

I Choose Self-Control

A person without self-control is like a city with broken walls.
Proverbs 25:28 ESV

From ancient history we can see that walls were built to defend and fortify cities, they kept the residents safe, and the enemies out. When there are no walls to a city anything can get in or out.
Self-control, is like a spiritual wall, that protects us, it gives us the power to restrain from doing what is wrong, and choosing what is right, and pleasing to God. If we want to rule and reign in life, we have to first learn to rule ourselves.
All of us at different points in our lives, face internal battles, but we can win, through the power of the Spirit.
Paul said that we could do all things through Christ who strengthens us, which means we have the ability to change, and to live a victorious life.
Maybe today your weakness is food, drink, anger, gossip, social media, or sexual addiction, whatever it is, realise you can resist, every temptation, and conquer through Christ Jesus.
Ask God to help you today, in your time of prayer say, heavenly father I choose self-control.

You are more than the sum total of your feelings and perfectly capable of that little gift from Jesus called self-control
Lysa Terkeurst

Personal reflections

....

....

....

....

....

....

....

....

....

....

....

....

....

....

....

....

....

....

....

....

Grace

That in the ages to come He might show the exceeding riches of His grace in His kindness toward us in Christ Jesus. For by grace you have been saved through faith, and that not of yourselves; it is the gift of God.
Ephesians 2:7-8

God, in his kindness has saved us by his grace, it is a gift from God, there will never be a moment in all eternity when you, and I, will not know his grace, for as the bible says, we stand in the grace of God.

Grace is more than we deserve, and greater than we could imagine, grace, is more than enough for anything we face in life.

Grace, has been defined as the unearned, unmerited, undeserved favour of God which is shown towards us.

We cannot earn it, we do not deserve it, but we receive it, freely through Jesus.

It is not based on who you are, it is based on who God is. He is a God of Grace, and he always promises you grace.

Every time the apostle Paul wrote a letter to the churches he worked with, he started, and ended it by saying, "Grace to you, and peace from God, our Father, and the Lord Jesus Christ."

From the beginning of our lives, to the end of them, there is never a shortage of grace, it is always freely available to us.

Maybe you are thinking today about wasted years, poor choices in life, maybe the mess you find yourself in now, God answers and says, "My grace is sufficient for you, my power is perfected in your weakness," his answer for your need, is the provision of his grace.

His grace, gives you the power to endure, and overcome anything you face in your life.

Get saturated afresh in the grace of God, ask and receive of his grace today.

Personal reflections

....
....
....
....
....
....
....
....
....
....
....
....
....

Gods Favour is with You

To proclaim the year of the Lords favor
Luke 4:19 NIV

You will arise and have mercy on Zion; For the time to
favor her, Yes, the set time, has come.
Psalms 102:13

Jesus came to declare, that this is the year of the Lords favour, so we can confidently believe, that this is our set time, to see an intervention of the favour of God. Whether you realise it or not, you are highly favoured by God. Divine favour is God's approval, and his exceptional kindness towards you, it also means he will bless the work of your hands, and offer you advantages, because you are his child.

For the Lord God is a sun and shield; the Lord bestows
favor and honor. No good thing does he withhold from
those who walk uprightly.
Psalm 84:11

Divine favour, releases provision for the people of God, which is not based on luck, or chance, but Gods goodness towards us.
Psalm 35 says, "God delights in the prosperity of his servants," he promises to meet all your needs, according to his riches in Christ Jesus.

God wants you to be successful, and know his blessings, in all areas of your life.

Surely, Lord, you bless the righteous; you surround them with your favor as with a shield.
Psalm 5:12 NIV

A shield is not an offensive weapon, but a defensive weapon, it defends us from attack.
God promises to protect us from the attacks of the enemy, his favour is like a spiritual shield surrounding us. Do not worry about your health, or be fearful for your future, because God promises protection for his people.
If you are unsure about this, read Psalm 91, and remind yourself, that every promise in that Psalm, is for you.

Personal reflections

....
....
....
....
....
....
....
....
....
....

Be Content

"Not that I speak in regard to need, for I have learned in whatever state I am, to be content."
Philippians 4:11

Contentment isn't something you find at a particular destination, it's something you practice every day on your way to it. And even if you miss the right path from time to time, you still enjoy the scenery along the detour.
Bob Gass

Paul learnt that whatever season of life he was in, he would be content. Contentment is an attitude we can have, that it is not governed by external circumstances. Paul was joyful in jail, and content, because he knew God was in charge, and God was still in control of his destiny.

We can also live like Paul, instead of grumbling, and carrying disappointment, or feeling frustrated, because things are not changing as quick as we want them to, we can ask God to help us be content.

One dictionary defines contentment as, being happy and satisfied with your life, satisfied and willing to accept a situation, until God moves on your behalf. It is the assurance that God will work all things together, for your good.

I don't think contentment comes naturally, we don't grasp it through a sermon, or a text book, I believe we learn it through the lessons of life, through circumstances we face, where we choose to endure, and trust in God.

Make the decision not to get upset, or despondent today, with where your life is at, your steps have been ordered by God.

So shake off any complacency in your life.

Until God opens the next door, praise him in the hallway
Unknown

Now godliness with contentment is great gain.
1 Timothy 6:6

Personal reflections

....
....
....
....
....
....
....
....
....
....
....
....

Knowing God's Will

And do not be conformed to this world, but be transformed by the renewing of your mind, that you may prove what is that good and acceptable and perfect will of God.
Romans 12:2

God does not play games with your life, his will is not a mystery, and he certainly does not want you to think you have to live in confusion, about your destiny. Unfortunately, many people struggle with not knowing what God wants them to do with their life, or at times they just don't know how to make the right choice.

I believe we can search, and find the answers in God's word.

The word of God, is the will of God, it renews our minds, when we study the word, and allow its truths to transform us, we can know Gods perfect will.

I opened a bible recently and noticed in the back of the bible, a number of scripture verses with a future plan, for myself, and my wife Anna. The writing was dated eight years earlier, and I can say, everything we wrote down, God has brought it to pass. God revealed his will through his word, we believed it, and we have seen it happen.

But the Helper, the Holy Spirit, whom the Father will
send in my name, he will teach you all things and bring
to your remembrance all that I have said to you.
John 14:26

When the Spirit of truth comes, he will guide you into all
the truth, for he will not speak on his own authority, but
whatever he hears he will speak, and he will declare to
you the things that are to come.
John 16:13

God reveals his will, through the Holy Spirit, Jesus said that he would send the helper, and he would show us things to come, our heavenly father does not want to keep us in the dark, or allow us to think that our future has to be shrouded in mystery. The Holy Spirit is here to help us make right choices in life, he teaches us, guides us, speaks to us, gives us peace and assurance, about the decisions we make.

It seemed good to the Holy Spirit and to us
Acts 15:28

God also uses people to confirm the will of God for your life, wisdom can be found through godly relationships that you have, a true friend will always be honest to tell you, not what you want to hear, but what you need to hear.
Many years ago, I got to know a family who were planning to move to Scotland, they had never

had a word about Scotland before, but a Christian had given them a word to move, and it was now becoming a pressure to them.

I remember sitting down with them and asking, if they ever had any desire to move to Scotland, they said no. I then asked if they had any peace, and they said no. After our chat they did not move to Scotland. God used me, to help them discern what was, and what wasn't, the will of God for their lives, we all need people like that in our world.

Personal reflections

....

....

....

....

....

....

....

....

....

....

....

....

....

....

....

Be Who God has Created You to Be

Gods amazing grace has made me who I am
1 Corinthians 15:10
The Passion Version

Be the best version of you, and don't try to be anyone else, you are unique, special to God, and fearfully and wonderfully made. You don't have to compare yourself to others, or feel pressurised to be someone you are not, God made you an original, and has a unique plan, that only you can fulfil. So let's stop feeling insecure, or trying to live up to false expectations we put on ourselves.

Today, is the day, to remind yourself what God thinks about you, and see yourself as God sees you. God uses imperfect people, but by his grace he makes us more like Jesus.

We are all eternally valuable, and loved by God, so today, let go of the internal baggage, that weighs down your soul, and ask the Holy Spirit to change you from the inside out.

Love God, but also learn to love yourself.

Wisdom

But the wisdom from above is always pure, filled with peace, considerate and teachable.
James 3:17
The Passion Translation

Success in life comes from experiencing and growing in wisdom, today we do not need earthly wisdom, we need the wisdom of God.

Wisdom, is a way God gives you divine common sense, it's also how he gives you understanding in what to do, wisdom is more than knowledge, knowledge will give you the facts, but wisdom will give you the solution.

For example, if I arrived in the UK for the first time, and needed to get to London, I would not be able to travel without understanding how to get to the destination, if someone gave me a road map, I would then have the facts, and see the full picture, then I would know how to get to my destination. That is what wisdom does, it brings a solution to your problems.

As believers we have the right and privilege to ask and then expect wisdom from God.

You will receive an impartation of the wisdom of God, when you ask in faith, this promise is for you.

*If any of you lacks wisdom, let him ask of God, who gives
to all liberally and without reproach, and it will be given
to him.*
James 1:5

Maybe you need answers, or have choices to
make, so draw on the wisdom of God today, it
will reveal the answers you need.

*That the God of our Lord Jesus Christ, the Father of
glory, may give to you the spirit of wisdom and revelation
in the knowledge of Him.*
Ephesians 1:17

Personal reflections

....
....
....
....
....
....
....
....
....
....
....
....
....
....

Kingdom Now

Your kingdom come.
Your will be done
On earth as it is in heaven.
Matthew 6:10

Jesus told us to pray, and believe, that his kingdom would come, on earth as it is in heaven. God's kingdom, is an everlasting kingdom, that will not be destroyed, it declares that God rules and reigns over everything.

His kingdom has come, and it has invaded planet earth, it will be fully seen, with the return of Jesus.

Our assignment today, is to bring his rule, and authority into our everyday life, and to take dominion over the unseen forces of darkness.

His kingdom gives us power, and authority, to enforce the will of the father, Jesus said, "Whatever we bind on earth is bound in heaven, whatever we loose on earth is loosed in heaven."

Everyday, we have the opportunity to release the authority, and power of heaven, because through Jesus we rule, and reign in life.

A few years ago a friend of mine, Trevor, was working on a building site, while he was working, his friend fell off the scaffold and split his head open on the ground. Immediately Trevor went over to him, and laid his hands on his head and commanded healing in Jesus name. The man was unconscious, but Trevor continued to pray, within a few minutes the bleeding had stopped, the man regained consciousness, and was completely healed. Trevor, took authority over the situation and commanded healing, in Jesus name, God's kingdom had come, and God's will had been done.

We also have to take authority over circumstances, and events that at times come crashing into our world.

Through prayer today, bind the powers of darkness that are attacking your life, take authority, and believe things will change, you are a child of the king.

Personal reflections

....

....

....

....

....

....

....

....

....

....

Faith Moves the Mountain

And Jesus replying said to them, have faith in God constantly. Truly I tell you, whoever says to this mountain be lifted up and thrown into the sea and does not doubt at all in his heart but believes that what he says will take place it will be done for him.
For this reason I am telling you, whatever you ask for in prayer, believe trust and be confident that it is granted to you and you will get it.
Mark 11:22-24 Amplified Version

Fight the good fight of faith
1 Timothy 6:12

If you have mountains, or obstacles that you are facing today, faith in God will move them.

Trust in God, puts the miracle into motion.

We have to walk by faith, and not by sight, we fight the good fight, of faith, because through Jesus, we win.

Please do not plead, or beg God, it never works, be confident, and speak the word to that situation, or obstacle.

Jesus said, "All things are possible to him who believes." The key is believing what the word of God says, about your circumstances. Throw off doubt and unbelief today, and choose to trust God.

Speak to your mountain, and it shall be moved.

Faith sees the invisible, believes the incredible, and receives the impossible
Corrie Ten Boom

Personal reflections

....
....
....
....
....
....
....
....
....
....
....
....
....
....
....
....
....
....
....
....
....
....

Above Every other Name

*Therefore God exalted him to the highest place
and gave him the name that is above every name,
that at the name of Jesus every knee should bow,
in heaven and on earth and under the earth,
and every tongue acknowledge that Jesus Christ is Lord,
to the glory of God the Father.
Phillipians 2:9-11*

Jesus, has been given the name, that is above every other name, and our saviour has been exalted, to the highest place in the universe.

The authority in that name, makes every other name bow, not only in the future but also in the present.

Cancer, arthritis, shame, or condemnation, whatever name seeks to attack and destroy our lives, is not greater than the name of Jesus.

Remember his name, is above every other name, and it has been given to us, to use in our lives too.

Jesus said twice in John 14:13, "That if we ask anything in his name he would do it." Therefore, we need to pray, and believe in his name, and results will follow.

I have seen countless miracles and answers to prayer, when I prayed and used the name of Jesus.

On one occasion, I sat with a couple that were told that they could not have children, the woman had a number of miscarriages, and the doctors said, it was impossible for them to have a child. We prayed together, and agreed in Jesus name, that a healthy child would be born, and believed that this was the will of God. Within two years she gave birth to a healthy baby girl, God hears, and answers prayer.

His name is our inheritance, and has greater power, than any problem.

Whatever you face right now, ask in his name, and it shall be done.

And whatever you ask in My name, that I will do, that the Father may be glorified in the Son. If you ask anything in My name, I will do it.
John 14:13

Personal reflections

....

....

....

....

....

....

....

....

....

You can Hear God

In the last days, God says,
I will pour out my Spirit on all people.
Your sons and daughters will prophesy,
your young men will see visions,
your old men will dream dreams.
Even on my servants, both men and women,
I will pour out my Spirit in those days,
and they will prophesy.
Acts 2:17-18

As Christians, our spiritual nature is prophetic, being a prophetic people means, that we can hear, and sense, in a variety of ways, how God is speaking to us. This may be through a still small voice, through a dream, or a vision, or a continuing burden we feel, whatever method God chooses, he wants to speak to you and speak through you.

We have to allow the Holy Spirit to teach us, and train us, to discern when God is speaking, not our emotions, or thoughts in our head, but the voice of God.

Jesus said, "My sheep hear my voice and they follow me.:

When I was a child my grand mother had a radio with a tuner, whenever the tuner was not on the channel properly, there was a distorted sound of white noise coming from it, I realised that I had to be sensitive with the tuner, and tune it into the right frequency, to find the radio channel, then I would have perfect sound.

Maybe there is a distortion in you hearing God at the moment, heaven might seem silent.

Well today, clear some things from your diary, draw near to God, and he will draw near to you.

By spending time in God's presence, praying in tongues, and worshipping God, we open ourselves up to hear his voice, with clarity.

I can say from experience, that when I give God first place in my life, and give him quality time, he speaks, and communicates with me, because my walk with him is based on relationship. My priority each day is spending time with God, which makes me sensitive to know when he is speaking. Expect the Holy Spirit to tune you into his frequency today, and prepare yourself to hear him speak.

Personal reflections

....
....
....
....
....
....
....
....

Healing Flows

Are you fed up with living with sickness
and disease?
Have you got questions about whether God
really heals today?

Healing Flows shows that God has already
revealed his will to us, in the Bible.
It will show you that God's will has always
been to heal us, from sickness, and disease.

As you read, I pray that the Holy Spirit,
will reveal the truth of God's word to you.

As you discover the miraculous power of
God to set you free from pain and sickness.

ISBN 978-1-326-73962-1

Soul control

We have been created to live in a physical body, but God also created us as spiritual beings.
Your mind, will, and emotions are as important as the body that surrounds them.

Maybe you are one of the countless people, who suffer from emotional scars, rollercoaster moods, or negative mindsets. Do you long for a transformation, and a change in your thought life?

If that is the case, Soul Control will help, and instruct you to live the abundant life God has intended. The greatest battles we face are not external, but internal.

A healthy soul creates a healthy life.

ISBN 978-0-244-10818-2

Salvation Prayer

Maybe through reading this book, you have realised you need a real experience with God.
Below are some simple steps to receiving Jesus Christ, as your Lord and Saviour.

Prayer

God desires a relationship with us. Through prayer, we communicate with the one who knows us completely, and loves us perfectly.
Prayer, is a two-way communication where we not only talk to him, but he also speaks to us.

God Loves You

God loves you and wants you to know him, so he can fill you with peace, and give you eternal life forever.
God loved the people of this world so much, that he gave his only son, so that everyone who has faith in him, will have eternal life and never die.
Jesus said, "I came so that everyone would have life, and have it in its fullest."

We are Separated from God

All of us have sinned and fallen short of God's holiness. Sin is choosing to say, or do, or think things that are against Gods will. The result of

unforgiven sin is death. Gods gift is eternal life, given by Jesus Christ our Lord.
There is only one way to reach God.

Jesus Christ Died for our Sins
Jesus Christ is God's Son, he is the only one who can bring us back to God. Jesus died on the cross, and rose from the grave. He paid the penalty for our sin, and bridged the gap between God, and people.
There is only one God, Christ Jesus is the only one who can bring us back to God. Christ died once for our sins. An innocent person died for those who are guilty.
Christ did this to bring you to God.
God has provided the only way, and we must make the choice.

We Must Receive Christ
We must trust Jesus Christ to forgive our sins, and receive him as our Lord, and Saviour.
As many as received him, to them he gave the right to become children of God.

Would you like to give your life to Jesus Christ right now?

If so, you can pray the following prayer, and accept Jesus as your Saviour:

Non-Governmental Public Action

Series Editor: **Jude Howell**, Professor and Director of the Centre for Civil Society, London School of Economics and Political Science, UK

Non-governmental public action (NGPA) by and for disadvantaged and marginalised people has become increasingly significant over the past two decades. This new book series is designed to make a fresh and original contribution to the understanding of NGPA. It presents the findings of innovative and policy-relevant research carried out by established and new scholars working in collaboration with researchers across the world. It is international in scope and includes both theoretical and empirical work.

The series marks a departure from previous studies in this area in at least two important respects. First, it goes beyond a singular focus on developmental NGOs or the voluntary sector to include a range of non-governmental public actors, such as advocacy networks, campaigns and coalitions, trades unions, peace groups, rights-based groups, cooperatives and social movements. Second, it is innovative in stimulating a new approach to international comparative research that promotes comparison of the so-called developing world with the so-called developed world, thereby querying the conceptual utility and relevance of categories such as North and South.

Titles include:

Barbara Bompani and Maria Frahm-Arp (*editors*)
DEVELOPMENT AND POLITICS FROM BELOW
Exploring Religious Spaces in the African State

Dena Freeman (*editor*)
PENTECOSTALISM AND DEVELOPMENT
Churches, NGOs and Social Change in Africa

Jude Howell and Jeremy Lind
COUNTER-TERRORISM, AID AND CIVIL SOCIETY
Before and After the War on Terror

Jenny Pearce (*editor*)
PARTICIPATION AND DEMOCRACY IN THE TWENTY-FIRST CENTURY

Tim Pringle and Simon Clarke
THE CHALLENGE OF TRANSITION
Trade Unions in Russia, China and Vietnam

Andrew Wells-Dang
CIVIL SOCIETY NETWORKS IN CHINA AND VIETNAM
Informal Pathbreakers in Health and the Environment

Thomas Yarrow
DEVELOPMENT BEYOND POLITICS
Aid, Activism and NGOs in Ghana

Non-Governmental Public Action Series
Series Standing Order ISBN 978-0-230-22939-6 (hardback) and
978-0-230-22940-2 (paperback)
(*outside North America only*)

You can receive future titles in this series as they are published by placing a standing order. Please contact your bookseller or, in case of difficulty, write to us at the address below with your name and address, the title of the series and the ISBN quoted above.

Customer Services Department, Macmillan Distribution Ltd, Houndmills, Basingstoke, Hampshire RG21 6XS, England

---

Also by Dena Freeman

INITIATING CHANGE IN HIGHLAND ETHIOPIA: Causes and Consequences of Cultural Transformation

PERIPHERAL PEOPLE: The Excluded Minorities of Ethiopia (*edited with Alula Pankhurst*)

Pentecostalism and Development

Churches, NGOs and Social Change in Africa

Edited by

Dena Freeman

First published 2012 by
PALGRAVE MACMILLAN

Palgrave Macmillan in the UK is an imprint of Macmillan Publishers Limited, registered in England, company number 785998, of Houndmills, Basingstoke, Hampshire RG21 6XS.

Palgrave Macmillan in the US is a division of St Martin's Press LLC, 175 Fifth Avenue, New York, NY 10010.

Palgrave Macmillan is the global academic imprint of the above companies and has companies and representatives throughout the world.

Palgrave® and Macmillan® are registered trademarks in the United States, the United Kingdom, Europe and other countries.

ISBN 978–1–137–01724–6

This book is printed on paper suitable for recycling and made from fully managed and sustained forest sources. Logging, pulping and manufacturing processes are expected to conform to the environmental regulations of the country of origin.

A catalogue record for this book is available from the British Library.

A catalog record for this book is available from the Library of Congress.

10 9 8 7 6 5 4 3 2 1
21 20 19 18 17 16 15 14 13 12

Printed and bound in the United States of America

Contents

Foreword

I am delighted to have been invited to write a foreword to this exciting book, more especially since my own work in rural Zambia in the 1960s,[1] and the re-study by Han Seur in the 1980s,[2] highlighted the role that religious beliefs and practices played in shaping local social change and development. In that particular case, it was the Jehovah's Witnesses who were committed to building the 'New Kingdom on Earth' which 'the righteous ones' would inherit – not unlike the expectations of the Pentecostals who are the focus of this book.

In more recent years we have witnessed a renewed interest in questions of religiosity and its role in the making of 'modern' society. Early in the 2000s a network of development institutions, including the World Bank, several national aid programmes and key non-governmental organisations (NGOs), such as Oxfam, Care, Save the Children, Caritas and Tearfund, initiated discussions with leaders of various world faiths and religious organisations with a view to exploring common ground between 'secular' and 'faith-based' modes of development thinking and practice. A key forum for these discussions has been the World Faiths Development Dialogue, whose principal concerns are to link issues of material and spiritual wellbeing to questions of development and poverty, and to encourage the sharing of perspectives between persons of different religious conviction. These issues – in part prompted by the problems of an increasingly polarised politico-religious world – present a major challenge to all those involved in development work.

Yet, ten years on, there remain serious gaps in our understanding of how precisely people's religious beliefs, values and practices underpin, supplement, challenge or redesign state or international models of development. 'Development', of course, is a field of study and practice in which it is difficult to judge what works and what does not, since it is composed of a differentiated set of value judgements, practices and justifications advanced by a heterogeneous set of social actors who often espouse conflicting or contradictory values, reasoning and interests. The process of intervention itself is usually a messy business, since defined goals (for one reason or another) are hardly ever effectively achieved as intended, in part because of unpredictable conditions, but mostly

because they are not shared by the targeted beneficiaries, nor supported by other key players in the field.

Against this backdrop, this book provides an in-depth understanding of the interplay between Pentecostalist beliefs, socio-economic conditions and future ambitions of committed believers in several regions of Africa. A dominant theme is the rise, impact and reshaping of African Pentecostal churches in the face of the global propagation of neoliberalism and the 'rolling back' of the nation state. But rather than giving prominence to how external development institutions engage with and seek to incorporate religious bodies into their plans for development, the greater part of the contributions explores the intermingling of spiritual and material objectives and ontologies from the standpoint of the churches and their devotees, thus highlighting how congregations and church leaders create space for the pursuit of their own 'development' goals and initiatives.

From the early 1980s a new wave of Pentecostal movements swept across the African continent, promoting new conceptions of belief, personhood, salvation, emotion and ambition that contrasted markedly with existing mainstream Protestant churches and Catholic orders. Their brand of Christianity was far removed from that of the Calvinists and the 'this-worldly asceticism' described by Max Weber as the first step towards the eventual 'disenchantment' of the world. The arrival of this new Pentecostalism brought with it a strong evangelical style associated with the need to be 'born again' into the Christian faith and immersed in its spiritual and codified morality. Accordingly, the everyday lives of these new Pentecostals were to be congruent with Christian values and guided by a strong sense of there being no sharp line between the sacred and the secular. In similar vein, and running counter to most African family systems, the Pentecostals were encouraged to accord women significant space and status to develop their own skills and aspirations so that they might also, like their male counterparts, achieve positions of responsibility within the church as well as within wider organisational networks, including key NGOs and government bodies. Thus, as elucidated in several of the chapters, we encounter cases of women from humble origins eventually moving into key positions in the church and from there to national and international bodies devoted to promoting women's affairs that often address the problems of poorer families or those suffering from AIDS or other debilitating illnesses. In Kenya, for example, there exist a number of female-led and -founded Pentecostal and charismatic churches (and spin-off organisations) where members are able to develop their own relations with the staff of NGOs that fund

gender-related programmes. Through such activities they often build contacts with government officers and party political personnel who need to maintain strong connections with the public at large.

This book also represents a major contribution to our understanding of processes of religiosity in the context of the uncertainties and crises of present day social, economic and political life. It focuses especially on the congruence between neoliberalism and the Pentecostalist drive towards personal salvation and the creation of new 'godly' arenas of influence and power. It is in this context, where the state scales down its responsibility for human welfare and the poorer sectors that faith-based initiatives – in this instance undertaken by Pentecostalist organisations – become critically important, and more especially so given the fragile nature of present day post-colonial structures in much of the African continent. A further implication of this fragility is that the majority of African countries are highly dependent on the largesse of international aid programmes. Given these conditions, it is no surprise that much of the discourse articulated among African populations is directed towards issues that identify the forces of divine destiny in human affairs, in particular the threats posed by evil spirits in everyday life. In several cases this is matched by the tendency of certain revivalist movements to seek their own regimes of power and enrichment and thus institute more autonomous forms of sovereignty both within the nation state or vis-à-vis well-funded NGOs, and in some cases transnationally through the networks of fellow Pentecostal believers. Thus, as well as stressing the healing process and deliverance from destructive forces, many of these Pentecostal churches provide innovative ways of responding to prevailing economic conditions and, in some cases, they resort to certain modes of political activism. An added dimension here, of course, is the socio-economic composition of specific church congregations, whose membership varies in terms of social status, household assets and income, and educational levels. Thus, at one end of the scale we encounter local Pentecostal congregations that cater primarily to relatively poor farming households or the poorer sections of the urban working classes, while at the other end we encounter upwardly mobile middle-class elements with a relative degree of affluence.

On a more analytical level, the ethnographic case study material, richly explored in this volume, provides a fruitful input into current debates about how to theorise and develop methodologies for elucidating contemporary modes of religiosity in an 'ultra-modern' world where religion is paradoxically both 'significant and insignificant'.[3] Indeed

one might argue, as many of the chapters do, that the analytic distinction between religion and development collapses in the study of Pentecostal movements since the tools for both personal development and economic growth are given by the churches themselves, and that by following religious principles there is a way of addressing misfortune of various kinds – medical or physical, financial or social.

This collection points the way to a fuller understanding of how faith-based groups, and their beliefs and practices concerning 'the good society', shape socio-economic behaviour and organising practices, and vice versa. Linked to this are important questions concerning how and to what extent faith-related components facilitate and/or inhibit the mobilisation, accumulation and redistribution of resources and opportunities, as well as how they promulgate new forms of collective action. Adopting an ethnographic approach allows us to understand better the encounters, negotiations and accommodations that take place between and within different faith groups in different development scenarios. The intricacies and complexities involved are many and require detailed comparative research, and not merely from the standpoint of their theologies and ethics. This book then is a must for all those working within the field of development.

Norman Long
Professor Emeritus
Department of Sociology of Development
Wageningen University

Notes

1. Long, Norman. 1968. *Social Change and the Individual*. Manchester: Manchester University Press.
2. Seur, Han. 1992. Sowing the Good Seed. PhD Thesis, Wageningen University.
3. See Beckford, James and John Walliss. (Eds). 2006. *Theorising Religion: Classical and Contemporary Debates*. Aldershot: Ashgate.

Acknowledgements

This volume grew out of a conference which I organised in Jerusalem in January 2010, entitled 'Salvation, Transformation and Modernity in Africa: Development NGOs and Pentecostal Churches as Contemporary Agents of Change'. This sought to address key theoretical issues about development, globally driven social change and the role of religion, particularly Pentecostal Christianity, in society during times of change. All of the chapters in this book started as presentations at this conference, with the exception of that by James H. Smith, which was added at a later date. It has been a pleasure to work with all the contributors and I thank them for their hard work and patience throughout the rounds of editing and revision.

The project was an initiative of the Van Leer Jerusalem Institute and I would like to express my sincere gratitude to them for hosting, funding and providing invaluable logistical support for the conference. Many thanks in particular to Prof. Gabriel Motzkin, Director of the Institute, Shulamit Laron, Director of Public Events, and Dr Tal Kohavi, Director of Publications. Without their support the conference would not have been possible. I would also like to thank the Department of Sociology and Anthropology at the Hebrew University of Jerusalem, where I was then a Lecturer, for giving me the opportunity to organise the event. And I extend my great appreciation to Prof. Norman Long for generously writing the foreword to the volume, and to Christina Brian at Palgrave Macmillan for her support and encouragement throughout the production process.

The original conference was held in honour of Prof. Shmuel Noah Eisenstadt, Israel's leading sociologist and a major international theorist of processes of modernisation and religious change (among many other things). He was a senior fellow at the Van Leer Jerusalem Institute for over 40 years and we were privileged to have his presence at the conference. His provocative questions and comments have influenced much of the analysis in this book. Sadly, he passed away shortly after the conference, and this book is dedicated to his memory.

Contributors

Jean Comaroff is Bernard E. and Ellen C. Sunny Distinguished Service Professor of Anthropology at the University of Chicago, and was founding director of the Chicago Center for Contemporary Theory, USA. She is also an honorary professor at the University of Cape Town, South Africa. Her scholarly work, much of it in collaboration with John L. Comaroff, has been primarily concerned with society and history in southern Africa, with particular focus on religion, medicine and body politics; capitalism and its cultural mediations; and crime and the politics of democratisation. Her recent publications include *Ethnicity, Inc.* (2009) and *Theory from the South, or How Europe Is Evolving toward Africa* (2011).

Dena Freeman is Lecturer in the Department of Anthropology, University College, London, UK. Her current work focuses on Pentecostalism, development and social change in Ethiopia, building on her earlier research on ritual and political life in a traditional rural community. She is the author of *Initiating Change in Highland Ethiopia: Causes and Consequences of Cultural Transformation* (2002), and co-editor, with Alula Pankhurst, of *Peripheral People: The Excluded Minorities of Ethiopia* (2003). She is currently exploring how NGOs engage with the market and working on a book about values and value chains.

Päivi Hasu is Lecturer at the University of Jyväskylä, Finland, and currently holds an Academy of Finland Research Fellowship with the research project 'Religion and Globalization: Evangelical Christianity and Development in Africa' in the Department of Political and Economic Studies, University of Helsinki. She has previously worked on historical anthropology, ritual and forms of Christianity in Tanzania.

Ben Jones is Lecturer in the School of International Development at the University of East Anglia, UK. His work focuses on the Teso region of eastern Uganda. He is the author of *Beyond the State in Rural Uganda* (2009), which was awarded the Elliott P. Skinner prize by the American Anthropological Association. His current research looks at the relationship between a newspaper, the *Guardian*, and a

development NGO, AMREF, in implementing a development project in northern Teso.

Damaris Parsitau is Lecturer in African Christianities at Egerton University, Kenya. Her current research focuses on Christian–Muslim relations, faith-based humanitarianism, and the impact of post-election violence on faith-based organisations and women in Kenya. She is widely published in reputable books and journals and has held visiting research fellowships at the universities of Cambridge and Edinburgh.

Charles Piot is Professor of Cultural Anthropology at Duke University, North Carolina, USA, where he also has a joint appointment in African and African American studies. His recent book, *Nostalgia for the Future: West Africa after the Cold War* (2010), explores shifts in Togolese political culture during the 1990s, a time when the NGOs and charismatic churches took over the biopolitical, filling the gap left by the withdrawal of the state from social and developmental terrains. His new project is on the gamesmanship of Togolese applying for the US diversity lottery.

James H. Smith is Associate Professor of Socio-Cultural Anthropology at the University of California, Davis, USA. He has conducted extensive research projects in Kenya on local understandings of development, neotraditionalism and the relationships among religion, witchcraft and development. More recently he has been conducting research on coltan mining and the digital age in the Eastern Democratic Republic of Congo. He is the author of *Bewitching Development: Witchcraft and the Reinvention of Development in Neoliberal Kenya* (2008) and is co-editor, with Rosalind Hackett, of *Displacing the State: Religion and Conflict in Neoliberal Africa* (2011).

Rijk van Dijk is an anthropologist working at the African Studies Centre, Leiden, the Netherlands. He has done extensive research and published on the rise of Pentecostal movements in urban areas of Malawi, Ghana and Botswana. He is the author of *Young Malawian Puritans* (1993) and has co-edited seven books. His current research deals with Pentecostal engagements with the domains of sexuality and HIV/AIDS in Botswana in relation to economic development and prosperity. He is also Chair of the International Research Network on Religion and AIDS in Africa and Editor-in-chief of *African Diaspora: A Journal of Transnational Africa in a Global World*.

1

The Pentecostal Ethic and the Spirit of Development

Dena Freeman

The practice and discipline of development was founded on the belief that religion was not important to development processes.[1] As societies developed and modernised, it was assumed that they would also undergo a process of secularisation. The irrelevance of religion for development is a cornerstone of 'modernisation theory', with its narrow focus on economic growth, which dominated development theory and practice from the 1950s to the 1980s (Deneulin & Rakodi 2011: 46). From the 1980s onwards there has been a broadening of scope within development studies, with the expansion of work on the multi-dimensional nature of poverty (e.g. Kakwani & Silber 2007) and the theoretical reorientation of development's aims from economic growth to more holistic concerns for human wellbeing and environmental sustainability – first through the livelihoods approach in the 1980s (e.g. Chambers & Conway 1991, Scoones 1998), and then in Amatya Sen's human development approach in the 1990s (Alkire 2005, Sen 1999), and more recently with interest in development and wellbeing (Gough & McGregor 2007). During the progression through these different approaches there has been increasing appreciation for the importance of non-material matters – such as beliefs, values and morality – in the development process (e.g. Goulet 1997). This has led in recent years to a return to the question of religion and a huge surge of interest in the role of religion in development (Berger 2004, 2009, Deneulin 2009, Deneulin & Rakodi 2011, Goody 2003, Rakodi 2007, Selinger 2004, Ter Haar & Ellis 2006, Tomalin 2008, Ver Beek 2002). This book seeks to make a contribution to this new field by exploring the developmental consequences of Pentecostal Christianity in contemporary Africa.

There has, of course, long been a connection between religion and development, as evinced in the twin activities of colonialism and

1

missionisation. And religious institutions are, of course, a key part of civil society, being the most prevalent form of associational life in Africa today (Gifford 1994: 533). Nevertheless, two recent changes in the religious and development landscapes are forcing scholars to assess their current interconnections more closely. First, alongside the rise of non-governmental organisations (NGOs) and their increasing role as the implementers of secular development interventions, there has been a recent blurring of the distinction between church and NGO, as many mainline churches established development wings following the expanded flow of aid money to civil society organisations in the 1980s and 1990s (see below). This 'NGO-isation' of the mainline churches (Gifford 1994: 521) has been matched by a parallel growth in faith-based organisations (FBOs) not necessarily directly linked to any particular church or mosque, but inspired by religious teachings and approaches. Noting the significance of these trends, there have been a growing number of studies of faith-based Christian and Muslim NGOs (Dicklitch & Rice 2004, Hefferan 2007, Kaag 2008, McDonic 2004), including some excellent ethnographic accounts (Bornstein 2005, De Temple 2006, Kamsteeg 1998), as well as discussions of donor experiences and strategies for engaging with this type of development organisation (Benedetti 2006, Clarke 2006, Marshall & Van Saanen 2007).

Second, there has been a massive 'Pentecostal explosion' that has radically altered the religious landscape in much of the developing world. Millions of people in Africa have joined Pentecostal churches in the past 30 years. This movement does not separate religion from development, and for the most part does not set up development wings or FBOs. It does, however, bring with it a radically new conception of development and broadcasts it to its followers with tremendous energy and efficiency. African Pentecostals see development in terms of 'What God wants for Africa' and most recently in terms of the gospel of prosperity. What God wants for Africa, they claim, is a continent blessed with health, wealth and abundance, where people work hard, pray hard and live upright moral lives. What the devil wants for Africa, however, is underdevelopment, poverty and suffering. And thus, along with hard work, development requires a 'war against the demons', a notion that captures hearts and minds much more energetically than the NGOs' rhetoric of the 'war against poverty'. This religious view of development is made explicit in sermons, preaching and religious literature, and it is broadcast to followers, and indeed many others across the continent, through films and teleserials made by Pentecostals (Pype 2009).

It is this second change in the religious and development landscape that is the subject of this book. Our first aim is to explore the internal

model of 'development' that drives Pentecostal organisations and to assess the implications of their activities for broader development goals. Second, we also set out to compare Pentecostal churches and secular NGOs as different types of contemporary development agent and to explore the different ways in which they operate and the different ways in which they bring about change in Africa. At the heart of our enquiry in this book is an exploration of processes of individual and social change, and their relevance to understandings of the successes and failures of development.

This introduction first describes the context of post-1980s Africa, providing the background contextualisation within which the massive rise of both development NGOs and Pentecostal churches must be understood. It then discusses the transition from state-led development to development-by-NGO, and critiques the mode of operation of NGOs and their effectiveness as agents of change. The next section considers the rise of the Pentecostal churches and provides an overview of the way in which they engage with people and reformulate subjectivities, moralities and social relationships. The following section turns to a discussion of Max Weber's *Protestant Ethic and the Spirit of Capitalism* (2008 [1904–1905]), arguably the most important study of subjectivity and economic change in the modern social sciences, and considers its relevance to the contemporary situation of the Pentecostal ethic and the spirit of development in Africa. Finally, before outlining the subsequent chapters, this introductory chapter closes with a perhaps somewhat surprising conclusion: that Pentecostal churches are often rather more effective change agents than are development NGOs. This is because they focus on some key aspects of change that secular NGOs continue to ignore – they are exceptionally effective at bringing about personal transformation and empowerment, they provide the moral legitimacy for a set of behaviour changes that would otherwise clash with local values, and they radically reconstruct families and communities to support these new values and new behaviours. Without these types of social change, I argue, it is difficult for economic change and development to take place.

Africa since 1980: debt crisis, structural adjustment and neoliberalism

In the 1980s Africa started a transition into a new era. After the initial enthusiasm following independence in the 1960s and the modest successes achieved by predominantly socialist governments in the first decade of post-colonial reality, most African countries took loans in

the 1970s to fund large infrastructural projects in the quest to develop their countries. By the 1980s, with high oil prices, rising inflation and collapsing commodity prices, these loans had spiralled into huge debts which jeopardised many African economies. The response was a policy of structural adjustment, instigated by the World Bank and the International Monetary Fund (IMF) and implemented by governments throughout Africa (and elsewhere). As is well known, structural adjustment programmes (SAPs) forced countries to liberalise and integrate their economies into the global economy (Curry 1997, Federici 2001, Walton & Seddon 1994). An emphasis was placed on private sector development, by lowering corporate taxes, reducing business regulation, devaluing the currency and encouraging the privatisation of state-owned enterprises. At the same time social spending was massively cut, with welfare programmes drastically reduced, subsidies and services cut to a minimum and the number of government workers slashed (Bond & Dor 2003: 1). The state was effectively 'rolled back' and reduced, while it was hoped that the market would expand and lead to the generation of wealth through business and enterprise.

The 'social costs' of adjustment were huge, and despite some recognition of this even by the World Bank and the IMF and talk of 'adjustment with a human face', there were very few examples of policies that effectively mitigated against them (Walton & Seddon 1994). Most people in most countries in Africa suffered a drastic fall in their material standard of living in the post-1980s era and poverty increased across the continent (Riddell 1992). In sub-Saharan Africa as a whole, per capita incomes dropped by 21 per cent in real terms between 1981 and 1989 (Manji & O'Coill 2002: 567). Prices of essential goods skyrocketed, incomes dwindled, jobs disappeared, services were cut and many people struggled to make ends meet (Ferguson 2006, Walton & Raggin 1990). The worsening conditions brought about by these austerity measures led to protests and 'IMF food riots' in many African countries (Bush 2010: 122, Logie & Woodroffe 1993: 43, Riddell 1992: 59, Simutanyi 1996: 827, Walton & Seddon 1994). It was at this time and in this context that the phenomenal growth of both NGOs and Pentecostal churches came about.

The rise of the NGOs

As international donors forced structural adjustment onto African governments, they also changed their way of offering development aid. As part of the so-called New Policy Agenda there was a drastic

reduction in foreign aid given directly to African governments as bilateral assistance, and a concomitant increase in the amount channelled through international and domestic NGOs (Edwards & Hulme 1996b: 961). This change in aid funding, combined with the new political space opened up by the weakening of the state, has led to what has been termed a 'global associational revolution' – an explosion of NGOs, civil society organisations and grassroots associations around the world (Fisher 1997, Salamon 1994). Since the 1980s the number of NGOs worldwide has skyrocketed. In 1995 there were almost 29,000 international development NGOs in existence, with an estimated US$5 billion in aid channelled through the NGO sector, and nearly US$3.5 billion going to NGOs in Africa. This represents just under one-fifth of the total aid to the continent (Chege 1999, Hearn 2007).

Countries throughout the African continent, then, have experienced a rapid increase in the number of NGOs, both international and domestic, operating in their countries during this period (Dicklitch & Rice 2004: 660), leading to what has been called the 'NGO-isation' of African society (Hearn 1998). In Kenya, for example, the NGO sector grew from 511 registered NGOs in 1996 to 2511 in 2003 (World Resources Institute 2005), while in Tanzania it grew from fewer than 20 in the early 1980s to around 3000 at the turn of the century (Hasu, this volume). Likewise, in Ethiopia the number of NGOs grew from fewer than 60 at the end of the 1980s to nearly 2000 in 2007 (Rahmato et al. 2008: 12).

NGOs are generally understood to be private, not-for-profit organisations which are independent of both government and business. There is a huge variety in the types of organisation that are grouped together under the banner 'NGO'. These organisations differ from each other in the levels at which they operate (local, national, international), in organisational structure, in membership base and in overall goals. The term NGO has been applied to groups providing social welfare services, organisations promoting development initiatives, social action groups struggling for social justice, groups lobbying for environmental protection and groups providing legal research and advocacy, to name just a few. In size and scale, NGOs range from small, loosely organised groups with a few unpaid staff members to huge organisations with multimillion dollar budgets and hundreds of salaried employees (Fisher 1997). Development NGOs can be broadly grouped into three categories: those that focus on humanitarian relief and charity, those that focus mainly on small-scale local development and those that focus on empowerment and social justice (Elliot 1987, Korten 1990). Most of the chapters in this book consider the second category of NGOs, those

with a focus on small-scale local development, and there are examples of international NGOs (chapters by Piot [5], Smith [6] and Freeman [7]), local NGOs (Parsitau [9]), community-based organisations (Jones [8]) and voluntary associations (Parsitau [9]).

For much of the post-1980s period NGOs have been the 'favoured child' of the international development agencies. They have become the new frontline of 'development', seemingly striving to help poor populations to transform themselves and improve their lives. Fighting a global 'war against poverty', these new organisations promise empowerment, participation and salvation from a life of struggle and misery. Seen as politically neutral, values-based civil society organisations with close links to the grassroots, NGOs have often appeared as the ideal development agent. They have been seen as a 'magic bullet' with the capacity to improve the effectiveness of development interventions by shifting from a top-down, state-led approach to a bottom-up approach that emphasises the involvement of poor people themselves.

The characteristics that were most expected to make NGOs effective agents of change were a focus on participation and empowerment and a close working relationship with the community (Fisher 1997: 442, Hearn 2007: 1096). It was believed that NGOs, as grassroots organisations, would be able to stimulate the participation of local people in their own development and empower them to take up new activities that would increase their wellbeing and lead to economic growth. And by working at the community level it was hoped that whole villages and societies could be transformed. However, as we shall see later, NGOs have mainly failed to live up to their expectations and have been disappointingly ineffective in bringing about social and economic change in Africa.

NGO performance: making a difference?

In recent years a critical literature has developed questioning the role of development NGOs in broader international and national political contexts. The rapid increase in funding to NGOs by governments and international organisations that has spurred their growth has also changed their very nature. Whereas before the neoliberal turn NGOs were primarily voluntary civil society organisations that defined their own mission and values, raised their own funds from the public and worked with a high degree of independence; the shift towards increased donor funding from governments, bilaterals and the World Bank from the 1980s onwards has led to many NGOs becoming more like subcontractors to foreign governments and organisations, implementing their

agendas and competing with each other for the privilege of doing so (Hearn 1998, Klees 2002, Manji & O'Coill 2002, Matanga 2010). Rather than being grassroots organisations accountable to local people, Southern NGOs have been shown to be dominated by Northern NGOs and donors, accountable to foreign stakeholders and increasingly implementing projects that address foreign agendas and concerns (Dicklitch 1998, Edwards & Hulme 1996a, 1996b, Hulme & Edwards 1997, Igoe & Kelsall 2005, Michael 2004, Tvedt 1998). The extent of the power imbalance between Northern donors and Southern peoples and NGOs has led some scholars to describe the NGO-isation of Africa as a form of re-colonisation and to see development NGOs as a new type of secular missionary (Anderson & Rieff 2005, Hanlon 1991, Manji & O'Coill 2002). Thus development NGOs, even Southern ones, cannot really be seen as 'local' organisations and are not straightforwardly accountable to the people that they serve.

At the same time it has become apparent that development NGOs are not nearly as effective as they were once hoped to be, and there is a growing disillusionment with their performance (Lewis 2001). In particular, NGOs have been found to be less than successful in stimulating local participation and bringing about the empowerment of poor people, precisely the processes at which they were initially expected to excel (Cooke & Kothari 2001). In theory, participatory approaches to development seek to include local knowledge in development planning and to make people central to development by encouraging their involvement in the interventions that will affect their lives. As Botchway has commented, 'meaningful participation implies at a minimum the process in which local communities discover the possibilities of exercising choice and becoming capable of managing what they understand as development' (Botchway 2001: 136). In practice, NGOs have found this very hard to do, especially when project planning is in fact largely guided by the agenda of external stakeholders, as discussed above.

For many NGOs encouraging participation and empowerment often boils down to using techniques of participatory rural appraisal (PRA) when identifying local problems, issues and stakeholders, and/or organising local committees to manage part of the project and take ownership of it after the NGO has left. Both processes have their problems and lead to only very limited notions of 'participation' and 'empowerment'. One challenge facing participatory approaches is that they are premised on the notions of individualism and equality and yet are often used in traditional settings where traditional power structures give different voice to different categories of people, often privileging chiefs, elders

and local elites (Aryeetey 1998). As Smith's chapter (6) shows in detail for southeast Kenya, participatory processes such as community planning units tend to get hijacked by local elites, thus leaving local youth excluded from decision-making processes and ultimately from resources.

It is also now widely known that local committees set up by NGOs rarely manage to function as expected or to continue in operation after the end of the project. For many beneficiaries these committees are simply a means to access resources, and when the inflow of external resources dries up the purpose of the committee disappears. As Jones' chapter (8) shows for a range of committees set up by various NGOs in northern Uganda, these committees are never truly owned by the local community and do not become established in the community landscape. They tend to remain extrinsic to local communal life and lack the moral valence that might make them meaningful long-term institutions. Once the NGO leaves, the committees disappear, and thus many NGO projects have proved remarkably unsustainable in the medium to long term.

While there is much rhetoric about how NGOs can empower poor people, there is very little discussion of what empowerment actually means and how it can be achieved. NGO models of empowerment seem to focus primarily on education, skills and access to resources. It is very rare to find an NGO that explicitly seeks to transform individual subjectivities. As Parsitau's chapter (9) shows with regard to women's NGOs in Kenya, empowerment for development NGOs is mainly about economic empowerment or legal empowerment, rather than a fundamental transformational experience of the self in which a person begins to see herself and her life in a whole different light and starts to act accordingly. Some NGOs even manage to bring about short-term improvements in economic conditions while disempowering their beneficiaries in the process. Piot's chapter (5) gives the example of a Danish child sponsorship NGO in northern Togo which – intentionally or unintentionally – humiliates its beneficiaries by making them write and rewrite letters in French to European sponsors, making them walk for hours back and forth to the project office where the latest versions of their letters are marked with red pen and sent back for further revision. While this process of letter writing ultimately leads to the inflow of resources and is for this reason tolerated by the local people, it is experienced as frustrating and humiliating and serves to remind people that they do not have the means or the ability to improve their lives, but are instead dependent on distant Europeans. And once the project came to an end, the situation in the village reverted back to

how it was pre-project, and very little development can be said to have taken place.

For these reasons, and several others, NGOs have largely disappointed development theorists and failed to bring about significant social and economic change in Africa. After an optimistic start they have proved to be no 'magic bullet' to Africa's problems. Most surprisingly, they have failed to live up to the buzzwords so often associated with them – despite the rhetoric and the intentions, NGOs rarely succeed in fostering participation or empowerment, they are rarely local grassroots organisations accountable to their beneficiaries, and they consistently fail to become embedded in local communities. In these respects, as we shall see later, they are rather different from Pentecostal churches.

For some theorists, NGOs have failed to bring about significant change because they remain part of the mainstream development ideology, promoting a spirit of development resolutely based on modernisation, capitalism and Westernisation. These more radical post-development theorists, as van Dijk discusses at length in his chapter (4), question this whole 'spirit of development'. Instead they seek alternatives to development, looking for models of progress and improvement that are rooted in local traditions, rather than in Western capitalist forms (Escobar 2007, Nederveen Pieterse 1998). Pentecostals, as we will see later, can be seen to offer a third approach to development – different from both the mainstream development and the more radical post-development views. While they embrace the mainstream capitalist 'spirit of development' with its desire for wealth and commodity consumption, they maintain a magico-religious worldview in sharp contrast to mainstream development's rational secularism. And while they acknowledge the existence of traditional practices and values, they seek to break away from them, in stark contrast to the post-development theorists who seek to base new models of the future in these traditional pasts. The Pentecostal model of change concurs with neither development nor post-development views. It offers a new and different way to think about and enact social change. Before discussing these dynamics in more detail, let us first provide a brief overview of Pentecostalism in Africa today.

Pentecostal and charismatic Christianity in Africa

The post-1980s period has also witnessed – alongside the rise of NGOs – the phenomenal growth of a new religious movement: what has come to be known as Pentecostal and charismatic Christianity. From humble

beginnings as an early twentieth century revivalist movement among America's poorer socio-economic groups, Pentecostalism has spread across the globe to become what is broadly believed to be the fastest growing Christian movement today (Anderson 2004: 1, Burgess & van der Maas 2002, Hollenweger 1997). In just over 100 years Pentecostal Christianity, and its charismatic and neo-charismatic relatives, has won over half a billion souls worldwide (Barrett 2001), representing almost 28 per cent of organised global Christianity (Barrett & Johnson 2002) and constituting what David Martin (2002) has called 'the largest global shift in the religious market place' in recent years.

By far the majority of these new Pentecostal and charismatic converts are to be found in the non-Western world, particularly in Latin America, Asia and Africa. Africa alone is estimated to have 126 million Pentecostals and charismatics, constituting some 11 per cent of the continent's total population. The vast majority of them, some 109 million, have joined since 1980 (Barrett & Johnson 2002: 287). Christianity is, of course, not new to Africa, and the growth of Pentecostal Christianity in recent years must also be seen in the context of the ongoing process of the appropriation of Christianity throughout the continent (Gifford 1995, 1998). Birgit Meyer (2004) has argued that, broadly speaking, there has been a shift over the course of the twentieth century from mainline missionary churches that brought European styles of Christianity and rejected traditional African religion, to African Independent Churches that creatively combined Christian and African religious elements in syncretic mixtures, to the new Pentecostal and charismatic churches which, as we shall see later, offer a form of Christianity that fits well with African sensibilities and which acknowledges the validity of traditional African beliefs – in witches, spirits, ancestors – while at the same time providing a way to break from them.

Many scholars and Pentecostal leaders alike have linked this sudden growth of Pentecostalism in Africa with the economic crisis of the 1980s and the subsequent SAPs that led to the worsening material conditions of life for many people at this time. Ruth Marshall (1991: 25), for example, quotes from a book written by a Nigerian Pentecostal pastor, entitled *Hope for the SAPped Generation*, which proclaims that:

> Fear and lack of confidence in the future are becoming the common currency of the day ... We no longer trust anything or anyone. Those we trusted have mortgaged us and held us to ransom for foreign loans which we did not benefit from ... Everything – absolutely

everything – is on the decline and on the verge of collapse... No jobs, no money, no food, no clothing, no personal dignity.

This sense of collapse and despair was echoed in many African countries at this time (Akoko 2007, Maxwell 2005, Meyer 1998b). Despite their foreign roots, Pentecostal churches, unlike development NGOs, were a local, home-grown response to this situation. And with the economic situation showing little sign of improvement, it is not surprising that Pentecostal and charismatic churches continue to grow and flourish. At present it is estimated that, globally, there are approximately 9 million new members per year – over 25,000 a day – with the vast majority hailing from the global South (Barrett & Johnson 2002: 284).

There is a huge variety of different Pentecostal and charismatic churches and it is difficult to generalise across them all. Nonetheless, it is broadly accepted that there are three broad categories, or waves, of Pentecostal and charismatic Christianity: classical Pentecostal, charismatic and neo-charismatic (Anderson 2004, Hollenweger 1997). Classical Pentecostal refers to churches with links to the early American and European Pentecostal churches and which stress the importance of speaking in tongues, or glossolalia, as evidence of baptism by the Holy Spirit. Examples include the Assemblies of God, the Church of God in Christ and the Pentecostal Church of God. Charismatic Christians are those members of mainline Christian denominations – Lutheran, Presbyterian, Catholic and so on – who began to experience the gifts of the Holy Spirit in the form of speaking in tongues, spiritual healing, miracles and the like. This 'Pentecostalisation' of mainstream Christianity started in the 1960s and there are now charismatic churches across virtually all Christian denominations (e.g. Coleman 2000, 2002, Csordas 1992, 2007). The third wave, or neo-charismatics, is the broadest category, serving much as a catch-all for the vast number of non-denominational or post-denominational churches and fellowships that have exploded onto the scene since the 1980s. Neo-charismatics have been particularly creative and innovative in their adaptation of Pentecostal doctrine and styles to new settings and contexts. Examples could include Mensa Otabil's International Central Gospel Church, David Oyepedo's Winner's Chapel, the Rhema Church and the Vineyard Fellowship (Bialecki 2008, Luhrmann 2004). Churches from all three waves are flourishing today in Africa and are discussed in the chapters of this book.

Pentecostal and charismatic Christianity has been characterised as a 'frankly supernatural and experientially robust' form of Christianity

(Robbins 2004: 120). It places an emphasis on strict moralism, combined with exuberant and ecstatic prayer. At its core are four key elements of doctrine, often known as 'Full Gospel' theology, which stress that (a) Jesus offers salvation, (b) Jesus heals, (c) Jesus baptises with the Holy Spirit and (d) Jesus is coming again (Dayton 1987: 19–23, Robbins 2004: 121).

While there is a huge amount of variation between different Pentecostal and charismatic churches in Africa today, in different countries and between urban and rural settings, there are nonetheless a number of characteristics that are shared by many of these churches throughout the continent. The chapters of this book provide rich ethnographic detail about particular churches in all their idiosyncrasy and variety, but it is useful here to provide a brief overview of some of the key characteristics of contemporary African Pentecostal and charismatic Christianity.

The most readily visible aspect of Pentecostal and charismatic Christianity in Africa is the ecstatic, spirit-filled church service, which frequently involves speaking in tongues and outbursts of ululations, as well as lively singing and dancing. These church services often last for two to three hours, sometimes all night and in many cases take place several times per week. They are emotionally charged, high-volume gatherings, with pastors 'amped up' by sound systems, words to hymns and songs projected karaoke-style, and congregants frequently being moved to stand up, extend their arms upwards and exclaim 'hallelujah!' Pentecostal worship is incredibly participatory – there is no sitting quietly at the back. Congregants frequently have to engage in call and response, share their hopes and fears with their neighbours or come up to the front to tell good news stories or to ask for blessing. There is a phenomenal power in this combination of euphoria and participation.

Personal transformation is a key theme in these churches, as indeed with all evangelical and 'born again' churches. Perhaps more than most, though, the Pentecostals and charismatics are extremely effective in bringing about dramatic changes in subjectivity (see particularly chapters by van Dijk [4], Freeman [7] and Parsitau [9]). They focus on a 'revision of consciousness' (Martin 1990: 287), a 'remaking of the individual' (Maxwell 1998: 352), a 'reorientation of persons' (Barbalet 2008: 75). There is an emphasis on making a break with the past (Meyer 1998a), which in many cases means attempting to break off from any form of traditional religion or ritual practice. The key element in this transformation of subjectivity, however, is a shift from seeing oneself as a victim to seeing oneself as a victor. Many people, particularly the urban

poor, first come to Pentecostal churches feeling wretched, despised and hopeless. Their self-esteem is low and they feel powerless to change their situation. Through their engagement with pastors and other church members, in study, prayer and healing, these people begin to see themselves as valued individuals, part of God's people, a 'somebody' rather than a 'nobody'. Most important of all, they begin to move beyond a passive fatalism and come to realise that they have agency in their lives (Maxwell 2005).

Pentecostal belief has been shown to bring about a dramatic restructuring of families, as believers loosen ties with the extended family and focus on the nuclear family as the central unit of production and consumption. There is also a concomitant reformulation of gender relations. With alcohol consumption, smoking and extramarital relations cast as immoral, many Pentecostal men are effectively 'domesticated' and they turn the focus of their energy and resources to their family (Maxwell 1998, van Dijk 2002b). And, as discussed in depth in Parsitau's chapter (9), women's status is often enhanced by the equalising power of the Holy Spirit – available to anyone – and the gifts that it brings, although ultimate gender ideologies tend to remain rather conservative, with women entreated to remain subservient to their husbands. Pentecostalism also challenges traditional power structures and modes of social organisation and instead emphasises individualism and personal achievement (see chapters by Smith [6] and Freeman [7]).

Another key feature of many Pentecostal and charismatic churches in Africa is an emphasis on spiritual healing and deliverance. This might come through prayer or the laying on of hands, but the belief in the ability to heal 'in the name of Jesus' is widespread. It is often linked to a parallel belief in the devil and his role in putting obstacles in the way and causing suffering. Thus healing is often related to exorcism and 'spiritual warfare', where evil spirits are cast out of the sufferer in noisy deliverance services with much crying, weeping and wailing. In many cases the devil is associated with traditional African religions, which are then recast as forms of devil worship. In this framework, then, it is impossible to elaborate self-consciously syncretic religious forms, combining traditional and Christian elements. Instead it is necessary to try to 'make a break with the past' and make every effort to separate oneself from former social networks and to actively shun traditional cultural practices. Despite the challenges of doing this in practice, this push to break with the past is paradoxically one of the main attractions of Pentecostalism. As we shall see later, and throughout this book, Pentecostalism is one of the few modalities – religious or secular – that

both demands and legitimises radical behaviour change, including the restructuring of families, communities and social relations.

Pentecostals place a strong emphasis on moral purity and ethical behaviour. They refuse, in theory and often in practice, to give or receive bribes or to engage in other forms of corruption. They observe strict injunctions against theft and lying, and place particular emphasis on honesty and reliability, clean and smart appearance and marital fidelity. While not everyone can live up to these high standards, it is widely believed, both inside and outside Pentecostal communities, that Pentecostals are in general more honest, trustworthy and hard-working than other people. In many countries in Africa it is not uncommon to hear employers, of whatever religious persuasion, preferring to hire born-again staff to work in their homes or businesses (Marshall 1991: 29). And, as Jones' chapter (8) shows, in situations of extreme moral breakdown, such as after the violent insurgency in northern Uganda in the late 1980s and early 1990s, Pentecostalism can be very appealing because of its strong moral framework.

Since the 1980s there has been the emergence of another feature that is now extremely common in very many, although not all, Pentecostal and charismatic churches in Africa, and that is some form of the prosperity gospel. While earlier forms of Pentecostalism promoted a rather ascetic approach to the material world, shifts since the 1980s in both the classical Pentecostal churches and, more particularly, in the new charismatic and neo-charismatic churches have led to a fundamental realignment with regard to views about the material life and this-worldly concerns. The new view, first espoused in America, but taken up with phenomenal enthusiasm in post-1980s Africa, promises an 'economically advantageous redemption' (Bialecki et al. 2008: 1149). Salvation, in this view, can take place in this life because Jesus wants his people to enjoy abundance and prosperity (Akoko 2007, Marshall 1991, Maxwell 1998, Meyer 1998b, Ukah 2005, van Dijk 2005). Churches that preach the prosperity gospel encourage their members to pray to Jesus for wealth and abundance, and also to do their part in the bargain, by engaging in business and working hard. Sermons are often blatantly materialistic. The Ghanaian Pentecostals studied by Meyer were told by their pastor to 'close their eyes and fill in a cheque in their minds', which they should then send up to heaven where 'God would sign [it] ... and they would, in the future, receive the money requested' (Meyer 1998b: 762–763).

Members are encouraged to give quite substantial proportions of their new-found wealth to the church, through tithes and various offerings,

with the belief that 'give and you shall receive'.[2] Tithing is central to the Pentecostal moral economy and serves as a new form of taxation in places where churches, rather than governments, provide most social services. Many churches also engage in business activities themselves, as a way to raise church funds, and in some notable cases run newspapers, radio stations and even banks, gyms and universities. One of the results is that many of these churches, particularly those in major urban centres, are phenomenally rich. Their pastors whizz around in fast cars, dress in expensive suits and sport the latest mobile phones. Congregants are encouraged to copy this style of opulent abundance, and material success is taken as a sign of God's blessing. This enthusiasm for material wealth is not without its dilemmas, often associated in Africa with witchcraft and, in some cases, although most certainly not all, churches acknowledge traditional fears of wealth accumulation and create practices that purify potentially dangerous commodities and legitimise accumulation by good Christians (Meyer 1998b). In all these ways, then, Pentecostal and charismatic churches create new social, economic and moral structures and act to transform both the subjectivities and the lifestyles of their followers. Let us now consider in more detail their influences on economic behaviour.

Weber's legacy: the Protestant Ethic and the Pentecostal ethic

One of the key questions regarding the impact of Pentecostalism on development is whether it can be seen to bring a 'Protestant ethic' to the people of non-Western countries. Many theorists have indeed suggested a continuity between Weber's Protestant Ethic of the sixteenth and seventeenth centuries and the Pentecostal ethic of today. In a review of the anthropology of Christianity, Bialecki et al. claim that 'in the prosperity gospel...it seems that we have a new Protestant ethic to match a new, neoliberal spirit of capitalism' (Bialecki et al. 2008: 1149–1150). Bernice Martin has called the spread of Pentecostalism in Latin America a 'new mutation of the Protestant Ethic' (Martin 1995, see also Martin 1998, 2006) and the Comaroffs have referred to 'new Protestant ethics and spirits of capitalism' (Comaroff & Comaroff 2000, 2001). Regarding Africa, several scholars have claimed that Pentecostal Christianity leads to increased entrepreneurial activity and saving, as Weber's thesis would suggest (e.g. Garner 2000, Maxwell 1998, Meyer 1998b, 2007, Schlemmer 2008). Others, however, have vehemently denied the relevance of Weber's thesis to contemporary Pentecostalism. Paul Freston has argued that Pentecostalism is 'quite unlike the popular Puritanism of the "Protestant ethic" [because] it separates wealth and

salvation, [and] thus... [lacks] the psychological mechanism (anguish about eternal destiny) which supposedly impelled the Puritan in his rational search for prosperity' (Freston 1995: 132). He even goes as far as to say that 'Prosperity Theology represents an advanced stage of the *decline* of the Protestant ethic' (ibid.: 131, my emphasis). And with regard to Africa, Paul Gifford has argued that, with very few exceptions, Pentecostal Christianity does not offer a new work ethic, an inner-worldly ascetic or the deferral of gratification that Weber's thesis would suggest, but rather promotes a new appetite for consumerism (Gifford 2004). The debate over whether, to what extent and how Pentecostal Christianity plays a role in establishing a type of 'Protestant ethic' in today's Pentecostal converts has been described by Joel Robbins as 'the key debate in discussions of [Pentecostal and charismatic] economic culture' (2004: 136). It is worthwhile, therefore, to consider the issues in some detail.

In his famous book, Weber (2008 [1904–1905]) argued that there was an elective affinity between the spread of Protestant Christianity and the growth of capitalism in sixteenth and seventeenth century Europe. He did not claim that Protestantism caused the development of capitalism or that the Protestant view of the world and the capitalist view of the world were the same. Rather, he sought to show that Protestant belief led to an ethic of hard work and limited consumption that had the *unintended consequence* of leading to successful enterprise and capital accumulation, and thus the further growth and spread of capitalist economic practice. The key Protestant belief in question was the doctrine of predetermination, whereby it was believed that God had pre-chosen the elect who would go to heaven, and that it was impossible to know or influence His decision. Unable to deal with the anxiety that such a doctrine promoted, many Calvinist Protestants came to see success in this-worldly affairs as a sign of God's grace in their lives, and thus a hint that their future lay in heaven.

Since then anthropologists have mainly applied Weber's ideas to non-Protestant societies, particularly when looking at issues of economic development and modernisation in non-Western countries in the 1950s and 1960s. At this time a number of studies were undertaken exploring how various religions affected orientations to economic development, with the aim of understanding why some countries modernised more rapidly than others (Bellah 1957, 1963, Geertz 1956, 1962, Nash 1965, Spiro 1966, Stone 1974). Some of the most influential of these studies were brought together by S.N. Eisenstadt in his edited collection, *The Protestant Ethic and Modernisation* (Eisenstadt 1968). After

this spurt of activity, interest in the Weberian thesis largely declined in anthropology, with some important exceptions (e.g. Gellner 2001, Grombich & Obeyesekere 1989, Roberts 1995). Surprisingly, there is a marked lack of in-depth anthropological work that applies Weber's ideas to contemporary Protestantism. This section, and indeed much of this book, seeks to fill this gap.

Different contexts

An initial look at early modern Europe and late modern Africa might suggest that the context of the contemporary growth of capitalism in the latter is not so different from the context of the original growth of capitalism in the former. Pre-modern European societies were largely based on subsistence agriculture and feudal arrangements, were frequently plagued by famine and disease and were often at war. The growth of capitalism took place against the decline of feudalism and the development of the sovereign state, processes rather similar to those that took place in late twentieth century Africa.[3] In Europe the Protestant Reformation was a key part of this transformation. It is easy to see the temptation to interpret the spread of Pentecostalism in contemporary Africa as a parallel African Reformation.

Nonetheless, it is also important to consider the very real differences between the contexts in which capitalism and Protestantism developed in sixteenth century Europe and in twentieth century Africa. First, capitalist modernisation in Africa is largely, although not entirely, taking place under the impact of external forces rather than internal initiative. In most countries capitalist modalities were first introduced through the processes of colonisation and missionisation, and today this process continues through the activities of multinational corporations, international NGOs and Western-dominated global financial institutions such as the World Bank and the IMF. To a very great extent, capitalism as an economic and cultural system has been parachuted into Africa from the outside. This is quite different from the context of internally driven scientific advance, technological discovery and cultural renaissance in which sixteenth century European capitalism developed (cf. Eisenstadt 1968, Martin 1995). And while European capitalism developed in the context of early modern state formation, contemporary capitalism in Africa is spreading in a context of the 'rolling back' of the state.

Second, European industrial capitalism was built with the capital produced during the earlier period of merchant capitalism, when huge amounts of capital were generated by colonial extraction and nascent international trade. Early European capitalism was thus supported and

facilitated by the inflow of wealth from the colonies. Contemporary capitalism in Africa has not been supported by a similar inflow of wealth.[4] Rather, in sharp contrast, it has been seriously challenged by the huge outflow of wealth to repay international loans. Contemporary Africa is a net exporter of capital (Ellis 1996: 24). This contrast is profound and significant.

Third, the nature of early industrial capitalism and late twentieth century neoliberal consumer capitalism is very different. Capitalism is not a singular 'thing'. Early European capitalism focused on industrialised production, particularly in the factory. Early capitalist entrepreneurs invested in expensive machinery and required a large number of workers – the proletariat – to carry out routine productive operations in a disciplined and rationalised way. In return they offered them secure employment, regular salaries and often housing and basic education. The development of capitalism in Africa followed a somewhat different trajectory, with more emphasis on agriculture and less on industrialisation. In contemporary late-modern neoliberal capitalism, particularly in Africa, jobs are in scarce supply and when offered tend to come with no job security, piece rates instead of salaries and very few other benefits. In the contemporary situation, workers are likely to move from job to job, often with long periods of unemployment in between. Many jobs, moreover, are likely to be in the service sector rather than in production, calling for a rather different personal orientation and set of skills. And furthermore, contemporary neoliberal capitalism increasingly stresses consumption over production and sets up a world where desires are satisfied and identities are forged through consumption activities (Miller 1987). Again, the contrast is profound.

Fourth, and finally, there is the very different religious context of sixteenth century Europe and late twentieth century Africa. Protestantism in Europe developed against the backdrop of Catholicism, a form of Christianity which in its philosophy – if not always in its practice – placed little value on this-worldly matters and promoted an ascetic ideal, culminating with monks living in monasteries far removed from worldly concerns. This is in sharp contrast to the religious context in Africa throughout much of the twentieth century, where many people belonged to mainline Christian denominations – Protestant and Catholic – or to African Independent Churches, and also retained, to a greater or lesser extent, beliefs and practices associated with pre-colonial traditional African religions. These traditional African religions emphasised the importance of making offerings and sacrifices to the ancestors

or the spirits in order to receive blessing – generally understood as health, wealth and fecundity – and to minimise misfortune. In these worldviews, then, the spiritual and the material were intimately entangled and wealth and this-worldly success were key values and concerns. Thus it is not so much the case that the prosperity gospel 'draws Pentecostals right into the "world"', as Meyer (2007: 19) has argued, but rather that it recasts and re-legitimises their already being there, in a way that other Christian denominations could not.

Differences between Calvinist and Pentecostal Protestantism

As we might expect, late twentieth century Pentecostal Protestantism, particularly the rapidly growing sector that is influenced by the prosperity gospel, is itself rather different from sixteenth century Calvinist Protestantism. We will discuss three major differences that are pertinent to our discussion here: differences in philosophy, theology and mode of embodiment.

Most obviously, there is a major difference in philosophy regarding the value of this-worldly goods and pleasures. Sixteenth century Calvinist Protestantism was deeply ascetic, whereas late twentieth century Pentecostal Protestantism is blatantly materialistic. While Weber's Calvinists found themselves accumulating capital and possessions unintentionally, today's African Pentecostals explicitly desire material wealth and abundance (cf. Comaroff & Comaroff 2000, Maxwell 1998, 2000, Meyer 2007). For many this desire is quite modest – to be able to eat three meals a day, to have enough money to send their children to school – while for others in the upwardly mobile middle classes it might be more extravagant, with desires for fast cars, expensive suits, fine jewellery and the latest mobile phones. In all cases though, these materialist desires are explicit and acknowledged, and are not only sanctioned, but promoted, by the Pentecostal churches.

While the Calvinists may have seen God in everything, they did not believe that God would directly intervene in this-worldly affairs. This-worldly success may have come to be seen by many as evidence of God's grace and proof that you were following the divine plan, but there was no notion that God would directly intervene in these matters Himself. Today's African Pentecostals offer a very different theology. For them, God is intimately involved in everyday matters and in direct communication with them through the Holy Spirit, which gives the gifts of tongues, healing and prophecy. God might save you from a traffic accident by making you forget something in your office and leave late that day, or heal you from an illness that you have been suffering from for

years. While the God of the Calvinists was transcendent, the God of the Pentecostals is astoundingly immanent.

Finally, the modes of embodiment of Calvinist and contemporary African Pentecostal Protestantism are extremely different. Calvinism was severely rational: emotions were to be controlled and repressed, and the mode of worship shunned music. This is in sharp contrast to the emotion-filled exuberance of lively Pentecostal worship, where music and song, and frequently movement and dance, enliven the church service. The emphasis on embodied religious experience, conceptualised as the embodiment of the Holy Spirit, leads to a very different embodied religious experience for Pentecostals as compared with Calvinists.

A Pentecostal ethic?

With these significant differences in historical context, type of capitalism and type of Protestantism, it is clear that we should not expect a simple repetition of Weber's argument in the spread of Pentecostalism in contemporary Africa. Weber's key point, however, was that in order for a new economic system – capitalism – to be taken up by people, there had to be shift in their values and subjectivity in order to motivate new behaviours and to make the new economic system seem moral, and that Protestantism unintentionally did this. Can Pentecostalism be seen to play the same role with regards to neoliberal capitalism and development in Africa?

The studies in this book indicate that Pentecostalism does indeed play a similar role in Africa today. It is a form of Protestantism that not only fits with African sensibilities, but also stimulates a transformation of behaviour that can lead to success, or at least upward mobility, in the contemporary neoliberal economy. It motivates new behaviours and renders them moral. It is the notion that 'God wants you to have abundance' and that this is the divine plan that motivates these new behaviours, not an anxious quest to find evidence of one's election for salvation in the next world. Nevertheless, the consequences are the same: hard work, saving and a limitation on certain types of consumption. While African Pentecostals certainly do not shun consumption to the extent that Weber's Calvinists did, they most certainly do limit and constrain it. Restrictions on the consumption of alcohol and tobacco and injunctions against extramarital relationships and visits to prostitutes have a huge impact on spending patterns among Pentecostals compared with others. There is a marked limitation of 'wasteful consumption' and a reorientation towards investment and accumulation. And while Calvinism moralised hard work and saving as an ascetic

practice in itself – a good way to fill your time so you are not tempted to sin – Pentecostalism makes it moral because this is the way to achieve God's plan for you: to become rich and abundant right here on earth.

Furthermore, for many Africans one of the main barriers to accumulating wealth is the pressure to participate in traditional practices, such as rites of passage or rituals of commensality, and the constant demands for financial support from poorer kin. Redistribution, in one form or another, is inherent in most traditional African religions and moral systems, and it makes personal accumulation virtually impossible. By linking these traditional practices with the devil, as shown most clearly in the chapters by van Dijk (4), Piot (5) and Freeman (7), Pentecostalism makes avoidance of them, and separation from more distant kin, intensely and aggressively moral, and thus enables the emergence of previously impossible behaviours.

There is a different emphasis in the Pentecostal ethic in urban and in rural settings. In urban settings, with a rapid influx of people newly disembedded from tightly knit communities in the countryside, Pentecostalism initially played an important role in providing new forms of community and morality in the new social setting. Many Pentecostal churches continue to play this role for newly arriving migrants and for the urban poor that have as yet remained on the peripheries of town life. Other Pentecostal churches have branched out and focused their attentions on the middle class. In post-structural adjustment Africa, this population has had to struggle increasingly to find employment, particularly as government jobs have been cut. Those jobs that are available demand workers that are diligent, flexible and that can work with minimal supervision. Pentecostalism helps produce such disciplined subjects, ideal for the neoliberal economy (cf. Martin 1995).

In today's economy, however, the route to wealth and prosperity at a greater scale is not through employment, but through business. Many of the new Pentecostal churches play a major role in stimulating business behaviour, empowering people to be courageous and aim high and in encouraging their members to start enterprises, large and small. Paul Freston (1995: 132), for example, quotes a Pentecostal pastor telling his congregation: 'It's not enough just to give the "sacrifice" (a special offering) and cross your arms. You have to leave your job and open a business, even if it's only selling popcorn on the street. As an employee you'll never get rich.' In a manner not that different from Western secular motivational speakers, such as Anthony Robbins or Stephen Covey, Pentecostal leaders are encouraging people to take

risks and follow their dreams. And as van Dijk's chapter (4) shows in detail, they are increasingly also giving them the business management tools needed for these endeavours.

In rural settings the situation is significantly different. Most people are living by subsistence agriculture and remain marginal to global capitalist practices and values. Many are ensconced in traditional communities and the redistributive practices inherent in them. In these contexts, as Freeman's chapter (7) discusses in detail, capitalism is most often being promoted by NGOs, in the guise of market-led development or 'making markets work for the poor'. In other words, development, in the rural context, is these days predominantly about trying to stimulate a shift from traditional to capitalist economic practices. NGOs seek to do this by promoting the production of cash crops, facilitating the establishment of value chains and giving trainings on business and marketing. But what they do not do is consider whether people's motivations and values fit with these behaviours. In very many instances they do not, and these projects fail. For such projects and practices to take hold, a radical shift in values is necessary. And in recent years, as Pentecostalism has begun to spread out to rural areas, it is the Pentecostal churches that provoke this shift in values, bringing new motivations and legitimising new types of behaviour. It is here, then, that the Pentecostal ethic most clearly supports the spirit of development.

The power of Pentecostalism

I have argued that Pentecostalism does indeed bring about a Pentecostal Ethic, similar to Weber's Protestant Ethic, which supports and legitimates the spread of capitalism. One question remains: Why does Pentecostalism do this so much better than mainstream Protestantism, which has, of course, been present in much of Africa since the nineteenth century? I offer three suggestions to explain the contemporary power and popularity of Pentecostalism, compared with mainstream Protestantism.

First, Pentecostalism incorporates a holistic ontology that fits well with the lived experience of many Africans and accords with most traditional African ontologies. Indeed, the dualistic worldview and ascetic ideas of mainstream Protestantism always seemed rather strange and somewhat irrational to most Africans and could never be fully embraced despite decades of mainstream Protestant and Catholic intervention (Meyer 2007: 13). What Pentecostal Protestantism offers is a form of Protestantism that fits with certain key African sensibilities. But at the

same time as acknowledging the existence and power of spirits and demons, it simultaneously provides a route for believers to distance themselves from them – to make a break – and it is in this that it has its particular appeal, as well as its fundamental difference from other forms of Christianity, as Joel Robbins (2004) has so cogently argued.

Second, there is the important role played by charisma and ecstasy. While there have been numerous descriptions of Pentecostal charisma, most scholarly *analysis* of Pentecostalism to date has either ignored its charismatic nature or been strongly influenced by anthropological theories of charisma that emphasise its role in constructing liminal stages in rituals which, although they temporarily challenge the social order, ultimately re-establish it (Gluckman 1954, Turner 1968, 1969). Thus the charismatic outbursts regularly witnessed in Pentecostal churches have been seen as cases of catharsis and examples of ritual communitas in many of the deprivation theory approaches to Pentecostalism (e.g. Austin 1981). Instead, following Weber, I would suggest that Pentecostal charisma and ecstasy play a fundamental role in transforming embodied subjectivities and in creating the felt *experience* of newness which makes the rhetoric of rebirth feel *actual* (cf. Csordas 2002, Maxwell 2005). Such charismatic experiences make possible a fundamental rupture in the social order and then lead to the possibility of the establishment of a new order (Keyes 2002: 249). What other forms of Protestantism may seek to do with sober words, stories and prayer, Pentecostalism achieves far more effectively with its exuberant rituals, exorcisms and gifts of the Spirit.

Third, Pentecostalism is becoming far more popular than other forms of Protestantism in contemporary Africa because it is itself constituted in part through the logic of neoliberal capitalism and is thus actively and creatively marketed. Contemporary evangelism, in the hands of Pentecostals and charismatics, has harnessed new media and technologies and combined them with the logic of consumer advertising to spread the word far and wide, through music, films and teleserials, by tape cassettes, DVDs, online chat forums and Facebook (Hackett 1998, Meyer 2002, 2006, Pype 2009). Appropriating contemporary marketing methodologies that combine advertising with entertainment, today's Pentecostals and charismatics have created a form of evangelism which is energetic, enticing and ubiquitous. They have become experts at 'advertising Jesus', marketing Him to the masses and thus growing their churches.

NGOs and Pentecostal churches: contrasting models of development and different modes of implementation

We have seen how the Pentecostal ethic supports and legitimates the spirit of development - the development of economic behaviours which enable people to better function in the neoliberal economic setting of contemporary Africa. And we have seen how secular development NGOs seem to be surprisingly less successful in this endeavour. Let us complete the analysis, then, by summarising the similarities and differences between these two development styles and trying to make explicit the reasons why their capacity to bring about change is so strikingly different.

Both Pentecostal churches and secular development NGOs are products of the contemporary neoliberal turn and its reconfigurations of self, society and economy. Born in the same circumstances, and addressing similar societal issues, Pentecostal churches and secular development NGOs thus have much in common. Most obviously, both provide services and welfare that used to be provided by the state, and both are part of translocal networks and confer translocal sensibilities (Corten & Marshall-Fratani 2001, van Dijk 1997, 2002a). Both operate in and are attuned to a strongly market logic. New Pentecostal churches and new NGOs appear at dizzying speeds, with new offerings and new innovations adapting to meet local demand. There is strong competition within each sector, and sometimes between them. Local churches and NGOs are often established by young charismatic leaders, and both often seek to challenge traditional and established power structures. Both are driven by values and are inspired by a particular vision of society and the 'good life' that they try to bring about. Both invocate a state of crisis and offer routes to salvation, whether it is salvation of the soul or of the soil. Both offer deliverance, from sin or from underdevelopment. And both wage wars against evil, be that conceptualised as Satan or as poverty.

Why, then, do the Pentecostal churches seem to be rather more successful in bringing about change that is effective, deep-rooted and long-lasting? I would suggest that there are four main reasons. First, although Pentecostal churches and secular NGOs both exist within a market logic, their funding sources are considerably different and this leads to some highly significant differences in their modes of operation and accountability. While most NGOs receive much of their funding from external stakeholders, such as foreign governments and international donors, and thus have to respond to the demands of stakeholders far removed

from the people that they actually serve, Pentecostal churches are almost entirely funded by their followers, through tithes and other offerings. Thus a church's survival and fortune depends on it attracting a large, and preferably wealthy, congregation. One consequence of this funding arrangement is that for churches to succeed they must be responsive to the demands of the 'religious consumer' and continuously adapt to follow trends. Third wave, neo-charismatic churches can be the most responsive of all, having no links to the more centralised and regulated forms of the mainline denominations. NGOs, in contrast, are often neither responsive nor accountable to the people they supposedly serve, instead having to report back to national and international donors.

Second, Pentecostal churches focus on transforming individual subjectivities. And they have become experts in this area. The 'transformative capacity' (Eisenstadt 1968) of Pentecostalism is quite astonishing. As several of the chapters in this book show, converts learn to see themselves and their lives in a new light. They reject passive, fatalistic beliefs and reclaim their agency. And in very many cases this new sense of empowerment leads to new behaviours and new types of social relations – both of which enhance economic development and foster upward social mobility. While NGOs and secular development theory are beginning to become interested in the connection between personal change and social change, and to place more emphasis on empowerment (Fisher 1997, Friedmann 1992, Kauffman 1990), they currently lack the tools to bring about personal transformation to anywhere near the same degree as the Pentecostals. While Pentecostals focus very strongly on the individual, most development NGOs tend to think more at the community level. While Pentecostals seek to bring about personal transformation, NGOs tend to be more interested in structural transformation.[5] When it comes to bringing about social and economic change it seems that approaches that focus on individuals are rather more effective.

Third, Pentecostal churches are rather better than NGOs at fostering participation. Church members find themselves actively involved in church activities from the start – whether it is participating in bible study, singing in the choir or running numerous other church activities. Pentecostal pastors are adept at getting people involved and helping them to feel part of the church community. Decision-making is very often democratic and all sectors of society are included, even women and outcaste groups. As such, Pentecostal churches are indeed locally owned organisations, run by the people for the people, in a way that most development NGOs simply are not. And because of this,

Pentecostal churches quickly become embedded in local communities and are seen as moral and meaningful institutions.

The fourth reason has to do with the way that Pentecostalism and secular development ideologies relate to the past and to traditional African religions and cultural practices. As discussed above, NGOs and secular ideologies of development largely ignore religion and culture altogether. They operate in a rational ontology, assume a society of Western-type individuals and pay little attention to traditional values, practices or forms of social organisation. In doing so, they fail to offer people a way to legitimately change any of these traditional forms or to extricate themselves from them. In contrast, Pentecostalism, with its holistic ontology which incorporates spirits and ancestors and witches, profoundly recognises the social and cultural reality in which people live, and, moreover, offers people a way to legitimately – morally – remove themselves from these traditional social and cultural forms, to reshape important social relations and to behave in a way which focuses more on individualism and accumulation.

It is for these reasons, as the chapters of this book show in rich ethnographic detail, that Pentecostal churches are often more successful in bringing about social and economic change than are secular development NGOs. And when these two types of organisation work together, or in parallel, in the same community, the overall potential for change is phenomenal.

Outline of the book

Part I. Pentecostalism and the neoliberal turn

The three chapters in Part I explore the rise of Pentecostal Christianity in the context of the major socio-economic transformations of neoliberalism. In the opening chapter (2), Jean Comaroff describes the epochal shift in the relations between capital, labour, consumption and place that characterises global neoliberal capitalism, with business increasingly liberated from regulatory control, states being rolled back and the division of labour becoming increasingly globalised. For many people in the developing world these changes are experienced as increasing instability, peripheralisation and inequality, coupled with widening gulfs between aspiration and possibility. Noting that the interplay between economics and religion has never been severed, and discussing the contemporary relevance of Weber's Protestant Ethic, she identifies two major dimensions of religious change that have emerged in dialectical tension to these socio-economic shifts. Both indicate a

move towards holism and a reconnection of the binary oppositions that laid the bedrock of the modernist project. The first is a sociological shift towards breaking down the dichotomy of church and state or religion and society. In the Pentecostal worldview, religion cannot be relegated to the private sphere, but rather God is in everything, from business to politics to entertainment. Second, there is a related ontological shift, reconfiguring the boundaries between sacred and secular, spiritual and material, self and society and emotion and cognition. Comaroff eloquently argues that these religious shifts emerge from a loss of faith in modernist conceptions of the world, as people find them inadequate to explain their lived reality or to offer routes to success. The new religious holism of Pentecostalism, in contrast, has something to offer to both the winners and losers of neoliberalism. For the rich it acknowledges aspirations and assuages guilt, and for the poor it offers welfare services and healing.

Päivi Hasu takes up this latter theme in her chapter (3) about Pentecostal churches in Tanzania. She provides a detailed study of two very different Pentecostal congregations in Dar es Salaam. Efatha is a rapidly growing, independent church catering to the entrepreneurial middle class. Drawing on the theology of Ghanaian 'religious superstar' Mensa Otabil, Efatha preaches a self-consciously materialist form of salvation, and encourages its congregants to work hard, empower themselves and enjoy abundance and economic prosperity. A central tenet of belief for Efatha congregants is 'give and you shall receive', and large amounts of money are given to the church in weekly collections and tithes and in the purchase of shares in the Efatha Foundation. With this money Efatha now owns and runs its own TV station, bank and newspaper, allowing it to spread its message further and to utilise business at the very heart of its evangelical activities. In stark contrast, the Glory of Christ Tanzania Church has a predominantly poor and underprivileged congregation, and it focuses on healing activities and deliverance from satanic forces. This church in particular is known for its ability to return people from the state of being zombies (*misukule*), people who are thought to be taken to carry out nocturnal unpaid labour for witches, while their bodies lie in bed at night. Victimised and slaving away for their capitalist owners in an occult economy that mirrors the emerging neoliberal one, these zombies wake up listless and exhausted. The Glory of Christ Tanzania Church organises services, consultations and vigils to drive away these satanic forces and to restore their victims to health and wellbeing. It helps its congregants to reconceptualise their problems (such as failure at school, teenage pregnancies) as the actions of demonic

forces and gives them support and direction in life. Through these two very different churches, Pentecostalism is able to cater to the spiritual needs of both the rich and the poor, the winners and the losers in the neoliberal turn. In both cases it seeks to bring about massive transformations in ontology, subjectivity and behaviour, creating new individuals, more able to deal with the social and economic situations in which they find themselves.

Basing himself in post-development theory, Rijk van Dijk also looks at the transformation of subjectivity and behaviour in his rich ethnographic study of the 'embedded development thinking' in Ghanaian Pentecostal churches, both in Ghana and in Botswana. Van Dijk's churches cater mainly to the upwardly mobile middle classes and particularly to Ghanaian migrant business-people in Botswana, who primarily own and run shops, beauty salons and car repair businesses. The chapter (4) focuses on how these churches seek to change selfhood and behaviour in two key areas – sexuality and relationships and business and enterprise. In the area of sexuality, the church offers counselling services to young couples and promotes 'Christian courtship' and 'abstinence pledges'. It promotes a marked 'break with the past' regarding sexual behaviour and carries out extensive AIDS education. Church counsellors speak frankly with youth about sexual matters and try to convince them that premarital abstinence is the way to a happy and healthy life. With regard to business and enterprise, these churches promote an ideology of hard work, empowerment and pro-activity. Similar to the Efatha church in Tanzania, the Ghanaian churches draw on the teachings of Mensa Otabil, and promote a form of salvation through the market. Rather strikingly, they back this up with business trainings and seminars, and the active promotion of such modernist skills as time management, planning and budgeting. They thus actively give their congregants the skills and outlook necessary to succeed in a market economy. Van Dijk argues that the analytic separation between religion and development, which has characterised development and post-development discourse since the 1950s, must be collapsed in the study of these Pentecostal movements, where the tools of development and economic growth are often being given by the churches themselves.

Part II. Pentecostal churches and secular NGOs: different routes to salvation

The five chapters in Part II seek to compare and contrast Pentecostal churches and secular NGOs as different types of development organisation operating in a variety of settings. The first three chapters

focus mainly on the similarities and complementarities. Piot's chapter (5) discusses the rise of the Pentecostal churches and development NGOs in post-Cold War, neoliberal West Africa, focusing particularly on Ghana and Togo. His analysis moves between the cities and the villages, and he shows how both the Pentecostals and the NGOs employ a 'spiritual cartography' whereby Satan (Pentecostals) or poverty and backwardness (NGOs) are to be found in the villages, while Christ (Pentecostals) and modernity (NGOs) are to be found in the towns. 'Salvation' or 'development' can only be achieved through a marked 'break with the past'. He also shows how both types of organisation make important use of affect and emotion: the Pentecostals with their emotionally laden prayer services and rousing speakers who make people feel good and motivate them to take control of their lives, and the NGOs, particularly BØRNEfonden, a Danish child sponsorship agency working in Togo, who use affect in the creation of (pseudo-)personal relationships between Western sponsors and 'their' African child.

Moving to East Africa, Smith discusses very similar themes in his chapter (6) on Taita, a rural area of Kenya where the neoliberal turn has led to a massive influx of both Pentecostal churches and secular development NGOs. Smith's analysis of the similarities and differences between these two types of organisation echoes Piot's, indicating the continent-wide nature of this social–economic–religious transformation. He also goes further, and begins an analysis of how Pentecostal churches and secular development NGOs interact with each other, as in practice many are present in the same communities and work with the same individuals. He explores what happened when Plan, a secular development NGO began operations in Taita, with its established Catholic Church of the older elites and the new Pentecostal church of the rather revolutionary youth. He shows that while the Pentecostals and the NGO shared a desire to break down old and corrupt power structures and create a more transparent and democratic society, they failed to fully align with each other because of their different understandings of the past and of 'tradition'. Plan considered recent power structures to be corrupt and unequal, but harkened back to an imagined past where they believed that traditional leaders presided fairly over community issues. For the Pentecostals, these very traditional structures were what were corrupt and unequal, and they sought to overthrow them, not reinstate them. Plan sought out local leaders to work with and ended up handing over much of the management of their projects to the Catholic elite, thus inadvertently reinforcing local power structures. When they realised what had happened and began to suspect that

funds were being siphoned off, they tried to place young Pentecostals onto the community committees. However, the Catholic elders refused to show them the accounts, and eventually the Pentecostal youth pulled out. Despite the desire to break down traditional power structures, the traditional elite managed to win this particular power struggle. Soon afterwards Plan left Taita, and the Pentecostals decided to form their own NGO.

Freeman's chapter (7) also explores what happens when Pentecostal churches and development NGOs operate in the same community, focusing on the village of Masho in the Gamo Highlands of southern Ethiopia. Using her ethnography to discuss both Marxian and Weberian theories of change, she shows how in this case the Pentecostal church and the development NGO, respectively, offered the two necessary ingredients for rapid social transformation – a change in values and subjectivity, and a new opportunity for enterprise. While on their own it is likely that neither organisation would have had much impact in Masho, the fact that they were operational there at the same time and that the changes they brought about could feed off each other, led to staggering social change in a very short time, including the successful development of a market-based apple enterprise and rapid conversion to Pentecostal Christianity.

The final two chapters explore some of the key differences between Pentecostal churches and secular NGOs as development actors. Jones' chapter (8) offers a fascinating analysis of the various institutions set up by the Pentecostal Assemblies of God church and various development NGOs in Teso, Uganda. Teso is a poor rural area, only marginally involved in national or international markets. Its most significant recent history is the violent insurgency that took place between 1986 and 1993, in which tens of thousands of people died. In the period after the insurgency, the Pentecostal church and various NGOs entered the area. Seeking to draw a line after this period of terrible social and moral collapse, many people were attracted to the Pentecostal church with its demand to 'make a break with the past'. It offered law and order, tight morals and meaning for a traumatised people terrified of further violence. Its institutions, both the church itself and the various committees it established, have become enduring features of Teso community life. In contrast, argues Jones, the activities of the NGOs failed to offer meaning or morality to the people of Teso, and thus their institutions – water committees, marketing associations, rural innovation groups – remained extrinsic to community life and disbanded as soon as the project finished or the NGO left.

In the final chapter (9), Parsitau looks at the transformation of gender relations by Pentecostals and NGOs in Kenya. While both types of organisation desire women's empowerment and carry out a wide range of activities to bring it about, they differ markedly in their views about quite how much women should be empowered and whether they should take on leadership positions or ultimately remain subservient to their husbands and men in general. While the NGOs push for full gender equality but fail to achieve it, the majority of the Pentecostal churches do not accept women into leadership positions and preach the biblical notion that woman should be man's helpmate. This intransigence, and their lack of acceptance of women in 'non-traditional roles' (unmarried, divorced, single mothers) has, however, spurred a breakaway movement of women-only church organisations, run by women, for women. Parsitau explores the various gender dynamics of both the Pentecostals and the NGOs and considers the extent to which either succeeds in bringing about a transformation of gender relations in Kenya.

Notes

1. This introduction has benefited from input and inspiration from all the contributors and also from detailed comments from Maurice Bloch, Jean Comaroff, Deborah James and Norman Long.
2. The amount of money raised by these churches worldwide is quite astounding, topping US$30 billion in 2000 (Barrett and Johnson 2002: 287).
3. And in both cases there was a marked increase in concern about witches and witchcraft, further suggesting the parallels in these two situations.
4. Wealth that has flowed into Africa in recent years in the form of foreign direct investment has led to wealth flowing out again in the form of profits and revenues to foreign investors. Very little of the revenue generated from mineral and resource extraction, to take the most significant example, has entered into wider African society (Ferguson 2005).
5. Although some NGOs are beginning to place more emphasis on the individual – particularly in micro-finance and enterprise projects – there is still a tendency to think at the level of the collective, such that even in these projects individual beneficiaries are often organised into savings groups, enterprise associations or cooperatives. In any case, even when they focus on the individual they consider material opportunities and economic conditions, and not on subjectivity.

References

Alkire, Sabina. 2005. *Valuing Freedoms: Sen's Capability Approach and Poverty Reduction.* Oxford: Oxford University Press.
Akoko, Robert. 2007. *'Ask and You Shall Be Given': Pentecostalism and the Economic Crisis in Cameroon.* Leiden: African Studies Centre.

Anderson, Allan. 2004. *An Introduction to Pentecostalism: Global Charismatic Christianity*. Cambridge: Cambridge University Press.

Anderson, K. and Rieff, D. 2005. Global Civil Society: A Sceptical View. In H. Anheier, M. Glasius and M. Kaldor (Eds). *Global Civil Society 2004/5*. London: Sage Publications.

Aryeetey, Ellen. 1998. Consultative Processes in Community Development in Northern Ghana. *Community Development*, 33(4): 301–313.

Austin, Diane. 1981. Born Again … and Again and Again: Communitas and Social Change among Jamaican Pentecostalists. *Journal of Anthropological Research*, 37(3): 226–246.

Barbalet, Jack. 2008. *Weber, Passion and Profits: 'The Protestant Ethic and the Spirit of Capitalism' in Context*. Cambridge: Cambridge University Press.

Barrett, David. 2001. *World Christian Trends, AD 30–AD 2200*. Pasadena: William Carey.

Barrett, David and Todd Johnson. 2002. Global Statistics. In Burgess, Stanley and Eduard van der Maas (Eds), *The New International Dictionary of Pentecostal and Charismatic Movements*. Michigan: Zondervan.

Barrett, David, G. Kurian and Todd Johnson. 2001. *World Christian Encyclopedia*. Oxford: Oxford University Press.

Bellah, Robert. 1957. *Tokugawa Religion: The Values of Pre-Industrial Japan*. Boston: Beacon Press.

Bellah, Robert. 1963. Reflections on the Protestant Ethic Analogy in Asia. *Journal of Social Issues*, 19(1): 52–60.

Benedetti, Carlo. 2006. Islamic and Christian Inspired Relief NGOs: Between Tactical Collaboration and Strategic Diffidence. *Journal of International Development*, 18: 849–859.

Berger, Peter. 2004. Max Weber Is Alive and Well and Living in Guatemala: The Protestant Ethic Today. Paper prepared at the conference on the Norms, Beliefs and Institutions of Twenty First Century Capitalism: Celebrating Max Weber's 'The Protestant Ethic and the Spirit of Capitalism', Ithaca, New York, 8 October.

Berger, Peter. 2009. Faith and Development. *Society*, 46: 69–75.

Bialecki, Jon. 2008. Between Stewardship and Sacrifice: Agency and Economy in a Southern Californian Charismatic Church. *Journal of the Royal Anthropological Institute (N.S.)*, 14: 372–390.

Bialecki, Jon, Naomi Haynes and Joel Robbins. 2008. The Anthropology of Christianity. *Religion Compass*, 2(6): 1139–1158.

Bond, Patrick and George Dor. 2003. Neoliberalism and Poverty Reduction Strategies in Africa. Discussion paper at the Regional Network for Equity in Health in Southern Africa.

Bornstein, Erica. 2005. *The Spirit of Development: Protestant NGOs, Morality and Economics in Zimbabwe*. Stanford: Stanford University Press.

Botchway, Karl. 2001. Paradox of Empowerment: Reflections on a Case Study from Northern Ghana. *World Development*, 29(1): 135–153.

Burgess, Stanley and Eduard van der Maas (Eds). 2002. *The New International Dictionary of Pentecostal and Charismatic Movements*. Michigan: Zondervan.

Bush, Ray. 2010. Food Riots: Poverty, Power and Protest. *Journal of Agrarian Change*, 10(1): 119–129.

Chambers, Robert and Gordon Conway. 1991. Sustainable Rural Livelihoods: Practical Concepts for the 21st Century. IDS discussion paper 296.

Chege, S. 1999. Donors Shift More Aid to NGOs. *Global Policy Forum.* www.globalpolicy.org/ngos/issues/chege.htm

Clarke, Gerard. 2006. Faith Matters: Faith-Based Organisations, Civil Society and International Development. *Journal of International Development,* 18: 835–848.

Coleman, Simon. 2002. The Faith Movement: A Global Religious Culture? *Culture and Religion,* 3: 3–19.

Coleman, Simon. 2000. *The Globalisation of Charismatic Christianity: Spreading the Gospel of Prosperity.* Cambridge: Cambridge University Press.

Comaroff, Jean and John Comaroff (Eds). 2001. *Millenial Capitalism and the Culture of Neoliberalism.* Durham: Duke University Press.

Comaroff, Jean and John Comaroff. 2000. Privatising the Millenium: New Protestant Ethics and the Spirits of Capitalism in Africa, and Elsewhere. *Afrika Spectrum,* 35(3): 293–312.

Cooke, Bill and Uma Kothari (Eds). 2001. *Participation: The New Tyranny?* London: Zed Books.

Corten, André and Ruth Marshall-Fratani (Eds). 2001. *Between Babel and Pentecost: Transnational Pentecostalism in Africa and Latin America.* Bloomington: Indiana University Press.

Csordas, Thomas. 2007. Global Religion and the Re-Enchantment of the World: The Case of the Catholic Charismatic Renewal. *Anthropological Theory,* 7(9): 295–314.

Csordas, Thomas. 2002. *Body/Meaning/Healing.* New York: Palgrave Macmillan.

Csordas, Thomas. 1992. Religion and the World System: The Pentecostal Ethic and the Spirit of Monopoly Capital. *Dialectical Anthropology,* 17: 3–24.

Curry, Timothy. 1997. The LDC Debt Crisis. *In History of the Eighties – Lessons for the Future, Volume 1: An Examination of the Banking Crisis in the 1980s and Early 1990s.* Federal Deposit Insurance Corporation.

Dayton, D. 1987. *Theological Roots of Pentecostalism.* Peabody: Hendrickson.

De Temple, Jill. 2006. 'Haiti Appeared at My Church': Faith-Based Organizations, Transnational Activism and Tourism in Sustainable Development. *Urban Anthropology,* 35: 155–181.

Deneulin, Severine. 2009. *Religion in Development: Rewriting the Secular Script.* London: Zed Books.

Deneulin, Severine and Carole Rakodi. 2011. Revisiting Religion: Development Studies Thirty Years On. *World Development,* 39(1): 45–54.

Dicklitch, Susan. 1998. *The Elusive Promise of NGOs in Africa: Lessons from Uganda.* Basingstoke: Macmillan.

Dicklitch, Susan and Heather Rice. 2004. The Mennonite Central Committee (MCC) and Faith-Based NGO Aid to Africa. *Development in Practice,* 14(5): 660–672.

Edwards, Michael and David Hulme (Eds). 1996a. *Beyond the Magic Bullet: NGO Performance and Accountability in the Post-Cold War World.* West Hartford: Kumarian.

Edwards, Michael and David Hulme. 1996b. Too Close for Comfort? The Impact of Official Aid on Nongovernmental Organisations. *World Development,* 24(6): 961–973.

Eisenstadt, Shmuel Noah. 1968. *The Protestant Ethic and Modernization.* London: Basic Books.

Elliot, Charles. 1987. Some Aspects of Relations between the North and South in the NGO Sector. *World Development*, 15: 57–68.

Ellis, Stephen. 1996. Africa after the Cold War: New Patterns of Government and Politics. *Development and Change*, 27: 1–28.

Escobar, Arturo. 2007. Post-Development As Concept and Social Practice. In Ziai, Aram (Ed.), *Exploring Post-Development: Theory and Practice, Problems and Perspectives*. London: Routledge.

Federici, Silvia. 2001. The Debt Crisis, Africa and the New Enclosures. *The Commoner*, N2: 1–13. http://www.commoner.org.uk/02federici.pdf

Ferguson, James. 2006. *Global Shadows: Africa in the Neoliberal World Order*. Durham: Duke University Press.

Ferguson, James. 2005. Seeing Like an Oil Company: Space, Security and Global Capital in Neoliberal Africa. *American Anthropologist*, 107(3): 377–382.

Fisher, William. 1997. Doing Good? The Politics and Antipolitics of NGO Practices. *Annual Review of Anthropology*, 26: 439–464.

Freston, Paul. 2001. *Evangelicals and Politics in Asia, Africa and Latin America*. Cambridge: Cambridge University Press.

Freston, Paul. 1995. Pentecostalism in Brazil: A Brief History. *Religion*, 25: 119–133.

Friedmann, John. 1992. *Empowerment: The Politics of Alternative Development*. Oxford: Blackwell.

Garner, Robert. 2000. Religion As a Source of Social Change in the New South Africa. *Journal of Religion in Africa*, 30(3): 310–343.

Geertz, Clifford. 1962. Social Change and Economic Modernization in Two Indonesian Towns: A Case in Point. In Hagen, E. (Ed.), *On the Theory of Social Change*. Homewood: Dorsey.

Geertz, Clifford. 1956. Religious Belief and Economic Behaviour in a Central Javanese Town: Some Preliminary Considerations. *Economic Development and Cultural Change*, 4(2): 134–158.

Gellner, David. 2001. *The Anthropology of Buddhism and Hinduism: Weberian Themes*. Oxford: Oxford University Press.

Gifford, Paul. 2004. *Ghana's New Christianity: Pentecostalism in a Globalising African Economy*. London: Hurst.

Gifford, Paul. 1998. *African Christianity: Its Public Role*. London: Hurst.

Gifford, Paul (Ed.). 1995. *The Christian Churches and the Democratization of Africa*. Leiden: Brill.

Gifford, Paul. 1994. Some Recent Developments in African Christianity. *African Affairs*, 93: 513–534.

Gluckman, Max. 1954. *Rituals of Rebellion in South-East Africa*. Manchester: Manchester University Press.

Goody, Jack. 2003. Religion and Development: Some Comparative Considerations. *Development*, 46(4): 64–67.

Gough, Ian and J. Allister McGregor (Eds). 2007. *Wellbeing in Developing Countries: From Theory to Research*. Cambridge: Cambridge University Press.

Goulet, Denis. 1997. Development Ethics: A New Discipline. *International Journal of Social Economics*, 24(11): 1160–1171.

Grombich, R. and G. Obeyesekere. 1989. *Buddhism Transformed: Religious Change in Sri Lanka*. Princeton: Princeton University Press.

Hackett, Rosalind. 1998. Charismatic/Pentecostal Appropriation of Media Technologies in Nigeria and Ghana. *Journal of Religion in Africa*, 28(3): 258–277.

Hanlon, Joseph. 1991. *Mozambique: Who Calls the Shots?* Oxford: James Currey.

Hearn, Julie. 2007. African NGOs: The New Compradors? *Development and Change*, 38(6): 1095–1110.

Hearn, Julie. 1998. The NGO-isation of Kenyan Society: USAID and the Restructuring of Health Care. *Review of African Political Economy*, 75: 89–100.

Hefferan, Tara. 2007. *Twinning Faith and Development: Parish Church Partnering in the US and Haiti*. Bloomfield: Kumarian.

Hollenweger, Walter. 1997. *Pentecostalism: Origins and Developments Worldwide*. Peabody: Hendrickson.

Hulme, David and Michael Edwards (Eds). 1997. *NGOs, States and Donors: Too Close for Comfort?* Basingstoke: Macmillan.

Igoe, Jim and Tim Kelsall. 2005. *Between a Rock and a Hard Place: African NGOs, Donors and the State*. Durham: Carolina Academic Press.

Kaag, Mayke. 2008. Transnational Islamic NGOs in Chad: Islamic Solidarity in the Age of Neoliberalism. *Africa Today*, 54(3): 3–18.

Kakwani, Nanak and Jacques Silber (Eds). 2007. *The Many Dimensions of Poverty*. London: Palgrave Macmillan.

Kamsteeg, Franz. 1998. *Prophetic Pentecostalism in Chile: A Case Study on Religion and Development Policy*. Lanham: Scarecrow.

Kauffman, L. 1990. The Anti-Politics of Identity. *Socialist Review*, 20(1): 67–80.

Keyes, Charles. 2002. Weber and Anthropology. *Annual Review of Anthropology*, 31: 233–255.

Klees, Steven. 2002. NGOs: Progressive Force or Neoliberal Tool? *Current Issues in Comparative Education*, 1(1): 49–54.

Korten, David. 1990. *Getting to the 21st Century: Voluntary Action and the Global Agenda*. West Hartford: Kumarian.

Lewis, David. 2001. *The Management of Non-Governmental Development Organisations*. London: Routledge.

Logie, Dorothy and Jessica Woodroffe. 1993. Structural Adjustment: The Wrong Prescription for Africa? *British Medical Journal*, 307: 41–44.

Luhrmann, Tanya. 2004. Metakinesis: How God Becomes Intimate in Contemporary US Christianity. *American Anthropologist*, 106: 518–528.

Manji, Firoze and Carl O'Coill. 2002. The Missionary Position: NGOs and Development in Africa. *International Affairs*, 78(3): 567–583.

Marshall, Katherine and Marisa Van Saanen. 2007. *Development and Faith: Where Mind, Heart and Soul Work Together*. Washington, DC: The World Bank.

Marshall, Ruth. 1991. Power in the Name of Jesus. *Review of African Political Economy*, 52: 21–37.

Martin, Bernice. 2006. Pentecostal Conversion and the Limits of the Market Metaphor. *Exchange*, 35(1): 61–91.

Martin, Bernice. 1998. From Pre- to Postmodernity in Latin America: The Case of Pentecostalism. In Heelas, Paul (Ed.), *Relgion, Modernity and Postmodernity*. Oxford: Blackwell.

Martin, Bernice. 1995. New Mutations of the Protestant Ethic among Latin American Pentecostals. *Religion*, 25(2): 101–117.

Martin, David. 2002. *Pentecostalism: The World Their Parish*. Oxford: Blackwell.

Martin, David. 1990. *Tongues of Fire: The Explosion of Protestantism in Latin America*. Oxford: Blackwell.

Matanga, Frank. 2010. NGOs and the Politics of Development in Africa. *Development*, 53(1): 114–119.

Maxwell, David. 2005. The Durawall of Faith: Pentecostal Spirituality in Neo-Liberal Zimbabwe. *Journal of Religion in Africa*, 35(1): 4–32.

Maxwell, David. 2000. 'Catch the Cockerel Before Dawn': Pentecostalism and Politics in Post-Colonial Zimbabwe. *Africa*, 70(2): 249–277.

Maxwell, David. 1998. 'Delivered from the Spirit of Poverty': Pentecostalism, Prosperity and Modernity in Zimbabwe. *Journal of Religion in Africa*, 28(3): 350–373.

McDonic, Susan. 2004. Witnessing, Work and Worship: World Vision and the Negotiation of Faith, Development and Culture. PhD dissertation, Department of Cultural Anthropology, Duke University.

Meyer, Birgit. 2007. Pentecostalism and Neo-Liberal Capitalism: Faith, Prosperity and Vision in African Pentecostal-Charismatic Churches. *Journal for the Study of Religion*, 20(2): 5–28.

Meyer, Birgit. 2006. Impossible Representations: Pentecostalism, Vision and Video Technology in Ghana. In Meyer, Birgit and Annalies Moors (Eds), *Religion, Media and the Public Sphere*. Bloomington: Indiana University Press.

Meyer, Birgit. 2004. Christianity in Africa: From African Independent to Pentecostal-Charismatic Churches. *Annual Review of Anthropology*, 33: 447–474.

Meyer, Birgit. 2002. Pentecostalism, Prosperity and Popular Cinema in Ghana. *Culture and Religion*, 3(1): 67–87.

Meyer, Birgit. 1998a. 'Make a Complete Break with the Past': Memory and Post-Colonial Modernity in Ghanaian Pentecostalist Discourse. *Journal of Religion in Africa*, 28(3): 316–349.

Meyer, Birgit. 1998b. Commodities and the Power of Prayer: Pentecostalist Attitudes towards Consumption in Contemporary Ghana. *Development and Change*, 29: 751–776.

Michael, Sarah. 2004. *Undermining Development: The Absence of Power among Local NGOs in Africa*. Oxford: James Currey.

Miller, Daniel. 1987. *Material Culture and Mass Consumption*. Oxford: Blackwell.

Nash, Manning. 1965. *The Golden Road to Modernity: Village Life in Contemporary Burma*. New York: John Wiley & Sons.

Nederveen Pieterse, Jan. 1998. My Paradigm or Yours? Alternative Development, Post-Development, Reflexive Development. *Development and Change*, 29: 343–373.

Pype, Katrien. 2009. 'We Need to Open up the Country': Development and the Christian Key Scenario in the Social Space of Kinshasa's Teleserials. *Journal of African Media Studies*, 1(1): 101–116.

Rahmato, Dessalegn, Bantirgu Akalewold and Yoseph Endeshaw. 2008. CSOs/NGOs in Ethiopia: Partners in Development and Good Governance. Report for the Ad Hoc CSO/NGO Task Force, Addis Ababa.

Rakodi, Carole. 2007. Understanding the Roles of Religion in Development: The Approach of the R&D Programme. Working Paper No. 9, Religions and Development Research Programme, University of Birmingham.

Riddell, Barry. 1992. Things Fall Apart Again: Structural Adjustment Programmes in Sub-Saharan Africa. *Journal of Modern African Studies*, 31(1): 53–68.

Robbins, Joel. 2004. The Globalisation of Pentecostal and Charismatic Christianity. *Annual Review of Anthropology*, 33: 117–143.

Roberts, Richard (Ed.). 1995. *Religion and the Transformations of Capitalism: Comparative Approaches*. London: Routledge.

Salamon, Lester. 1994. The Rise of the Non-Profit Sector. *Foreign Affairs*, 73(4): 109–122.

Schlemmer, Lawrence. 2008. *Dormant Capital: Pentecostalism in South Africa and its Potential Social and Economic Role*. Johannesburg: Centre for Development and Enterprise.

Scoones, Ian. 1998. Sustainable Rural Livelihoods: A Framework for Analysis. IDS working paper 72.

Selinger, Leah. 2004. The Forgotten Factor: The Uneasy Relationship between Religion and Development. *Social Compass*, 51(4): 523–543.

Sen, Amartya. 1999. *Development as Freedom*. Oxford: Oxford University Press.

Simutanyi, Neo. 1996. The Politics of Structural Adjustment in Zambia. *Third World Quarterly*, 17(4): 825–839.

Spiro, Melford. 1966. Buddhism and Economic Action in Burma. *American Anthropologist*, NS, 68(5): 1163–1173.

Stone, Russell. 1974. Religious Ethic and the Spirit of Capitalism in Tunisia. *International Journal of Middle East Studies*, 5(3): 260–273.

Ter Haar, Gerrie and Stephen Ellis. 2006. The Role of Religion in Development: Towards a New Relationship between the European Union and Africa. *European Journal of Development Research*, 18(3): 351–367.

Tomalin, E. 2008. Faith and Development. In Desai, V. and R. Potter (Eds), *Companion to Development Studies*. London: Hodder Education.

Turner, Victor. 1969. *The Ritual Process: Structure and Anti-Structure*. Chicago: Aldine.

Turner, Victor. 1968. *The Drums of Affliction: A study of Religious Processes among the Ndembu of Zambia*. Oxford: Clarendon Press.

Tvedt, Terje. 1998. *Angels of Mercy or Development Diplomats: NGOs and Foreign Aid*. Oxford: James Currey.

Ukah, AF-K. 2005. Those Who Trade with God Never Lose: The Economies of Pentecostal Activism in Nigeria. In Falola, T. (Ed.), *Christianity and Social Change in Africa: Essays in Honor of J.D.Y. Peel*. Durham: Carolina Academic Press.

van Dijk, Rijk. 2005. The Moral Life of the Gift in Ghanaian Pentecostal Churches in the Diaspora: Questions of (in-)dividuality and (in-)alienability in Transcultural Reciprocal Relations. In Van Binsbergen, W. and P. Geschiere (Eds), *Commodification: Things, Agency and Identities*. Hamburg: LIT Verlag.

van Dijk, Rijk. 2002a. The Soul Is the Stranger: Ghanaian Pentecostalism and the Diasporic Contestation of 'Flow' and 'Individuality'. *Culture and Religion*, 3(1): 49–67.

van Dijk, Rijk. 2002b. Religion, Reciprocity and Restructuring Family Responsibility in the Ghanaian Pentecostal Diaspora. In Bryceson, D. and U. Vorella (Eds), *The Transnational Family: New European Frontiers and Global Networks*. Oxford: Berg.

van Dijk, Rijk. 1997. From Camp to Encompassment: Discourses of Transsubjectivity in the Ghanaian Pentecostal Diaspora. *Journal of Religion in Africa*, 27(2): 135–159.

Ver Beek, K. 2002. Spirituality: A Development Taboo. In Eade, D. (Ed.), *Development and Culture: Selected Essays from Development in Practice*. Oxford: Oxfam GB.

Walton, John and Charles Raggin. 1990. Global and National Sources of Political Protest: Third World Responses to the Debt Crisis. *American Sociological Review*, 55,6: 876–890.

Walton, John and David Seddon (Eds). 1994. *Free Markets and Food Riots: The Politics of Global Adjustment*. Oxford: Blackwell.

Weber, Max. 2008 [1904–1905]. *The Protestant Ethic and the Spirit of Capitalism*. Translated by Talcott Parsons. Miami: BN Publishing.

World Resources Institute. 2005. Awakening Civil Society. In *Decisions for the Earth: Balance, Voice and Power*. http://pubs.wri.org/pubs content print.cfm?ContentID=1898

Part I

Pentecostalism and the Neoliberal Turn

2

Pentecostalism, Populism and the New Politics of Affect

Jean Comaroff

The massive growth of evangelical churches across much of the planet in recent times is especially ironic from an African perspective. It is not merely that these movements underline what has become a truism: the enduring, even intensifying salience of the sacred in our ever more rationalised world – something that defies the telos of disenchantment, presumed by the great evolutionary theorists of modernity. It is also that the forms of religious life that have proved most adaptive to conditions on the continent in the twenty first century challenge many of the tenets of Protestant modernism promulgated by the likes of Max Weber, or by those who hoped to usher Africans into the 'civilized' world by way of conversion. What is more, the movements that have proved to be most popular in current times have been self-propagating in a manner that eluded earlier, laborious efforts to seed Christianity on African soil – like the effort by the European missions to cultivate self-possessed African converts, to tame their passions and to instil a message of salvation through patient toil.

The kind of church that resonates most evidently with African sensibilities in the present is of another sort. As in many other parts of the world, from the US to Ukraine, Sao Paulo to Seoul, the Pentecostal movements that have waxed most luxuriantly across the continent in recent times promote conceptions of belief, personhood and emotion that contrast markedly with the ontology of mainstream Protestant modernism. These 'born-again' faiths have affinities with enduring forms of African religiosity, to be sure, forms that have long contested European Christianity, or remade it in independent ways. They also have links with home-grown apocalyptic movements of an earlier vintage, those sparked in African contexts by early twentieth century American revivalism, both black and white – the Zionist churches in South Africa,

41

for instance (Comaroff 1985, Sundkler 1961), or the Watchtower movement in the Rhodesias and Nyasaland (Fields 1985). Indeed, such resemblances have suggested to some that Pentecostal awakenings should be understood, first and foremost, in term of distinctively local, African continuities.

Nevertheless, the shape, scale and self-consciousness of the most recent Pentecostal movements in Africa also share features with developments elsewhere in the world, features that, as David Martin (2008) insists, are profoundly contemporary. And, while they assert a foundationalism of a kind, these churches also tend also to be outspokenly *opposed* to 'African tradition' per se, even though they continue, in their very opposition, to underline its power. In fact, what these movements stress is less an unbroken continuity with indigenous forms of belief than a self-conscious, *born-again* return to fundamentals. In this their faith seems to be of a distinctly late modern sort, striving at once to be authentic and totalising, yet being locked, simultaneously, in an explicit struggle with the threat of falsity, counterfeit, doubt. Such belief is late modern, also, in its means: in Africa, as elsewhere, it puts its trust is an electronically enabled millennium, in digitally enhanced miracles, televisual intimacies and mass-mediated communitas – the better to restore a sense of return to an original oneness with God. Yet in their propensity to frame local spiritual impetus in technologically reproducible, global forms, these movements are also part of a longer history; they serve to tune particular dispositions and aspirations to larger-scale projects, even processes of radical transformation, much like the evangelical movements of an earlier colonial era.

But current religious movements differ from these earlier counterparts in telling respects. For if the complexity of self-consciously 'born-again' faiths cannot be fully explained in terms of local African traditions or conditions alone, they also seem to defy more conventional theories of religious modernity, such as those enshrined in Weber's *Protestant Ethic and the Spirit of Capitalism* (2001). The kind of belief represented by what are sometimes termed 'neo-Pentecostalist movements' – like the Universal Church of the Kingdom of God, for instance, to which I shall make frequent reference later – differs in crucial ways from Weber's iconic model of Protestantism. Originally from Brazil, but now one of the fastest growing organisations in south-central regions of the continent, the Universal Church propagates a media-savvy, emotionally hyped, frankly materialist brand of faith that contrasts sharply with this-worldly asceticism. It also presumes a rather different social-institutional context of operation, being oriented to rather distinct ideals of

personhood, family and enterprise in the world. Yet this contemporary brand of Protestantism, I would suggest, is no less integrally connected to the spirit of capitalism than was its Weberian precursor, albeit to capitalism in its late modern, post-industrial phase. In fact the Universal Church, and movements like it, have a great deal to teach us about the current social epoch, in Africa and beyond. Why is it that these forms of social organisation have succeeded when so many other, characteristically modern institutions and sensibilities have faltered? How might they bring about social transformation at a time when older models of state-centred economy and 'development' have significantly receded?

The spirit of liberalisation

As I have noted elsewhere (Comaroff & Comaroff 2008, Comaroff 2009), the sacred has become increasingly prominent in profane places in our world. 'Jesus is the answer', declare large, uneven letters beside a highway to Sun City, northwest of Johannesburg, anticipating global audiences to be drawn by the 2010 World Cup. Further south, an ad proclaims 'Cape Town For Jesus – the final countdown. Tickets still available'. Cape Town for Jesus indeed – or at least, for explicitly enchanted enterprise of one kind or another! In the inner city, evangelical street-sweepers, their crisp overalls identifying them as 'God's Cleaners', ply their brooms along sidewalks that front a diverse array of thriving religious denominations, including several bustling mosques. Swelling evangelical congregations hold services in shopping malls and amphitheatres. Like their counterparts elsewhere, they avoid traditional ecclesiastical symbols; they have no steeples or spires, no bell towers or pointed arches, not even a crucifix. As Rybczynski (2005) points out, they look less like places of worship than performing-arts centres, community colleges or corporate headquarters (none of which is totally inapt). In a similar spirit, cutting-edge congregations use slick websites and Facebook pages to reach out to potential followers in terms that shun lofty piety, offering 'Self Discovery, New Friends, Lots of Praise, Lots of Fun'.[1] Faith-based groups, in other words, move ever more assertively into the mundane reaches and registers of everyday life: into business, education, politics, popular entertainment – domains hitherto taken to be distinct from religion, properly conceived.

Neither is this merely an African phenomenon. In the UK and the US, Pentecostal corporations run a growing number of privatised prisons (Burnside et al. 2005). In America, mega-churches have become sites 'where Wall Street meets the pulpit', where pastor-CEOs preach a 'gospel

of entrepreneurship and sound business practices' – for many see this as a response to God's call, which enjoins his stewards to economically empower the humble.[2] Such faith is not embarrassed to invoke ambition, desire or the frankly corporeal: in California, the exercise chain, *Lord's Gym* promises to build body and soul 'without compromising a properly Christian atmosphere' (Comaroff 2006); its logo is a pumped-up Jesus, bench-pressing a huge cross under the message, 'His Pain Your Gain'. It seems that no instrument is too profane to act as a vehicle of salvation, rendering more and more ambiguous that key dimension of the ideological architecture of liberal Western modernity – the line between sacred and secular.

None of these developments are altogether new, of course. The civic ideology of modern Western nation-states might have stressed the separation of powers – of the public and the private, the sacred and profane – but these ideals have always been undermined in practice. By the end of the twentieth century these ideals had been seriously flouted in many places, and the boundaries dividing government, market and organised religion were under siege almost everywhere. This undermining takes different institutional forms in different contexts: in Euro-America, the institutional divisions implied by the Keynesian state, with its grand civic institutions of justice, health care, education and so on have been transformed by the impact of deregulation and privatisation, opening the way for faith-based initiatives of all kinds. In Africa, the fragile civil structures of many post-colonial polities have buckled under the impact of structural adjustment, and religious organisations have expanded concomitantly. Congregations have been expanding, often offering members what amounts to alternative citizenship. Post-apartheid South Africa, from which most of my examples here are drawn, combines features of both these tendencies: although government there remains relatively robust, and organised labour has put something of a brake on the state's liberalising ambitions, its rulers' efforts to succeed in the global economy have introduced many of the features associated with neoliberalism (from the outsourcing of public services and resources and to the corporatisation of policy of all kinds and, also, to a widening of the gulf between the enfranchised and the dispossessed). Along with this have gone sharp shifts in the experience of belonging: the rapid expansion of holistic religious communities expresses a reality pithily captured by a pastor in the Universal Church: 'When the film credits roll at the end of your life', he declared, 'they will not acknowledge the South African government, they will thank us at the Universal Church.'

Here, as everywhere, changes in the form of religious life must be seen in the first instance in light of local history – the relatively recent 'transition to democracy', for example, which entailed an uneasy juxtaposition of 'liberation' and 'liberalisation' (Comaroff & Comaroff 2001, Comaroff 2002). But I shall argue that these shifts also bear similarities to changes taking place, to a greater or lesser degree in many other contexts, and that they therefore suggest more epochal transformations. Most immediately, they resemble processes occurring in other polities that have undergone similar dramatic regime change in recent years (in Central Europe and Latin America, for instance), contexts in which new democracies have sought to shape themselves amidst processes of state deregulation. But there are also observable changes in South African religious life that seem to be even more widely distributed than this. For example, the embrace of Pentecostal faith across much of the world seems to have been abetted by post-Cold War geopolitical shifts on a global scale, even though the precise impact of these transformations varies with context and location. What, if anything, underlies this apparent correlation, and how do we approach the challenging pattern of similarity and divergence that it presents?

For my purposes here, I focus on two, interrelated dimensions of this religious shift and the underlying historical reconfigurations of which it is part. The first is sociological, the second a matter of ontology. But first, how, precisely, do these transformations actually manifest themselves?

Born-again theocracies

While many have remarked on the growing commitment, across the world, to ideologies and policies vested in the logic of the market, fewer have noted the strong, apparently contrary strain that has gone along with this: a new sense of the force of divine destiny in human affairs, whether it be Pentecostal or Latin, Jewish, Muslim or Hindu. In a recent ten-nation survey of Pentecostal and charismatic Christians, for example, the Pew Forum on Religion and Public Life found that adherents of 'renewalist' faiths made up 'at least half the population in Brazil, Guatemala and Kenya, and about one-third that of South Africa and Chile' (Pew Forum 2006). These constituencies, it adds, are prone to bringing their commitments into public debate, with real consequences for processes of government. Theologico-politics, a concern of seventeenth century rationalists like Spinoza (1883), is again a lively reality, it appears. Indeed, amidst a flourishing of confessions of all types, the hegemony of liberal humanism, what Asad (2003: 13)

terms 'the modern project', has been ever more assertively brought into question in recent times, largely in the name of revealed truths and Godly imperatives. These challenges have been explicitly framed, in some places, in opposition to prevailing notions of the secular; thus the American pre-millennial pastor, Tim LaHaye (LaHaye & Noebel 2000), attacks the hubris of 'liberal humanism' in so many words. But dissent often emerges as a less overt shift in sensibility, a loss of faith in key tenets of modernist ontology, like the persuasiveness of social idioms of thought, or secular constructions of truth, history or 'development' (cf. Harding 1994, Smith 2008). Along with this goes an ever greater readiness to see the intervention of spiritual forces in ordinary events, and an ever more audible appeal to absolutist truths. In fact, a deep suspicion of social, relativist and humanist understanding is shared by foundationalists across a range of creeds. There are connections to be noted – in form, if not in content – to the concerns of other opponents of liberal humanism, from political neo-conservatives to market funda- mentalists. The latter are also partial to asserting the end of history and the treachery of philosophy, preferring putatively literal readings of the law from pulpit and bench (Crapanzano 2000).

A related aspect of current revitalised faith, no less in tension with the modernist project, is the growing salience of revelation as a legitimate basis for truth, action and the interpretation of events-in-time. Mod- ern liberal theory might champion the separation of church and state, but organised religion and revitalised belief play an ever more palpable role in the workings of government – not only in places like Uganda and Nigeria, but also in the US, the UK and Italy (Muehlebach 2007). In addition, a host of born-again believers across the world *choose* to suspend 'free' choice when convicted by divine authority, manifesting a form of selfhood somewhat different from the deliberative Kantian subject that many see as basic to modern rationalism (cf. Blom Hansen n.d.); different, too, from the choosing subject presumed by liberal mod- els of democracy and consumer-oriented identity. It might be argued that these idealised selves have had only uneven purchase beyond the West, in African societies, for instance (though they certainly were hege- monic within the European civilising missions, and in the projects of modernisation and development that characterised newly independent African nations). True, the born-again faiths that flourish across the non- European world at present resonate with local ontologies and senses of being, orientations that often defy the dualistic categories of lib- eral modern orthodoxy. These movements tend also to propose new forms of commitment, communication and subjectivity that are, I have

noted, a product of current historical conditions. Born-again conviction lays emphasis, for instance, on self-production, but also stresses engagement with the authority of foundational texts and prophetic callings. It displays a widespread quest for ontological security; for sovereignty, for a firm basis for law and order, for authoritative knowledge – all of these being aspects of experience seriously disrupted by current social conditions, especially in the post-colonial world.

But there is more. Pentecostal movements do not merely question, from below, the tenets of liberal modernist knowing and being. They aim, also, to counter the signature institutional arrangements that have nurtured the modernist world view – and this is where their sociological dimension becomes evident. Canonised above all in the liberal nation-state as imagined commonality, these arrangements presume a clear separation between a secular, neutral public domain and the realm of private commitment, interest and belief. But in late modern times, born-again faiths have tended to challenge that divide in various ways, seeking to reshape the received order of things, challenging the 'impartiality' of state law, the legitimacy of secular government, and the perceived moral vacuity of public institutions. Many such faiths work to 'reclaim' the fragmented realms and plural cultural registers of liberal modern society, to imbue the profane reaches of everyday life with divine purpose. Commerce, government, education, the media, popular arts – nothing seems too trivial or debased to be invested with hallowed purpose in the world. The task, according to Ted Haggard, erstwhile president of the National Association of Evangelicals in the US, is to put 'God-in-everything', so 'anything can be holy' (Newton 2006). This impetus is evident, too, among Pentecostals in Africa. The Universal Church, for instance, extends the reach of the Spirit into ever more mundane facets of ordinary life: its places of worship spring up in shopping malls and at taxi ranks; they offer menus of pragmatic services, all day, every day. This trajectory represents an ironic, late modern return to a kind of pervasive spirituality that is practically integrated with ordinary life – much like the forms of religion outlined in classic anthropological accounts of African traditional culture (Goody 1962, Lienhardt 1961).

The totalising, 'worlding'[3] ambition of many Pentecostal movements has special salience in an age of widespread deregulation, not least in Africa. At a time when, under the sway of neoliberal policies, many states have relinquished considerable responsibility for schooling, health and welfare – in short, for the social reproduction of their citizens – religious organisations have willingly reclaimed this role, a

role they never fully lost, in many places, to the grand disciplinary institutions of the modern state (vide the enduring importance of Catholic care, or the cradle-to-grave guardianship of clan associations in Southeast Asia). The recent expansion of faith-based social services and pedagogy has strongly challenged the idea of the separation of powers that underlay the tenets, if not always the practices, of most twentieth century liberal democracies.

Add to this the fact that organised religion has made a vital place for itself in the domain of politics, the market, the mass media, seeking to bend them to its purposes. As I have noted, this evinces a shift from the division of institutional labour captured in signal modernist accounts, like those of Durkheim (1984 [1892]) and Weber (2001 [1904–1905]). It diverges, too, from the rationalised religiosity of modern Protestantism, which tended to scorn faiths that ignored the distinction between sacred and secular, or church and state, dubbing them idolatrous, heathen superstitions. Indeed, this was how colonial mission churches viewed most indigenous African religion, and also the domesticated Christianities (the Independent Churches in early-twentieth century South Africa, for instance) whose pragmatic healing, inspired leadership and holistic care were seen as 'syncretic', even a 'bridge... back to heathenism' (Sundkler 1961).

These days, religious holism is in the ascent, a tendency evident not merely within Christianity, but within Judaism, Islam and beyond. It is especially evident in Pentecostalism, and in contexts where born-again belief resonates with forms of spiritual pragmatism never fully captured by northern Protestant orthodoxy. What Paul Jenkins (2002: 3) terms the 'New Christian Revolution' is centred in Latin America, Africa and Asia, which together have a growing majority of the estimated 2.6 billion Christians worldwide. Evangelical Pentecostal churches are said to attract almost 20 million new members a year, having emerged as the major competitor of a Catholicism that is itself becoming markedly more charismatic. Here, too, it is not merely that faith-based initiatives are expanding, or that their sense of the gifts of Spirit has a major impact on ordinary understandings of self, identity, politics and history. These movements are also assuming increasingly state-like responsibilities, especially where states themselves have been compromised in their governing capacity.

Take the New Life Church in Mafikeng, South Africa, for instance, an offshoot of the organisation of the same name founded in Colorado Springs in 1984. New Life typifies a brand of upbeat, technically savvy faith that aspires to fill the moral void left by the withering of older civic

norms in the post-colony. The congregation, part of a global network, mixes a lively charismatic realism with frank materiality, a theology comfortable with this-worldly desire. The church offers everything from marriage guidance to financial counselling and AIDS outreach, casting pastoral care in a service-oriented key. It also aims explicitly to entertain: 'It might sound heretical', says the pastor, 'but we strive to make worship exciting, affecting. Our competition, after all, is the video arcade, the movie house, and the casino.' In New Life's sparkling sanctuary, a sophisticated sound stage replaces the altar. A large screen – part karaoke, part powerpoint – flashes the lyrics, monitored by a technician at the rear. The membership spans a relatively wide spectrum of race and age among the more humble classes, all drawn by the pulsating vitality, the readiness to acknowledge the legitimacy of lively, this-worldly appetites.

As this example underlines, mass media have played a vital role in extending the influence of revitalised faith in the world, not just because such media radically amplify the scale, speed and directness of its address, but because they have become integral to the way that revelation takes form in experience. To a large extent, in other words, radio, TV and the Internet have come to shape the very form in which the sacred is witnessed. Of course, mass media have been used to spread the Word since the advent of the printing press; evangelists in Africa and elsewhere have long been avid users of novel means of communication, from magic lanterns to movies. At the same time, the reach of popular religious broadcasting today seems unprecedented. In Africa, transnational Evangelical and Muslim groups (Hackett n.d., Meyer 2002, Schulz 2007) are taking advantage of the deregulation of state media to build broadcast enterprises that impact powerfully on the circulation of images and the creation of subjects and publics. The means of communication in general are ever more under the control of faith-based corporations here. Religious media conduct a growing proportion of business on the continent, from paid religious programming to Pentecostal video-cassettes, gospel CDs and tapes conveying the *baraka* of sheikhs (Soares 2004).

The qualities displayed by revitalised faiths, then, are both old and new, uniform and diverse, global and thoroughly domesticated. Movements of this kind hardly exhaust the contemporary religious terrain, of course. But older, established denominations that tend to question their values and motives have also had to respond to the stunning effectiveness of their *modus operandi*, and their seemingly irrepressible appeal, especially among the young. While there appears to be an elective affinity between Pentecostalism and the unruly vitality of

economic liberalisation, its pragmatic preaching also harks back to the original holiness impetus in Industrial Revolution Methodism, the 'positive thinking' fostered by late nineteenth century Christian Science, and the 'name it and claim it' Rhema doctrine, first popularised by Kenneth Hagin of the Assemblies of God in Texas in the 1930s. What is more, as I have stressed, these legacies have been thoroughly domesticated in particular socio-cultural contexts, resonating with long-standing local forms; the Universal Church in southern Africa, for example, engages vigorously with anxieties about witchcraft, though it treats witches as minions of the devil and vestiges of evil tradition. In addition, the 'free market faith' of many – if not all – Pentecostals jibes with African expectations that spiritual favour will express itself in pragmatic blessing. The Brazilian-born preacher at the large, inner-city headquarters of the Universal Church in Cape Town sometimes places an over-sized domestic closet, the 'Lord's Treasure Chest', on the podium: those who have faith, he declares, will receive the manifold goods it contains. Even more dramatic is the example of Miracle 2000, a South African pyramid scheme, whose born-again founder promised a 220 per cent return on investments in 42 days. The promise drew crowds from across the land to the founder's East Rand home. When the police cracked down on the scheme, hundreds of outraged believers marched on the High Court in Pretoria demanding the release of their 'Messiah'. They carried placards declaring 'Do My Prophet No Harm' (Bokaba 2000).

What, then, *does* make sense of the exuberant growth of 'new Christianity' in these times, particularly in Africa? What of its continuities with, and breaks from, the past? Talal Asad (2003) has argued that the process of holding the line between the secular and the sacred has been essential to the ideology of the modern liberal state and its modes of governance. Shifts in the nature of this state might well be implicated, then, in the kind of boundary breaching that comes with the rise of Pentecostalism. But as I have suggested, there has also been a widespread *popular* impetus, in the early twenty first century world, to redefine the place of religion in the civic order – a widespread effort to recover a sense of authenticity, to give birth, anew, to a sense of sovereign authority in the world. All this implies more thoroughgoing structural transformation. Indeed, there is much to suggest that the character of contemporary faith is integral to a reorganisation of core components of capitalist modernity as social formation, a worldwide process that has specific implications for post-colonial Africa. This shift has entailed an intensification of some signature features of the liberal modern order, and an eclipse of others, a process made manifest in the

changing credo and institutional form of liberal democracies across the world. These shifts vary in local manifestation and so, too, does the nature and impact of the religious revitalisation I have been describing here. Some scholars have argued, for example, that the challenge to secular hegemony has been less evident in Western Europe – the presumed heartland of liberal democracy – than elsewhere, although there is mounting evidence to suggest that this claim might need rethinking.[4] Indeed, there are grounds for identifying some very widespread trends in religious life across the world. How might this reconfigured social landscape speak back, with latter-day insight, to classic accounts of religion and modernity, like Weber's classic conception of the kinship between the Protestant Ethic and the Spirit of Capitalism?

The same again, but not quite: the neo-world order

What has come to be glossed as 'neoliberalism' has been characterised in a variety of ways, few of which capture the mix of continuity and rupture, intensification and transformation at issue. We appear to be witnessing an epochal shift in relations among capital, labour, consumption and place. For one thing, the generation of wealth is more reliant than ever before on abstract means – on the transaction of quasi-monetary instruments across space and time in an electronic economy. For another, primary production has been reorganised as the quest for a cheap, tractable workforce has eroded existing bases of industrial manufacture, has globalised the division of labour and has significantly liberated corporate enterprise from state regulation. The connection between sites of manufacture and consumption has become increasingly deterritorialised, being rendered opaque in a way that undermines the very idea of a national economy, one in which interest groups recognise each other as interdependent components of a commonweal. In Africa, where local and regional economies have historically been integrated into world markets more by means of primary extraction than industrialised production, the neoliberal era has brought further peripheralisation from mainstream enterprise, although it has also seen a thickening entanglement of points on the continent with informal, twilight transaction of all kinds and an ever more ruthless – and profitable – scramble by external powers for scarce resources. Secular models of economic rationality and development, under such conditions, are less and less plausible. The growth of electronic communications has further exacerbated these effects, intensifying the circulation of images, capital and objects across space and time, imploding prior borders and creating

novel associations – but also opening up more extreme socio-economic divisions, new gulfs between aspiration and possibility, experience and understanding.

In the upshot, the spheres of politics and economy do not map easily on to one another – as has become apparent to contemporary South Africans, struggling to come to terms with porous national borders, privatisation and a mounting sense that global economic pressures are drastically undermining the local workforce, and the promise of civic inclusion. These experiences unsettle efforts to re-imagine the nation as a unified entity, and complicate understandings of belonging, citizenship and attachment. They also erode commonsense assumptions about the relation between signifiers and signifieds, the real and the counterfeit, the sources of misfortune and evil.

It is such forces that structure the terrain on which revitalised religion takes shape. These spiritual movements, I stress, are not simple, autonomic responses to 'neoliberalism'. They are also vanguards of a vision which endorses earthly desire and entrepreneurial ambition – most overtly borne by a host of so-called prosperity gospels that thrive on the African continent. In this, revitalised movements often anticipate and reinforce the work of other agents of development, especially at a time when this work is driven less by state-centred models than visions of private enterprise. Neither are these movements translocal in an unprecedented sense; the Roman Catholic Church – arguably the original translocal non-governmental organisation (NGO) – has been 'global' for 2000 years. But, over the centuries, the nature of globalism has changed. Whereas the Christian commonwealth forged by colonial evangelists followed the map of a Eurocentric, international order, post-colonial spirituality evinces different translocal trajectories – electronic, economic, emotive – that link newly emergent centres and peripheries, and often pay scant attention to national borders. This process is exemplified by the south–south ministries of the Universal Church, that tie together what are, in many ways, structurally parallel populations in Brazil and southern Africa, thus to form a distinctive, post-colonial map of the universal–global. When disastrous floods hit Mozambique in 2000, the Universal Church in South Africa was the first on the scene with material assistance, bypassing the cumbersome formalities that delayed more conventional NGOs and relief organisations. In this sort of outreach, old diasporas are superseded by new: this is especially evident in the traffic in faith across the black Atlantic, with Nigerian churches flourishing in major American cities, and 'postmodern' African American evangelists, like T.D. Jakes, drawing

unprecedented audiences in cities like Nairobi (Lee 2005). Startling
new sacral economies are also apparent. The Yoruba-based Redeemed
Christian Church of God, for example, has established a worldwide network of parishes across Africa, Europe, the US, Australia and Southeast
Asia, its cutting-edge electronic and financial circulations tracing out a
novel kind of Christendom (Ukah 2008).

As I have noted, I am concerned in this account with two dimensions of the burgeoning relationship between new religious movements
and neoliberalism, broadly defined: the sociological and the ontological.
The first set of concerns, the sociological, focuses on what is perhaps the
most prominent feature of the fastest growing Pentecostal groups – their
tendency to take the form of theocracies, to embrace a wide array of
once secular activities and regulatory functions in the quest to reclaim
the world. The second order of issues, the ontological, concerns the
impetus of born-again faiths to counter the impact of relativism and
the loss of authoritative meaning. They seek to fix floating signifiers,
what scholars term 'postmodern semantic drift', by positing a theology
of revealed truth and a culture of affective realism.

Making us whole again

Across the ages religious utopianism has repeatedly sought to return
to holiness through wholeness (Douglas 1966). The prophetic movements that rallied black South Africans in the wake of overrule were a
clear instance of this impetus (Peires 1989); also, the Zionist churches
that have long offered cogent visions and unifying codes of conduct in
the wake of radical structural change (Comaroff 1985). Contemporary
mega-movements carry this project into the late modern era. They seek
to build Christendom anew by healing breaches deepened by economic
and political deregulation, forces that unhinge imagined communities
and received perceptions of locality and class. A recent study suggests,
for example, that even though they do not reject their national identity, the 'vast majority' of South Africans think of themselves primarily
as members of 'an ethnic, cultural, language, religious or some other
group', and 'attach their personal fate' to those groups (Gibson 2004: 2,
cf. Chidester et al. 2003).

The rise of evangelical organisations that resemble ethno-national
movements and 'surrogate governments' (Mahler 2005) are all of a
piece with these general historical developments. In South Africa, revitalised religious communities of various sorts – Muslim, Christian,
Jewish, nativist – are waxing at the expense of older, mainstream

denominations. For the most part, they are less concerned to pressure formal government than to create their own, relatively autonomous forms of sovereignty, their own regimes of order, power, enrichment. But this is not the case everywhere: Walter Ihejirika points out that some spokesmen for Nigerian Pentecostalism have declared the aim of a 'Total Take Over' of the country, this by establishing inroads from the fringes to the core of the national polity. '[We] are working while others are sleeping,' a leader of the national Pentecostal Fellowship announces: 'If you want to take over Nigeria you better win the students, win the market women, the media... the rich, the poor and the press.' Here religion is about world-making. It is inherently political, even if not always in a conventional sense. In West Africa (as the US) these expansionist movements tend to be centred on particular charismatic leaders, whose congregations and mega-churches, while frequently part of religious federations, remain organisationally independent (Ihejirika 2005). As is often remarked, the fact that Pentecostals stress personal religious experience rather than doctrine allows for considerable differences among them, though they remain linked in their foundational belief in Baptism of the Spirit and the reality of world-making power. As I have noted, widely shared goals (like extending God's dominion on earth by promoting Christian values, and returning religion to the schools, the courts and the market square) have made them a force that transcends local organisations in many places.

Newly holistic movements, I stress, are part of the neoliberal turn both *reactively* and *intrinsically*. In their readiness to take charge of welfare or education, they respond by assuming forms of social reproduction that late liberal governments cannot, or will not, provide. And while this is hardly a novel feature of religious movements, the process takes on specific late modern features, as I have noted, with the downsizing of government in many places. This is often presented, by faith-based activists, as a valued infusion of the public sphere with an ethics of sacrifice and service that was systematically eviscerated by the 'bloodless' liberal state (Muehlebach 2007). Religious movements also respond to, and enable the increasingly global division of labour. Their networks span continents, sustaining far-flung migrants with intimacy and communion in the absence of other kinds of cultural capital; the Akan-speaking churches that minister to migrants in Israel are a case in point (Sabar 2004). Again, this gives a late modern spin to longer-standing processes; African churches in colonial times played a similar role, albeit on a smaller scale (Welbourn & Ogot 1966). In general, the expansion of Pentecostal membership in current conditions makes evident a

certain organisational genius that thrives off the very socio-economic circumstances that have undercut more conventional forms of modern social aggregation rooted in class or locality. Widespread use is made in the movement of the so-called cell-group structure, in which networks of highly ritualised small units can proliferate, yet remain alike in their mode of professing faith. Multiplex, face-to-face congregations (offering everything from soup-kitchens to computer literacy, entertainment to financial credit) also fill the classic role of churches as places of sociality, affective engagement, 're-creation'.

A widely noted feature of this multiplexity is the readiness of Pentecostal churches to engage directly in business, not merely in propagating the faith and defining its values, but in economic enterprise way beyond the sanctuary. Here, again, they popularise the ethos of neoliberalism. Many churches take on explicitly corporate form, an orientation made plain in their architectural design (they often set up shop in store-fronts or former commercial premises). Many seek explicitly to harness what Connolly (n.d.: 33) has termed the creativity of capitalism, offering loyalty cards (like the Rhema Church in Cape Town) and founding banks, insurance companies and business schools (like the Redeemed Christian Church in Nigeria [Ukah 2008]). All this expresses a revived sense of Christian agency – and urgency – that propels Pentecostal world-making, a sense of activism-in-time most palpable by premillennial impetus to put market forces to the purpose of producing Christian value, to hitch commerce to a pursuit of God's kingdom on earth. Advocates of the Gospel of Prosperity are only the most literal in communicating a much more widely shared sensibility: many mainline denominations embody this same spirit in practice. How, if at all, might these features be connected to recent global changes in economy, society and the state; and what are the implications for Africa in particular?

In distinguishing neoliberalism from the classic liberalism that preceded it, Foucault stressed transformations in the relationship between state and economy (Lemke 2001: 200). Whereas before, the former directed and monitored the latter, the neoliberal turn makes 'the market itself the organising and regulative principle underlying the state'. Enhancing profitability and promoting entrepreneurial citizens have become both the end and the measure of good governance, in state and in church. As I have already remarked, in Pentecostal movements, this mode of operation breaks down the separations between moral, economic and political institutions, the better to embrace them all under a single, fundamental principle of productivity.

In this process of worlding, Pentecostals risk losing the critical tension between faith and context that makes it possible for each to hold the other accountable – as when critical churchmen in South Africa declared *apartheid* a heresy, or the clergy in Independent black churches decried the colonial racism that lingered in established denominations. As this suggests, the ever more porous boundaries between sacred and secular in many places also expresses a more profound transformation in the nature and site of politics itself, a shift from civic participation and collective mobilisation to more personal and partisan visions of securing the future. For the most part, current revivalist faiths offer a privatised, materially indexed salvation, and more immediate returns on spiritual investment ('Invest in the Lord, he pays rich dividends', goes the Universal Church mantra; another gospel show host on SATV recently quipped: 'There has never been a recession in the kingdom of God').[5] While apparently far removed from Weber's Puritans in many respects, they share the belief that profit is proof of compliance with divine design.

As these examples imply, the upsurge in born-again faith is also implicated, in complex ways, in ever more tangible polarisations of wealth and poverty, in the tension between intensified consumer desire and widening Gini coefficients in many countries, in the rise of marginal, informal economies amidst mass unemployment in many places. Pentecostalism works on both sides of Africa's widening socio-economic divides. In South Africa, the Rhema Bible Church, founded by the flamboyant Ray McCauley, claims a following of 20,000; it ministers to new black elites and white, middle-class followers, acknowledging their aspirations and assuaging their guilt (their young adults division is called Rema Dot God).[6] The Universal Church and its ilk, on the other hand, offer 'Gods and Services' to the more marginal – among whom Pentecostals are gaining ground not merely in relation to the mainline denominations, but also relative to the Zionist groups that have long ministered to the dispossessed.

I suggest, once again, that all this is testimony not merely to a significant reconfiguration of the institutional landscape of modern society, in Africa and the wider world. It speaks also to the salient shifts I have noted in the ontology of how the world works, how history is made, how human agents act. It is here that we find the intrinsic relation of born-again faith to the neoliberal turn. Mass conversions endorse an evangelical theology and mode of worship that is less and less in sync with secular social and political theory – or with the rationalist telos of modernisation and development. Notes

Malaysian Methodist theologian Hwa Yung (1995: 2): 'There is even less reason today for non-Western Christians...to allow their theologies to be domesticated by Enlightenment thinking, something which Western Christians themselves find increasingly dissatisfying.' For many, the impact of metaphysical forces is more palpable than intangibles like 'society', 'economy', 'history', whose structures of plausibility seem seriously undermined.

The rising temperature of public passion

I have noted the ever more overt role played by revelation in Pentecostal ontology, of the direct intervention of the divine in human affairs, both individual and collective – a kind of white heat that resets time and re-establishes truth. Among its many implications, such revelation implies a particular conception of the inspired human witness as the bearer of conviction, and as motivated actor in the world. Embodying such faith involves distinct performative conventions that have had noticeable effects on the culture of religious practice. In South Africa, for instance, a marked component of contemporary evangelical religious life across the social spectrum involves highly theatrical manifestations of feeling: often – in more charismatic movements – the demonstration of a self overwhelmed by the power of the spirit. In the case of older Protestant denominations, such emotive tendencies were strongly discouraged as transgressions of a dominant emotional economy of cool deism, of affect as the stuff that made possible the enactment of control, direction, grace. In its secular version, Durkheim and his followers famously saw such affect as presocial, embodied vitality (Victor Turner's [1967: 54] 'orectic pole' of the symbol) that – through the alchemy of ritual – made the obligatory desirable. In the early nineteenth century African mission field, the passionate, carnal sensibility that was seen to characterise the primitive also provided an opening for the moving power of God. Nonconformist evangelists spoke of God's Word as calling forth tears that could 'wash away all the red paint' of heathenism from their bodies (Comaroff & Comaroff 1991: 214).

But while they actively courted such emotionalism, the missions also laboured hard to develop a private, reflective person, with a conscience that has internalised the struggle between flesh and spirit. Outbursts of public emotion among those who had committed themselves to the civilising mission were read as signs of immature faith, of an absence of rational self-possession. A regime of sensory surveillance was installed by the gatekeepers of Protestant propriety in order to suppress the signs

of unmediated savage ardour (Comaroff & Comaroff 1997). Yet pious sublimation presumed incitement as its necessary supplement: the ever-present danger of backsliding into primitive promiscuity, magic, satanic desire that fuels the evangelical process.

The Pentecostal churches that are expanding at the expense of mainstream Christian denominations in many parts of the African continent at present operate with a somewhat different economy of affect. Not only do they encourage outbursts of enthusiasm as testimony to a radical invasion by the spirit; they express distrust of modes of piety and public action that lack animating fervour. In this, they resonate with more urbane sentiment, in this society and beyond: an increasingly palpable sense that secular liberalism 'lacks authenticity because it lacks passion'. Yet again, none of this is unprecedented. William Mazzarella (2009) is right to note that most visions of modernity have implied the idea of affective deficit. All the same, there does seem to be a heightened perception at present that passion is a scarce resource, serving as a unique, sought-after idiom of truth unclouded by rationalisation. At a time when both 'ideology' and 'politics' have increasingly been devalued as mere interested calculation, affect becomes evidence of a forthright relation between heart and deed; the truth or fakery of expressions of feeling become more significant than debate about their content.

This quality is evident, too, in the enactment of religious commitments. At least in the South African churches I know best, there has been a marked move (most striking in the more charismatic faiths, but relayed across a broad spectrum beyond them) to turn up the heat, to publicly perform a kind of conviction that Weber (2001: 82) termed 'hysterical': faith that seems to overwhelm reason, strategy, personal interest to flood the self with divine compulsion. 'Even the Lord Jesus Christ needed the Holy Spirit to live on earth', says a recent Sunday handout from the *Universal Church of the Kingdom of God*[7] in central Cape Town, 'The Spirit – like a driver – drives you to his Kingdom' (this in a context where cars embody post-apartheid personal agency *par excellence*, and altars in churches of this denomination are often adorned with BMW advertisements). Not only does this discourse presume a yearning for sovereignty (note the widespread nostalgia for father-figures, the appeal of authoritarian populism more generally in contemporary South Africa, and beyond).[8] The cult of affect at work here parallels closely that advanced by sophisticated, Deleuzian theorists like Brian Massumi, who speaks of affect (after Spinoza) as an embodied state that while it 'has affects', is also 'open[ed] up to being affected' (Zournazi 2007). Affect,

says Massumi, is our 'angle of participating in processes larger than ourselves', having a 'directness that...isn't necessarily self-possession'. Massumi insists that in contrast to emotion (a more limited, symbolically shaped, subjective feeling), affect 'needs no concept of mediation'. Enabling one to be captured from without, affect is increasingly summoned in the idiom of mass-marketed consumer desire, becoming the prime vehicle of subject-formation everywhere. This process works, Massumi insists, through contagion rather than persuasion, edging aside rational choice as a means of enrolling subjects to its cause. This resonates with the logic of purifying passion, espoused by those who advance Christianity as lifestyle. One senses a kinship, here, with early modern humoral understandings of 'passion' as arousal, evoked by the direct action of external forces on the corporeal self (Hirschman 1977) – a conception rather different from later understandings of 'emotion' as a privatised, pyschodynamic feeling.

Critics have disputed Massumi's commitment to the idea that affect – because it defies mediation – offers an escape from the determinations of language and culture (Mazzarella 2009), and I am largely in agreement with them. But what interests me here is the parallel between his view and popular understandings of affect in movements like those of African Pentecostalism. For many such Pentecostals likewise see passion as incarnate power and potential, being a force antithetical to lying and corruption because it is unmediated by conscious manipulation or control. For charismatics, of course, such affect is a manifestation of God. They strive, as have many believers before them, to recapture an original unity with God that is seamless, and actually dispenses with mediation of any kind. Again, the contrast with Protestant mission orthodoxy is marked.

The divine can only be known by way of mediation, of course. As Mazzarella (2009), Warner (2002) and others note, the 'fiction of premediated existence' derives precisely from this fact. What is more, to the degree that they disguise their own role as go-betweens in the production of divine intimacy, media often present themselves as the 'hot lines' to power. Many Pentecostals show an obsession with state-of-the-art communications: hence their appellation as 'electronic churches' (churches 'with karaoke and powerpoint').[9] Here sound systems sometimes replace altars, and mass mediation becomes integral to the nature of conviction (witness talk about 'downloading Jesus in one's life').

As several scholars have argued (Meyer 2004), devout vernaculars are also colonising the ground of urbane popular representation, especially

(if not exclusively) in the prodigious West Africa straight-to-video industry. These media of the miraculous apply the diverse possibilities of filmic fantasy to create a realist sublime – a mobilisation of what Kracauer (1960: 83) called the superior capacity of film to 'render visible things that have been imagined'. And here, as in many charismatic movements elsewhere, we see how an expansive, impassioned faith occults the sources of its own circulation, dispensing with concerns about sacred/secular divides. While its subject matter runs the gamut from crime and football dramas to witchcraft-horror, charismatic movies have become integral to the manner in which spirituality presents itself, both to African Pentecostals and to a much wider public (Meyer 2004). More than this: personal film and video draw ever more avidly on the same cinematic tropes to record the drama of the Spirit's work in the world. As has been noted in Brazil and elsewhere, the airing of glossy, camera-ready spectacles on high-tech religious channels makes evident the degree to which local understandings of ritual (funerals and healing rites, for instance) have been remade in the tropes of televangelical drama; Kracauer (in Hansen 1999: 70) remarked that cinematic expression plays in visceral ways with the paradoxes and limits of modern realism: 'in a flash' he noted, 'it passes from the objective to the subjective, and simultaneously evokes the concrete and the abstract'. This is evident, for instance, in the genre of slapstick; with its well-choreographed orgies of demolition, it both invokes and inverts the capitalist-modern relation of people to things.

Similar sorts of claims can been made for the burgeoning cinema of the late modern miraculous in Africa, where the surreal capacities of film become synonymous with the power of the Spirit, a power to dissolve and reform the mundane world. Birgit Meyer (2006: 11) invokes Derrida, in pondering whether one needs to believe in an age of such visual verisimilitude. Indeed, in saturating the lived world with the miraculous, these pious vernaculars reinforce other more embracing structural shifts that reverse disenchantment. To return to the irony with which I opened this chapter, they strive to return that world to the kind of unremarked, doxic commitment, the 'primitive' religious sensibility, that so unsettled missionary modernists.

But these efforts can never fully prevail, for the wider universe that contains them remains heterodox, fostering a late modern awareness of alienation from sovereign authority and foundational truth which, in turn, reproduces the need for a continuous reaffirmation of faith. The very assertion of belief is simultaneously a reinforcement of the existence of doubt, and this is a rather long-standing modernist conundrum.

Is this not just another instance of the fact that, while modernity seems to be changing, it remains essentially the same?[10]

Conclusions: ironic and otherwise

Weber argued that the Protestant Ethic sanctified the maximising ethos of early industrial society, serving to nurture cultural orientations that ensured that it flourished. Is the revitalisation of faith we are witnessing in Africa and the wider world merely a later chapter in the same long story, one that confirms an elective affinity between evangelicalism and capitalism?

Yes. And no. The historical relationship of Protestantism to capitalism is both less privileged, and more complex than Weber's model allowed. For one thing, his longer-term telos has not been confirmed; the prediction that capitalism would develop a secular autonomy, free of the need for Godly reinforcement, has proved wrong. It is evident that there has been a more intrinsic, enduring connection between capitalism and various strains of Protestantism (not to mention Catholicism and Judaism) than he recognised. What is more, colonialism – capitalism's occluded underbelly – cannot be left out of the equation. As African history attests, Christianity was integral to the making of colonial modernity on much of the continent, and was itself remade in the process. The historical dialectic that congealed as European capitalist modernity, albeit in various local guises, was far more complex than Weber allowed. This dialectic was mediated, in crucial respects, by Christian ideologies of labour, progress, salvation and also by the liberal politico-legal institutions that arose to secure and regulate industrial capitalism as a mode of production. The Protestant faith was transformed in different, context-specific ways in this process, but faith has remained a key aspect of the story. The interplay of religion and economy was never severed in the thoroughgoing manner implied by some more literal understandings of 'disenchantment'. All this was evident when European colonisers sought to modernise the rest of the world: humane imperialists like David Livingstone saw commerce, Christianity and civilisation as conditions of each other's possibility, much like latter-day Pentecostals, who encourage the faithful to aspire for salvation in terms of a gospel of desire and prosperity.

But as this last example suggests, many of the features of contemporary Protestantism – at least, in its avid, Pentecostal form – *are* new. This is not to say that they are mere reflections of the workings of 'free' market. *Per contra*, they are reciprocally involved, in intricate ways, with

economic forces sharpening in our times, forces whose impact are especially stark in post-colonial African contexts: the expanding scale and abstraction of transactions across the globe, the tension between the mobility of capital and the fixities of the nation state, the erosion of many of the institutional forms of liberal democratic society. They are also entangled in the ever more competitive quest for scarce resources and the growing inequities in wealth and power characteristic of the 'neo-world order'. The received dualities of modern bureaucratic states – sacred and profane, public and private, state and society – are being sundered by fresh forms of theodicy, by charismatic authorities who seek to counter the insecurities of the age, to intervene where Christian humanists – like those in South Africa who have championed truth, reconciliation and human rights – run up against the limits of liberalism. Ironically, in reforming itself in light of these conditions, born-again faith has overcome many of the obdurate cultural barriers that hindered modern Protestantism in its efforts to conquer non-European hearts and minds. Now, the most dynamic expansion of the church is occurring beyond the West.

As I have tried to show, then, these shifts in the nature of religious life are not adequately seen as either 'models of' or 'for' new socio-economic forms; rather, they are intrinsically, dialectically entailed with the transformations of the current moment. The institutional architecture associated with modern bureaucratic states is being cross-cut by a rebirth of sacred sovereignty that authorises new agglomerations, that builds new lexicons of feeling and visions of enterprise, at once pre- and post-modern. These manifestations both respond to socio-economic shifts and themselves promote innovative modes of world-making. The Spirit of Revelation is among us once more, ministering to those whose lives appear – in significant respects – to have outrun the logic of 'the modern project'. Its genius is to address the desires, dis-ease and displacement of our times, to make terror, violence, crime and pandemic into signs of redemption. As social theorists, we would be foolish to underestimate the world-making implications of this spirited enterprise.

Notes

1. 'Rhema Cape Town North Church Is on Facebook', www.en-gb.facebook. com/pages/Brackenfell-South-Africa/Rhema-Cape-Town-North-Church/117296411627723, accessed 12 September 2010.
2. 'The Business of Faith: Black Megachurches Are Turning Pastors into CEOs of Multimillion-Dollar Enterprises', *The Free Library*, 1 May 2006, www.

thefreelibrary.com/The+business+of+faith%3A+Black+megachurches+
are+turning+pastors+into . . . -a0145681346, accessed 3 September 2010.

3. I mean the term in the sense deployed by post-colonial literary critics (see, e.g. Spivak 1995) to imply the act of situating people, things or places within a particular, ideological vision of the world.

4. This is evident not merely in the challenge of what might be construed as immigrant religiosity in Western Europe (recall here the controversial remarks by the Archbishop of Canterbury to the effect that adoption of some aspects of *Sharia* law for relevant communities 'seems unavoidable' (Sharia Law in UK is 'Unavoidable', *BBC Radio 4 World at One*, 7 February 2008). The introduction of the Human Fertilization and Embryo Bill to the UK Parliament in the spring of 2008 drew unprecedented levels of home-grown Christian activism, and evoked considerable media attention. One extended BBC report noted that '[h]ard-line Christian activists are now mobilizing believers in an attempt to make an impact on society nationally', adding that 'well funded and politically active Christian groups [are] emerging as a significant voice in British politics' (*In God's Name*, Channel 4 Despatches, 19 May 2008, 8:00 PM).

5. SAMA Music awards, 2 May 2009. My thanks to Jeremy Jones for alerting me to this example.

6. See 'DOT.GOD Is on Facebook', www.facebook.com/group.php?gid= 6316676057, accessed 20 September 2010.

7. This church, a branch of the prolific and much-discussed *Igreja Universal do Reino de Deus* Brazil, has flourished in southern Africa in the past couple of decades (Comaroff & Comaroff 2002, Kramer 1999).

8. I think, here, of the theatrical invocations of masculine paternalism enacted by (now) President Jacob Zuma and his supporters at the time of his rape trial in 2006 (Motsei 2007); or the hugely popular Afrikaans song and video that in 2006 called upon a deceased Boer War general (de la Rey) to return to deliver his people from their current rudderless plight.

9. See Dennis A. Smith, 'Eine Bewegung jenseits der Modernität in Lateinamerika', *The World Association of Christian Communication*, 13 August 2004, www.wacc.org.uk/de/publications/media_development/2005_2/ moving_beyond_modernity_in_latin_america, accessed 5 June 2008. I first heard mention of churches with 'karaoke and powerpoint' in the US, with reference to Southern Baptist churches. Subsequently, I have heard the phrase used to refer to South African Pentecostal worship as well.

10. This is a paraphrase of Engels, as cited by Andre Gunder Frank (1971: 36).

References

Asad, Talal. 2003. *Formations of the Secular: Christianity, Islam, Modernity*. Stanford: Stanford University Press.

Bokaba, Selby. 2000. Hero's Welcome for Miracle 2000 Mastermind. *The Star* (Johannesburg). www.iol.co.za/general/newsprint.php3?art_id=ct200007312 04009474M624397, accessed 5 August 2000.

Burnside, Jonathan, Loucks Nancy, Adler Joanna R. and Gerry Rose. 2005. *My Brother's Keeper: Faith-based Units in Prison*. Cullompton: Willan Publishing.

Chidester, David, Phillip Dexter and Wilmot James (Eds). 2003. *What Holds Us Together: Social Cohesion in South Africa*. Cape Town: HSRC Press.

Comaroff, Jean. 2009. The Politics of Conviction: Faith on the Neoliberal Frontier. *Social Analysis* 53(1): 17–38.

Comaroff, Jean. 2006. The Force That is Faith. *WISER Review* 2: 6–7.

Comaroff, Jean. 2002. Second Comings: Neoprotestant Ethics and Millennial Capitalism in South Africa, and Elsewhere. In Gifford, P., D. Archard, T.A. Hart and N. Rapport (Ed.), *2000 Years: Faith Culture and Identity in the Common Era*. London: Routledge.

Comaroff, Jean. 1985. *Body of Power, Spirit of Resistance: The Culture and History of a South African People*. Chicago: University of Chicago Press.

Comaroff, Jean and John Comaroff. 2008. Faith. In Shepherd, Nick and Steven Robins (Eds), *New South African Keywords*. Johannesburg: Jacana Media.

Comaroff, Jean and John Comaroff (Eds). 2001. *Millenial Capitalism and the Culture of Neoliberalism*. Durham: Duke University Press.

Comaroff, Jean and John Comaroff. 1997. *Of Revelation and Revolution: The Dialectics of Modernity on a South African Frontier*, Vol. 2. Chicago: University of Chicago Press.

Comaroff, Jean and John Comaroff. 1991. *Of Revelation and Revolution: Christianity, Colonialism, and Consciousness in South Africa*, Vol. I. Chicago: University of Chicago Press.

Crapanzano, Vincent. 2000. *Serving the Word: Literalism in America from the Pulpit to the Bench*. New York: The New Press.

Douglas, Mary. 1966. *Purity and Danger: An Analysis of Concepts of Pollution and Taboo*. Harmondsworth: Penguin Books.

Durkheim, Emile. 1984. *The Division of Labour in Society*. New York: The Free Press.

Fields, Karen. 1985. *Revival and Rebellion in Colonial Central Africa*. Princeton: Princeton University Press.

Frank, Andre Gunder. 1971. *Capitalism and Underdevelopment in Latin America: Historical Studies of Chile and Brazil*. Harmondsworth: Penguin.

Gibson, James L. 2004. *Overcoming Apartheid: Can Truth Reconcile a Divided Nation?* New York: Russell Sage.

Goody, Jack. 1962. *Death, Property and the Ancestors: A Study of the Mortuary Customs of the Lodagaa of West Africa*. Stanford: Stanford University Press.

Hackett, Rosalind. n.d. Market Values. In Religious Tolerance Out: Assessing Media Liberalization in Africa. Paper presented at the conference on 'Religion in African Conflicts and Peacebuilding Initiatives', Jinja, Uganda. April 2004.

Hansen, Miriam. 1999. The Mass Production of the Senses: Classical Cinema as Vernacular Modernism. *Modernism/Modernity* 6(2): 59–77.

Hansen, Thomas Blom. n.d. Cool Passion: The Political Theology of Conviction. Call for papers for a seminar at the Amsterdam School of Social Science Research, 23–25 May 2007.

Harding, Susan. 1994. Imagining the Last Days: The Politics of Apocalyptic Language. *Bulletin of the Academy of Arts and Sciences* 48(3): 1–44.

Hirschman, Albert. 1977. *The Passions and the Interests: Political Arguments for Capitalism before Its Triumph*. Princeton: Princeton University Press.

Hwa, Yung. 1995. Critical Issues Facing Theological Education in Asia. *Transformation* 12(4): 1–6.

Ihejirika, Walter. 2005. Media and Fundamentalism in Nigeria. *World Association for Christian Communications*. www.wacc.org.uk/wacc/network/africa/african_articles/media_and_fundmentalism, accessed 9 October 2005.

Jenkins, Paul. 2002. *The Next Christendom: The Coming of Global Christianity.* Oxford: Oxford University Press.

Kracauer, Siegfried. 1960. *Theory of Film: Redemption of Physical Reality.* Oxford: Oxford University Press.

Kramer, Eric. 1999. *Possessing Faith: Commodification, Religious Subjectivity, and Community in a Brazilian Neo-Pentecostal Church.* PhD thesis, University of Chicago.

LaHaye, Tim and David Noebel. 2000. *Mind Siege: The Battle for the Truth.* Nashville: Word Publishing.

Lee, Shayne. 2005. *The Postmodern Preacher: The Rise of Bishop T.D. Jakes.* New York: New York University Press.

Lemke, Thomas. 2001. 'The Birth of Biopolitics': Michel Foucault's Lectures at the Còllege de France on Neo-Liberal Governmentality. *Economy and Society* 30(2): 190–207.

Lienhardt, Godfrey. 1961. *Divinity and Experience: The Religion of the Dinka.* Oxford: Clarendon Press.

Mahler, Jonathan. 2005. The Soul of the New Exburb. *The New York Times Magazine*, March 27, pp. 30–57.

Martin, David. 2008. Have Pentecostalism, Will Travel: How Sarah Palin's Religion Continues to Evolve Around the World. *Times Literary Supplement*, 17 September.

Mazzarella, William. 2009. Affect: What Is It Good For? In Dube, Saurabh (Ed.), *Enchantments of Modernity: Empire, Nation, Globalization.* Durham: Duke University Press.

Meyer, Birgit. 2006. Religion and Capitalism. *The Wiser Review* 2: 10–11.

Meyer, Birgit. 2004. 'Praise the Lord': Popular Cinema and Pentecostalite Style in Ghana's New Public Sphere. *American Ethnologist* 31(1): 92–110.

Meyer, Birgit. 2002. Pentecostalite Culture on Screen: Magic and Modernity in Ghana's New Mediascape. www.history.wisc.edu/bernault/magical/public.3.htm, accessed 9 October 2005.

Motsei, Mmatshilo. 2007. *The Kanga and the Kangaroo Court: Reflections on the Rape Trial of Jacob Zuma.* Auckland Park, Johannesburg: Jacana Media Pty.

Muehlebach, Andrea. 2007. *The Moral Neo-Liberal: Welfare State and Ethical Citizenship in Contemporary Italy.* PhD thesis, University of Chicago.

Newton, Greg. 2006. Free Market Christianity. In *Travelers: Theological Conversation for the Journey.* www.travelersjournal.blogspot.com/2006/03/free-market-christianity.html, accessed 5 May 2008.

Peires, Jeff. 1989. *The Dead Will Arise: Nongqawuse and the Great Xhosa Cattle-Killing Movement of 1856–7.* Johannesburg: Ravan Press.

Pew Forum. 2006. Spirit and Power: A 10-Country Survey of Pentecostals. The Pew Forum on Religion and Public Life, 5 October 2006. www.pewforum.org/Christian/Evangelical-Protestant-Churches/Spirit-and-Power.aspx, accessed 5 December 2009.

Rybczynski, Witold. 2005. An Anatomy of Megachurches: The New Look for Places of Worship. Slate, www.slate.com/id/2127615

Sabar, Galia. 2004. African Christianity in the Jewish State: Adaptation, Accommodation and Legitimization of Migrant Workers' Churches, 1990–2003. *Journal of Religion in Africa* 34(4): 407–437.

Schulz, Dorothea. 2007. Evoking Moral Community, Fragmenting Muslim Discourse. Sermon Audio-Recordings and the Reconfiguration of Public Debate in Mali. *Journal of Islamic Studies* 26: 39–71.

Smith, James. 2008. *Bewitching Development: Witchcraft and the Reinvention of Development in Neoliberal Kenya.* Chicago: University of Chicago Press.

Soares, Benjamin. 2004. Muslim Saints in the Age of Neoliberalism. In Weiss, Brad (Ed.), *Producing African Futures: Ritual and Reproduction in a Neoliberal Age.* Leiden and Boston: Brill.

Spinoza, Benedict de. 1883 (1670). *A Theologico-Political Treatise.* Part 1. Translated by A.H. Gosset. London: George Bell & Sons.

Spivak, Gayatri Chakravorty. 1995. Three Women's Texts and a Critique of Imperialism. In Ashcroft, Bill, Gareth Griffiths and Helen Tiffin (Eds), *The Post-Colonial Studies Reader.* London: Routledge.

Sundkler, Bengt. 1961. *Bantu Prophets in South Africa.* London: Oxford University Press for the International African Institute.

Turner, Victor. 1967. *The Forest of Symbols: Aspects of Ndembu Ritual.* New York: Cornell University Press.

Ukah, Asonzeh. 2008. *A New Paradigm of Pentecostal Power: A Study of the Redeemed Church of God in Nigeria.* Trenton: Africa World Press.

Warner, Michael. 2002. Publics and Counterpublics. *Public Culture* 14(11): 49–90.

Weber, Max. 2001. *The Protestant Ethic and the Spirit of Capitalism.* Translated by Talcott Parsons. London and New York: Routledge.

Welbourn, Frederick and Bethwell Ogot. 1966. *A Place to Feel at Home.* London: Oxford University Press.

Zournazi, Mary. 2007. Interview with Brian Massumi. www.theport.tv/wp/pdf/pdf1.pdf, accessed 10 May 2007.

3
Prosperity Gospels and Enchanted Worldviews: Two Responses to Socio-economic Transformation in Tanzanian Pentecostal Christianity

Päivi Hasu

Introduction

Following the remarkable global growth of Pentecostal churches, a body of research has developed that has been preoccupied with tracing the relationships between Pentecostalism, modernity and neoliberalism (Maxwell 1998, 2005, Meyer 1999, Gifford 2004, Robbins 2004). At the same time a parallel literature has developed that associates discourses about witchcraft in Africa with changing patterns of production and consumption and with new forms of wealth (Comaroff & Comaroff 1993, Geschiere 1997). In this literature, witchcraft has been accounted for in terms of moral economy; as a levelling force opposing new material inequalities, or conversely as a force in the accumulation of wealth and power (Geschiere 1997: 5). On the other hand, Pentecostalism has been shown to address issues of wealth and inequality, particularly through the so-called prosperity gospel, but also through its ideas of demonic agency (Maxwell 1998, Newell 2007: 463). An overlapping theme in studies of both witchcraft and Pentecostalism has been their associations with individualist ideologies of modernity and with transformations of social relations and kinship. Both the spread of Pentecostalism and the resurgence of occult beliefs and practices have been related to economic transformations and the neoliberal economy. Since the mid-1980s, following structural adjustment and economic liberalisation, there has been an increase in both Pentecostal churches and discourses of occult activity in Tanzania. Both have a bearing on ideas and possibilities of human agency and development.[1]

Pentecostal and charismatic Christianity is itself remarkably diverse, with significant differences existing between different churches and congregations. In this chapter, I examine two forms of Pentecostal and charismatic Christianity in urban Tanzania and the way they can, in their different ways, be understood to result from, and be responses to, the consequences of economic restructurings and neoliberalism. They both offer spiritual discourses that address the (im-)moral nature of capitalism and the possibility of personal, social and economic development. One appears to appeal to the 'winners' of neoliberalism, people who might be in a position to take an advantage of the changing circumstances; the other one appeals more to the underprivileged who are on the verge of losing all hope for a better future. It is the possible short-term and the long-term consequences of these discourses that are of interest. This chapter has three main aims. First, I show that the spreading of Pentecostal and charismatic churches in Tanzania cannot be understood without contextualising it in the recent economic reforms and their consequences, and that it is reasonable to talk about emergent Pentecostal and occult economies. Second, I address the changes and transformations that have taken place in the Pentecostal-charismatic gospel itself over the decades. Some of the most important transformations relate to the economic ethos of third-wave Pentecostal Christianity. Third, I discuss how the diverse forms of Pentecostal and charismatic Christianity transform the person and produce new kinds of subjects which are particularly adaptable to the changing social and economic circumstances.

In contrast to faith-based development organisations, development work per se is not the primary aim of churches, it is conversion, salvation and the creation of new persons, attitudes and personal morality by way of character building (Simensen 2006: 84). What I am suggesting is that Pentecostal discourses may have intended and unintended short-term and long-term consequences. In this chapter I focus on the different kinds of spiritual discourses and their implications for personal empowerment, social responsibility and possibilities of development in general. I address the idea of multiple modernities (Comaroff & Comaroff 1993, Eisenstadt 2000) by comparing two different versions of global Pentecostalism: one church that preaches a variety of the prosperity gospel and one that preaches a gospel based on demonology and deliverance. The two case churches, Efatha Church and the Glory of Christ Tanzania Church, are taken to illustrate the diverse socio-economic and spiritual ways that Pentecostal churches

encounter the consequences and requirements of neoliberal economic transformations.

Neoliberalism, development and Pentecostalism

Africa's primary experience of globalisation has been related to economic restructuring and its consequences for social reproduction and socio-economic differentiation (Barker 2007: 411). From the 1980s onwards, international economic policies linked development aid to reduced government spending, privatisation and market liberalisation. The structural reforms evoked strong hopes of improvements in social and economic living conditions, but it soon turned out that the 'blessings of neoliberalism' were distributed extremely unevenly and that only a few benefited. In Tanzania, despite macro-level economic growth, the economic reforms and the liberalisation of the economy have resulted in increased unemployment and a reduction in social services at the grassroots, as well as in increased differences in access to production, accumulation and consumption (Sanders 2001). While the structural adjustment policies were conceived originally as instruments for poverty alleviation, they have led to a rise of living costs in Tanzania and an increasing impoverishment of rural areas, thus reinforcing migration to urban centres. They also triggered a decrease in formal employment opportunities in the urban centres and a stagnation of salaries, and thereby increased the pressure on women to engage in income-generating activities (Dilger 2007: 63).

As part of the economic reforms, major donor countries changed their aid distribution policies, diverting aid money away from governments and channelling it more towards non-governmental organisations (NGOs). This has led to a dramatic increase in the number of NGOs, both religious and secular. Since the 1980s the number of NGOs has increased exponentially, from fewer than 20 in the early 1980s to around 3000 in the early 2000s (Jennings 2008: 92, Kontinen 2007: 65). Churches have long been involved in development in Tanzania. In the 1960s, when the Tanzanian state had established full control over development, the Protestant and Catholic churches decided to support the government's development objectives and played a vital role in securing acceptance in local communities for the state's policies (Jennings 2008: 65–66).[2] By the mid-1960s, the Christian Council of Tanzania had established itself as the central authority of the development projects of the main Protestant churches – Anglican, Lutheran, Mennonite and

Moravian – and in the early 1970s the Tanzanian Episcopal Conference established Caritas, with the responsibility for the development projects of the Catholic Church (Jennings 2008: 69–70). However, in this chapter I want to draw attention to a more recent, and rather different, way that Christianity is interfacing with development in contemporary Tanzania. Since the 1980s there has been a massive growth in Pentecostal and charismatic churches in the country. Although many of these churches fall outside of official structures of development aid, and although they run relatively few social projects themselves, they are significant public actors and their theological discourse has broad development-related implications in the societies and communities in which they operate.

Many scholars have interpreted Pentecostal doctrines as a means of enabling adherents to make the best of rapid social change. Pentecostal Christianity embeds neoliberalism particularly well as there is a certain degree of congruence between Pentecostalism and the requirements of neoliberalism. Maxwell (1998), for example, suggests that, for some, the doctrines bring about social mobility based on merit, while for others they provide codes of conduct that prevent them from falling into extreme poverty and destitution. In both cases they provide a way to come to terms with, and benefit from, modern capitalist values and institutions. Pentecostalism therefore appears to offer its adherents the chance to change their responses to the limiting conditions that neoliberal structures create (Maxwell 1998: 351, 2005: 28; Zalanga 2010). And as has been suggested by Dilger, Pentecostal churches not only offer moral and spiritual explanations about how modernity, the global market economy and the structural adjustment programmes have affected the lives of individuals and groups, they also provide new ways for followers to act in situations where they increasingly feel powerless and frustrated (Dilger 2007: 62).

Other scholars have criticised Pentecostal and charismatic churches as simply offering a form of escapism and for having no serious commitment to social and political reform (Simensen 2006: 84). It is therefore necessary to distinguish between first-wave classical Pentecostalism and third-wave neo-Pentecostalism. Apart from the mainline Protestant churches, the first independent, Canadian Pentecostal missionaries arrived in Tanganyika as early as 1913, soon followed by the Holiness Mission, Assemblies of God, the ELIM Pentecostal Church and Scandinavian missionaries from the Swedish Free Mission and the Finnish Free Mission. Scandinavian Pentecostal missionaries, in particular, have a long history in the practice of holistic mission – the ideal of integrating spiritual and social work. These early missions – representing classical

Pentecostalism – created hospitals, schools and clinics and provided other services across the country (Anderson 2004: 114). Today, the Free Pentecostal Church of Tanzania that has its roots in the Swedish Free Mission states that some of its objectives are to:

> Provide special social welfare and community activities as well as facilities hand in hand with the government, to include relief services, education, health programmes, orphanage care and service camps for destitute and handicapped persons.[3]

However, despite this early presence it was not until the 1980s that Pentecostal Christianity started to spread more rapidly and became a major player on the religious scene. Many of the churches that grew most in this period were third-wave, independent, neo-Pentecostal churches. Some of the largest and most influential include the Full Gospel Bible Fellowship led by Bishop Zachary Kakobe, Assemblies of God Mikocheni-B led by a Member of Parliament, Dr Gertrude Rwakatare, and the Word and Peace Organization (Wapo Mission) managed by Bishop Sylvester Gamanywa. Members of these churches and ministries usually joined from other Christian denominations, and some churches appear to attract Muslim converts as well. Some, such as Mikocheni-B, are known to attract the affluent urban middle class, whereas others are more appealing to the less fortunate urban population. In this chapter I discuss in detail two very different Pentecostal churches – Efatha Church and the Glory of Christ Tanzania Church – and I explore the implications that their theological discourse and practice have for ideas of development, empowerment and agency.

The economic ethos of classical, first-wave Pentecostalism has been significantly transformed in contemporary third-wave neo-Pentecostalism, which has more of an emphasis on miracles of prosperity and divine healing (Corten and Marshall-Fratani 2001: 5). The 'magical' approach to wealth and heavy emphasis on tithing seem to indicate that they do not promote the classic Protestant Ethic (Gifford 1998: 337, Robbins 2004: 137), but these emphases differ between one church and another. The prosperity gospel has spread a set of doctrines promising believers both physical health and material success on earth. Accordingly, illness and poverty are thought to be caused by sin, lack of faith or demonic influence (Gifford 2001, Robbins 2004). Instead of disenchantment, there has emerged the projection of universal 'spiritual warfare' between Godly and satanic powers (Gifford

1998: 328). The new churches encourage accumulation, individualism, entrepreneurship and showing off one's wealth in a way quite different to the classical Pentecostal ethos. An unintended consequence of this emphasis on individual wealth might be the legitimisation of the idea of unlimited accumulation of wealth and the recognition of competition as a creative strategy for getting ahead in life (Zalanga 2010: 49). Therefore, the individualistic economic ethos of Pentecostalism may advance individual accumulation at the expense of the social and moral obligations of kinship. This chapter deals with these two flip sides of the same coin – one Pentecostal church advancing individual prosperity, the other one presenting a spiritual criticism of the immorality of accumulation.

One of the key questions concerning the economic culture of Pentecostalism has been the extent to which this form of Christianity establishes a Protestant Ethic in today's converts similar to the one described in Weber's account of the development of capitalism (Weber 1904–1905 [2004]). Circumstances in the global South in the era of globalisation are, however, radically different from those in which capitalism originally developed in Europe. It has been argued that whereas earlier forms of popular Christianity helped African peasants and labour migrants come to terms with the demands of capitalist imperialism, contemporary Pentecostalism responds to another kind of socio-economic context and enables African adherents to come to terms with neoliberalism (Maxwell 2005: 28). Weber discussed a form of Protestant Ethic that negated the material world in favour of salvation in the world to come. Devotion to God took place through work in this world, and salvation was the result of discipline and life's systematic rationalisation. At the same time, it was the this-worldly ascetic ideal of rational action and retreat from the world that led to the generation of wealth (Weber 1904–1905 [2004]). The code of ethics in classical, first-wave Pentecostalism is rather similar to that described by Weber; it is said to produce a sober lifestyle, upward social mobility and individuals that are honest, disciplined and transparent. The goal of conversion is not financial; rather, economic gain is the unintended consequence of a changed life (Miller & Yamamori 2007: 162–165, 169). Yet empirical studies on the effect of conversion on economic status appear to be inconclusive (Brouwer et al. 1996: 235–236, Woodberry 2006). Weber's work further explored the phase of assumed emancipation from magic, a phase when people began to rely more on scientific investigations as the way to truth. Disenchantment referred to the process of emptying the world of magical or spiritual forces. This was ultimately to result in secularisation and the decline of belief in magic and God. As this chapter

will show, while contemporary third-wave neo-Pentecostalism can be seen to embody a new type of Protestant Ethic, it most certainly does not lead towards secularisation and the disenchantment of the world. In order to substantiate these claims, let us now consider in detail two very different Pentecostal churches in contemporary Tanzania.

Prophetic prosperity – Efatha Church

Efatha is an independent, vibrant and rapidly growing church located in Mwenge, Dar es Salaam, a church that rests solidly on the charisma and vision of its founder and leader, Josephat Elias Mwingira, who wants to be addressed as Apostle and Prophet.

Mwingira grew up a Catholic, but later attended the Mwika Lutheran Bible School in Kilimanjaro. Before being saved he was, among other things, involved in the mining business at the Mererani mining community outside Arusha, and it was there, in 1992, that he got the calling from God. He went on to set up Efatha Ministry, which was eventually officially registered in 1997. By 2007 there were over 300,000 followers throughout Tanzania. Efatha has also started churches in Kenya, Zambia and Malawi. The organisation is carefully planned according to Mwingira's visions, and he uses both spiritual and financial advisors to support him. A registered company, Efatha Foundation, was also established to administer investments. As is evident by the number of cars parked outside the church, most of his followers come from relatively well-to-do socio-economic backgrounds and many of them are small-scale entrepreneurs.

Mwingira claims that he was given a nine-point programme by God (Mwingira 2005). He was to start a Bible school to educate religious leaders. He was to arrange services to deliver people from the powers of darkness – witches, witch doctors, ancestral sacrifices, as well as all sorts of harmful traditional practices. He was to hold healing services with a holistic approach to healing; to treat social problems, even those affecting the entire country, as well as personal crises to do with illness, marriage, family and income. He was also to teach the word of God. He was to prepare singers, choirs and people able to perform prayers. He was to start schools and thereby educate new generations of saved leaders. This would take place at all levels, from nursery schools to universities. He was to start new churches and places of worship. He was to conduct seminars and meetings as well as to start new services of various kinds such as hospitals and radio and TV programmes. In June 2007, after a few years of fundraising, the church officially launched

a TV station of its own, Trinity Efatha Network Television (TRENET). In the same week the church inaugurated a bank of its own. The church also started a weekly Christian newspaper *Utatu* ('Trinity') and intends to start a radio station. Future visions include a university, hospital, airport and a phone company. When I interviewed Josephat Mwingira in June 2006 he proudly presented the first sketches of a ten-storey office building that Efatha is intending to construct.

Mwingira takes pride in announcing that Efatha does not rely on foreign aid, donations or funding but that all the funds are raised among its own Christians. The sums of the weekly collections, tithes and offerings are not publicised but the general understanding is that they can be up to 50 million Tanzanian shillings on a good week (in 2007; almost US$30,000). Congregants also purchased shares in the Efatha Foundation, with a rumoured value of 15 billion shillings. The principle of giving in order to receive is of supreme importance at this church. Constant emphasis is placed on the need to work hard and be successful in order to be able to make donations. One of Mwingira's central ideas is to lead Christians to hard work and self-reliance. Mwingira thinks of himself as a skilful manager of the economy and has often proclaimed: 'I am an economist.'

Efatha also organises conferences and seminars. At a particularly large conference in 2007, when the TV station and bank were launched, the Minister for Labour, Employment and Youth Development and the Minister for Lands, Housing and Human Settlements Development honoured the occasion with their presence. During the week international guests taught and preached to both leaders and lay Christians. The main speakers were Dr Mensa Otabil, a famous Ghanaian religious superstar, Dr Tayo Adeyemi, Nigerian-born leader of the New Wine Church in the UK and pastor Randy Morrison, Trinidad-born leader of the Speak the Word Church International in Minnesota, USA. It may not be accidental that there was not one white preacher present. The overarching theme of the week was the empowerment of Tanzanian Christians and their path from poverty to prosperity. For the conference of 2008 the church had prepared a billboard advertising the key messages of the same speakers: 'Receive anointing to do business and raise your capital' (Mensa Otabil), 'Receive the power to rule and to control beyond your own boundaries' (Tayo Adeyemi) and 'Live a life according to a plan, not a life from one problem to another' (Randy Morrison). Although Efatha also promotes prayer healing and deliverance, the focus of its teachings are about prosperity and empowerment.

Think like a winner and you will be one

Mensa Otabil is one of the most prominent Pentecostal leaders in Africa. He told his Tanzanian audience that he is also a businessman, a business consultant and the chancellor of a private university that he founded. He started his International Central Gospel Church in 1984 in Accra and draws about 7000 people to Sunday services, which are popular among the educated urban middle class. He has extensive media activities and is a popular speaker on TV. As well as being a churchman and the head of several hundred churches, he is also a business consultant. He is a board member of several Ghanaian and international companies, including companies dealing with pharmaceuticals and computers: 'I train businessmen. Not just Christian business men. I teach some of the top businessmen in West Africa. I run a consultancy for them. I train their top management staff from banks to mining, to multinational companies.' Otabil has published several books that are repeatedly referenced in Efatha's teachings. One of these, entitled *Four Laws of Productivity*, presents his four principles of prosperity: (1) be fruitful, (2) multiply, (3) replenish the earth and (4) subdue it. In another book, *Beyond the Rivers of Ethiopia: A Biblical Revelation on God's Purpose for the Black Race*, he instils pride into the black people who, according to him, are inclined to regard themselves as inferior to whites (Gifford 2004: 113).

Otabil's thinking initially appeared rather extreme to Tanzanian Pentecostals. He paid little attention to demonic forces in interpreting and explaining the emergence of poverty and underdevelopment. In his mind, underdevelopment is caused by human decisions and actions – rightly so, many might say. In the Tanzanian charismatic context, where godly miracles on one hand, and the satanic agency on the other, are significant aspects in conceptualising human fortunes and misfortune, Otabil's teachings were quite revolutionary, in that he preached personal, social and national transformation. While visiting Efatha in 2008 he proclaimed: 'This ministry (Efatha) is a ministry that God is using not only to save souls and heal the sick but also to transform the nation. Because the change in our hearts must result in a change in our lives and in a change in our society.'

Otabil's teachings in Dar es Salaam in 2007 were based on the book of Genesis. As he said, the first thing that one learns from that book is that God is a working God; his work produces results, he is a producing God, he is a creative God, he is a God who does things. And man has been created in his image, as a working and creating man. According to Otabil, Africa is the most anointed continent and Africans pray more

than any other people on earth. So why is Africa poor? How do you develop the nation? How do you develop the national economy? This is what Otabil preached to the Efatha congregation in June 2007:

> The answer is: switch on the light and you can see clearly, you can start solving problems. Light represents knowledge and understanding. If you do not know and understand you cannot solve the problem. Don't be ignorant; do not let anybody make you ignorant!

> I am fed up with underdevelopment! I believe God created us for something better.... You are going to see a new story in Africa. The old picture is gone and the new picture is here! You will see churches do things that you never thought churches would do. Preachers doing things you did not think preachers would do...Many of us Africans have grown up in an atmosphere of poverty and scarcity. An atmosphere of little thinking. An atmosphere of inferiority complex.... You have to ask God to change your environment for you from scarcity to abundance!

> The inferiority complex must change. Africans think that we do not deserve much. It started from the past, before the white people came, with our own forefathers. They did not value the life of others.... From the past to the present we have been reduced in value. When a black man sees a white man he instantly thinks the white man is wiser.... When God raises a leader among us we want to bring him down. In that atmosphere nothing grows.

> Most black people do not invest their money in the future. They spend and waste their money fast....If you are going to be rich you must save and invest! To save and to invest are the two important principles of prosperity....They have nothing behind them. We depend on others to do things for us. That must change! In Africa there is an environment of dependency!

> God has brought you into an atmosphere; a new atmosphere is being built in this house. It is not the atmosphere of the old Tanzania. It is not the atmosphere of scarcity but of abundance! Some of you will have more money than your government. Your government will borrow from America but you will give to America. You will start banks and own hotels, airlines and universities! You have so much ability inside you! You have businesses, books, hotels, airplanes, shipping lines, computer businesses consultancies, hospitals sitting inside you. As God created so will you create; new companies, businesses,

investments, franchises! You will invest in Hong Kong, Australia, Europe. Get ready! Your business will not end in Tanzania; it will go out of Tanzania! Not just to Kenya and Uganda because God is bigger than East Africa. Break the fear, be bold, be strong, stand out for God and see Him do mighty things for you! He will change the atmosphere! In this church I sense that this is a new atmosphere. God has brought you into the new. Forget about the old! In the past it was illegal to be prosperous in Tanzania. Those days are gone forever!

Godly miracles, satanic interventions or human development?

There were several areas of interest in Otabil's teachings in Dar es Salaam. First, he disregarded the agency of demons and the possibility of miracles that remain so prevalent in much of Tanzanian Pentecostal Christianity. Second, he placed an emphasis on detrimental cultural factors on the one hand, and empowerment and black consciousness on the other, in explaining and interpreting (under-)development. And lastly, he spoke about the importance of human labour, rationalism and disenchantment.

Otabil has made culture the prime focus of his theology and his criticism of the emergence of underdevelopment. But at the same time, he is a passionate advocate of empowerment and black consciousness. He is critical of many African cultural practices and suggests that they hinder development. Otabil differs from many other charismatics in his commitment to the mental liberation of black people. He has become well known for his brand of black consciousness to the point that his thinking has been coined as an 'African-Pentecostal liberation theology' (Larbi 2002: 155). Otabil also integrates spiritual power and rationality: in order to be successful, you need both. For Otabil, naturally, disenchantment it is not about secularisation. Rather, it refers to playing down the agency of demons in material affairs.

Otabil, like Mwingira, draws on many Weberian themes, such as the importance of labour, investment, rationality and non-existence of magic and miracles. Both insist that development comes from hard work and not from miracles. They focus on success, achievement, self-development and personal improvement. Their preaching presents an intriguing mix of born-again ideology of personal transformation, African consciousness and self-development discourse characteristic of management and consultancy literature (de Witte n.d.). Mwingira is different from many religious leaders in Tanzania who do not, in the same way, counsel their people to work hard, plan and order their lives properly. Drawing on the teachings of Otabil, Mwingira is part of a new

generation of religious entrepreneurs in Tanzania, bringing an uplifting and empowering message to middle class congregations seeking success and upward mobility.

However, the teachings about disenchantment, education and investment that are so appealing to the wealthy middle class are rather far away from the experience of poorer Tanzanians. Many members of that socio-economic group prefer to go to Pentecostal churches that focus on deliverance from demonic forces, as the second case illustrates.

'This is a people plundered' – the Glory of Christ Tanzania Church

During July and August 2008 several weekly Christian newspapers of Pentecostal background reported the miraculous return of zombies in different parts of Tanzania. Stories were written, in particular, about the pastors of the Glory of Christ Tanzania Church who had gone to perform prayers for people allegedly captured as zombies. Cases were also reported of people who refused to bury their dead relatives in expectation of their resurrection a few days later. The Glory of Christ Tanzania Church, also identified as the Church of Resurrection and Life, is widely known in Tanzania as the church that returns zombies. The church was founded by pastor Gwajima, a Sukuma by ethnic background, who grew up in the classical Pentecostal Church of Assemblies of God. However, Gwajima became discontented with the authority structures of his mother church and developed a vision for an independent church of his own. Gwajima studied at the East Africa pastoral theological school in Nairobi during the early 1990s and later started churches in Musoma and Mwanza. He was called by God to Dar es Salaam in 1997, where he set up his main church, which now has some 40,000 members. He has also managed to create international networks and establish church branches in Asia, particularly in Japan and South Korea, and has planned conferences in Indonesia, Taiwan, Pakistan and India. He has also preached in Switzerland, Germany, the US and throughout Africa.

At Glory many of the adherents come from underprivileged backgrounds and are 'people with many problems', as characterised by pastor Gwajima himself. Here, the heart of the gospel is delivering people from the powers of darkness in general and bringing back zombies (*msukule* in Swahili) in particular (Hasu 2009). In subjective testimonies the believers emphasise the experience of having been delivered from the state of being a zombie rather than the turning point of having become saved as such. At this church the focus is not on the prosperity gospel,

but on the destruction caused by satanic forces and the possibility of deliverance from them. Like so many other Pentecostal and charismatic churches in Tanzania, this church wages a continual spiritual warfare against witches, witchcraft and other satanic elements.

The demonology of the Glory church draws elements from the biblical narratives of the Old and New Testaments, but it also draws from traditional Sukuma understandings of witchcraft and the complexities of the occult in the coastal areas of Tanzania (Giles 1999, Mesaki 1993, Tanner 1970). Gwajima's general mission is based on a verse in the book of Matthew 10:8 – 'Heal the sick, raise the dead, cleanse those who have leprosy, drive out demons. Freely you have received, freely give' (The Bible, New International Version [NIV]). Gwajima draws extensively from the Bible to support his views about witches and also about resurrection. One of his favourite phrases comes from the book of Exodus 22:18: 'Do not allow a sorceress to live' (NIV). As for the description of zombies, Gwajima finds literal evidence from the Old Testament book of Isaiah 42: 22, which echoes the African perception of zombies as a form of exploitation:

> But this is a people plundered and looted, all of them trapped in pits or hidden away in prisons. They have become plunder with no one to rescue them; they have been made loot, with no one to say, 'Send them back'.
>
> (NIV)

Unlike at Efatha, with its emphasis on empowerment, here the emphasis is on healing and deliverance from destructive, satanic powers. This message creates an image of human agency as limited and conveys a fatalistic and subdued vision of the future.

The return of the zombies

Recent research on popular imagination and the occult has related imageries of witchcraft and zombies to historical processes of globalisation. Stories of zombies have been seen as imaginative moral frameworks for making sense of the incomprehensible logic of the contemporary global economy, with structural adjustment programmes, migration, expanding markets and new cultures of consumption (Comaroff & Comaroff 2002; Moore & Sanders 2001). In southern Africa, where zombies frequently appear in popular discourse, the phenomenon has been related to the exploitation of wage labour and the encounter between the local and the global within the culture of global neoliberalism.

In Central and West Africa, the connection has also been made to the slave trade (Austen 1993; Comaroff & Comaroff 1999, 2002, MacGaffey 1986, Shaw 1997). In Tanzania, witchcraft discourses and the Pentecostal gospel with its demonology and testimonies of witchcraft take place in the context of structural adjustment and the consequences of a neoliberal economy: growing inequality, poverty, unemployment and the collapse of health care systems (Dilger 2007: 62, cf. Comaroff & Comaroff 2002: 797). In fact, Sanders has argued that structural adjustment has provided the necessary and sufficient conditions for the rapid escalation of occult discourses in Tanzania (Sanders 2001: 162).

Most people giving testimony about having been *msukule* are young, underprivileged women. On the other hand, people suspected of practising witchcraft and taking others' *msukule* are often intimately related senior women such as the victim's paternal grandmothers or father's sisters, residing in rural areas and home villages. Seldom did the victims make accusations against town-dwelling relatives, neighbours or accidental acquaintances. As is well known, African witchcraft is explicitly associated with the domestic setting, and it is believed that the most dangerous attacks come from within the family (Ciekawy & Geschiere 1998, Geschiere 1997). In South Africa, by contrast, the creators of zombies are often thought to be unrelated neighbours (Comaroff & Comaroff 1999: 289). The Comaroffs have described zombification as a tension between generations, mediated by gender; elderly women are accused by young men for taking them as zombies, thereby destroying employment opportunities (Comaroff & Comaroff 1999). At Glory, the victims are most often young women. Here, the blame for the failure to make one's living in the urban setting is mostly put on village-dwelling relatives.

The zombies of Glory have many common features with zombies that we hear of from other parts of Africa. *Misukule* are zombies who are thought to have been taken to act as free nocturnal labour for their owners, who are said to be located in valleys, caves and pits. Most often the former zombies report that they have done nocturnal farming work with bare hands using their long fingernails as the only tools, but some also recount having been toiling in a mine digging gems or working at somebody's business as a shop assistant. Although the African idea of a zombie often suggests antisocial accumulation of wealth by the witch, the accent here seems to be more on the victimisation and exploitation of the victim's skills and energies.

The victims regularly state in their testimonies that there is no proper food available for the zombies and that their diet usually consists of husks and water. Instead they report having been cannibalistically fed human flesh and blood. The origin of this human flesh is – as a rule – said to be babies who died at birth in hospitals where the witches send their recruits. It is also frequently reported that the *misukule* are unable to speak as their tongue has been cut off. They are thereby unable to give voice to their affliction, a feature also reported elsewhere (Comaroff & Comaroff 1999: 289, 2002: 787, Mesaki 1993: 161).

At Glory it is taken for granted that witchcraft and possession are the fundamental causes of affliction, and therefore prayers and exorcisms are performed for people who are believed to have been taken *misukule*. Deliverance can take place during services, special consultations or at vigils organised at the church. During church services, deliverances take place during long prayers led by pastor Gwajima. Drawing on imagery from the Book of John, where Jesus raised Lazarus from the dead by calling him: 'Lazarus, come out!', pastor Gwajima banishes witchcraft and calls the souls of the bewitched to return. By mid-2008 the church claimed to have brought back at least 150 people from *msukule*.

'The shade of a stick doesn't hide you from the sun'[4] – Testimonies of Ex-Zombies

The gospel preached at this church and the shared worldviews of the congregants provide the framework within which people interpret and conceptualise their own spiritual, social and economic affliction. The accounts are often rather challenging to follow because they defy rationality and logic in any mundane sense. But in essence, it is possible to see the accounts as narratives of victimisation. Past lives that are perceived as traumatic, regrettable or shameful are re-conceptualised as having been victimised as a zombie. Recurrent themes and life events with which *msukule* experiences are associated include poor school performance, teenage pregnancies and ill health. And most of these narratives also emphasise problematic and strained kinship relations and perceived lack of social and material support.

Narratives tell about the experiences of having been captured as zombies and of their role as active cannibalistic agents of reproductive destruction. The testimonies of young women from the social margins portray them as victims, potentially dangerous agents in possession of occult knowledge, and as born-again Christians all at the same time. Let us consider the case of Neema.

When I met Neema in 2008 she was living in the church, sleeping on the church floor with many other people in a similar situation. She had been expelled from her home and now, 17 years of age, found herself vulnerable and alone. Originally from a Lutheran home in Kilimanjaro, she had passed standard seven of primary school but had then dropped out of school. She claims to have been taken *msukule* by an elderly clanswoman when she was 12 years old and in standard six. According to Neema, she lived with several other people 'under the waters', working for the old woman who wanted to become rich through her sugar cane business. Neema says that she received sugar canes to sell for 1000 shillings (US$0.60). Neema explained that the business was good, they made a lot of money and that it was her duty to attract customers by using a special magic potion prepared from hair. The circumstances as *msukule* were cannibalistic:

We ate blood and human flesh. There was a group that went to places like hospitals. Or to cause accidents. If they went to cause accidents they brought blood. If they went to hospitals they took small babies. And we ate flesh. For example, a certain woman may have felt the contractions but then they finished. And then they went and took the baby and replaced it with a thing like a doll.

Eventually, in her real life, Neema left her family home in Moshi and came to Dar es Salaam. She said she was ill and not quite herself because she had already been taken *msukule*: 'My soul was ill.' She also had headaches and chest pains and was taken to hospitals and given medication without result. Then her brother heard that there was a church where people were raised from the dead and where people returned from *msukule*. Her brother said that they should go there so that she could be prayed for; maybe she would be cured and get well again.

Neema described how, one day in the land of the witches, she heard somebody calling her name from afar. She heard the voice calling her: 'Neema come, Neema come!' Then she saw a white person resembling pastor Gwajima who came and took her hand and said that Neema had been tormented enough and that it had to stop. She then unexpectedly found herself at Glory church. At the beginning she was possessed by spirits (*mapepo*), but she was prayed for and since that day she has not had any more headaches or chest pains.

Since Neema's family drove her away from home she prayed to God that he would show her the way. None of her relatives came to see Neema at the church. She explained that she used to live with her

brother in Dar es Salaam but he kicked her out after she had been brought back from *msukule*. Everybody called Neema *msukule* and her father did not want to see her. However, Neema's narrative left it undecided what were the fundamental reasons for her abandonment.

Neema became saved when she was delivered. God saved her from the place where she was suffering by bringing her back to the world. She received Jesus as her personal saviour and wanted to serve God. She saw a clear difference in her life compared with what it had been before. Previously she was ill all the time and had no direction in her life. Now she had received Jesus and was not ill any more. She had joy in her life as well as direction. She wanted to go back to school and complete her education. Despite her bleak circumstances, Neema had begun to feel more hopeful about the future.

Conclusion

In Tanzania, Pentecostal and charismatic Christianity has been flourishing since the economic reforms of the mid-1980s. Pentecostalism in general is becoming ever more attractive to both the rising urban middle class and to the rural and urban poor. For many people, religious ideas are integral to their moral values and understanding of the world. These new churches are growing rapidly and their theological discourses, with development-related ideologies and impacts, are becoming ever more influential in many societies. Religion is a model of and a model for the lived reality. And the consequences of economic structuring and the failings of the state in service provisioning have, in their way, shaped the form and content of religious ethos. Pentecostal Christianity, with its prosperity gospel and deliverance practices, offers means to come to terms with changing social and economic circumstances. Conversion, salvation and the creation of new attitudes and personal morality transform the person, enabling them to make the best of the rapid social and economic change. Religious ideas inform the ways that contemporary economic circumstances are interpreted and acted upon in the neoliberal setting. Furthermore, the lived realities of Tanzanians give rise to and shape their Pentecostal beliefs and ideas about salvation, success and modernity.

The Ghanaian religious superstar, Mensa Otabil, emphasises empowerment, human agency and the significance of hard work in creating development and prosperity. In those teachings human responsibility and disenchantment replace demonic control. Development comes from hard work, not from miracles. The integration of spiritual

power and rationality is necessary; reason, knowledge and scientific thinking are considered vital. Pastor Mwingira, like Otabil, emphasises the importance of education and rationality in personal transformation. While recognising the importance of historical and structural factors, this gospel largely sees the solutions to poverty and suffering in terms of personal and individual transformation.

The gospel preached at Glory church offers a different cosmological framework with which to interpret spiritual, social and economic afflic- tion. Among the young women who attend this church, narratives of zombification are articulated in circumstances where kinship networks have failed to offer adequate support. In this setting, such accounts are commentaries about the moral economy of kinship relations, perceived social obligations and individual aspirations. Zombie imageries are diag- nostic of the predicaments of urban life by reference to the draining exploitation of rural kin in a situation where neither the rural communi- ties nor the urban economy are able to provide youth with employment, income or visions of the future. At Glory, I have suggested, narratives of witchcraft and zombies are gendered commentaries of, and reactions to, the consequences of the economic reforms, growing inequality, poverty and unemployment.

Notes

1. This research was part of the project *African Christian Identity: Construction of African Christian Identity as a Dialogue between the Local and the Global* funded by the University of Helsinki and the Academy of Finland. I thank Prof. Paul Gifford, Prof. Mika Vähäkangas, Dr Kim Groop and Mrs Mari Pöntinen for their generous comments on earlier versions of this paper. I am also grateful to Mr Geoven Festo Rwiza, Mr Fred Traziace and Miss Vivian Baitu for assisting me in the field. The fieldwork took place over four months between 2007 and 2008.
2. Islamic organisations such as the Aga Khan Foundation and the Aga Khan Development Network were also significant (Jennings 2008: 66).
3. http://www.fpcttanzania.org/PDF/FPCT_CONSTITUTION_EN.pdf (accessed 12 September 2010).
4. Swahili proverb, '*kivuli cha fimbo hakimfichi mtu jua*'. It means that those with limited abilities, due to weakness, poverty and so on, cannot be depended upon for protection.

References

Anderson, Allan. 2004. *An Introduction to Pentecostalism: Global Charismatic Christianity*. Cambridge: Cambridge University Press.
Austen, Ralph. 1993. The Moral Economy of Witchcraft: An Essay in Com- parative History. In Comaroff, Jean and John Comaroff (Eds), *Modernity and*

Its Malcontents: Ritual and Power in Post-colonial Africa. Chicago: University of Chicago Press.

Barker, Isabelle. 2007. Charismatic Economies: Pentecostalism, Economic Restructuring and Social Reproduction. *New Political Science* 29(4): 407–427.

Brouwer, Steve, Paul Gifford and Susan D. Rose. 1996. *Exporting the American Gospel: Global Christian Fundamentalism.* New York: Routledge.

Ciekawy, Diane and Peter Geschiere.1998. Containing Witchcraft: Conflicting Scenarios in Post-colonial Africa. *African Studies Review* 41(3): 1–14.

Comaroff, Jean and John Comaroff. 2002. Alien-Nation: Zombies, Immigrants, and Millennial Capitalism. *South Atlantic Quarterly* 101(4): 779–805.

Comaroff, Jean and John Comaroff. 1999. Occult Economies and the Violence of Abstraction: Notes from the South African Postcolony. *American Ethnologist* 26(2): 279–303.

Comaroff, Jean and John Comaroff. 1993. Introduction. In Comaroff, Jean and John Comaroff (Eds), *Modernity and Its Malcontents: Ritual and Power in Post-colonial Africa.* Chicago: University of Chicago Press.

Corten, Andre and Ruth Marshall-Fratani. 2001. *Between Babel and Pentecost: Transnational Pentecostalism in Africa and Latin America.* Bloomington: Indiana University Press.

de Witte, Marleen. n.d. Sound, Image and Charisma: Mediating Spiritual Power in Ghana. Unpublished PhD Dissertation. University of Amsterdam.

Dilger, Hansjörg. 2007. Healing the Wounds of Modernity: Salvation, Community and Care in a Neo-Pentecostal Church in Dar Es Salaam, Tanzania. *Journal of Religion in Africa* 37(1): 59–83.

Eisenstadt, Shmuel Noah. 2000. Multiple Modernities. *Daedalus* 129(1): 1–29.

Geschiere, Peter. 1997. *The Modernity of Witchcraft: Politics and the Occult in Post-colonial Africa.* Charlottesville: University Press of Virginia.

Gifford, Paul. 2004. *Ghana's New Christianity: Pentecostalism in a Globalising African Economy.* London: Hurst.

Gifford, Paul. 2001. Complex Provenance of Some Elements of African Pentecostal Theology. In Corten, Andre and Ruth Marshall-Fratani (Eds), *Between Babel and Pentecost: Transnational Pentecostalism in Africa and Latin America.* Bloomington: Indiana University Press.

Gifford, Paul. 1998. *African Christianity: Its Public Role.* Bloomington: Indiana University Press.

Giles, Linda. 1999. Spirit Possession and the Symbolic Construction of Swahili Society. In Behrend, Heike and Ute Luig (Eds), *Spirit Possession, Modernity and Power in Africa.* Oxford: James Currey.

Hasu, Päivi. 2009. The Witch, the Zombie and the Power of Jesus: A Trinity of Spiritual Warfare in Tanzanian Pentecostalism. *Suomen Antropologi – Journal of the Finnish Anthropological Society* 34(1): 70–83.

Jennings, Michael. 2008. *Surrogates of the States: NGOs, Development and Ujamaa in Tanzania.* Bloomfield: Kumarian Press.

Kontinen, Tiina. 2007. Learning Challenges of NGOs in Development: Co-operation of Finnish NGOs in Morogoro, Tanzania. PhD Dissertation, Department of Education, University of Helsinki. Helsinki: Helsinki University Press.

Larbi, Kingsley. 2002. African Pentecostalism in the Context of Global Pentecostal Ecumenical Fraternity: Challenges and Opportunities. *Pneuma* 24(2): 138–166.

MacGaffey, Wyatt. 1986. *Religion and Society in Central Africa: The BaKongo of Lower Zaire*. Chicago: University of Chicago Press.

Maxwell, David. 2005. The Durawall of Faith: Pentecostal Spirituality in Neo-Liberal Zimbabwe. *Journal of Religion in Africa* 35(1): 4–32.

Maxwell, David. 1998. Delivered from the Spirit of Poverty? Pentecostalism, Prosperity and Modernity in Zimbabwe. *Journal of Religion in Africa* 28(3): 350–373.

Mesaki, Simeon. 1993. Witchcraft and Witch-killings in Tanzania: Paradox and Dilemma. PhD Thesis, University of Minnesota.

Meyer, Birgit. 1999. *Translating the Devil. Religion and Modernity among the Ewe in Ghana*. Edinburgh: Edinburgh University Press.

Miller, Donald E. and Tetsunao Yamamori. 2007. *Global Pentecostalism: The New Face of Christian Social Engagement*. Berkeley: University of California Press.

Moore, Henrietta and Todd Sanders. 2001. *Magical Interpretations, Material Realities: Modernity, Witchcraft and the Occult in Post-colonial Africa*. London: Routledge.

Mwingira, Josephat. 2005. *Wito Wangu Na Kusudi Nililopewa*. Dar es Salaam: Central Printing Works.

Newell, Sasha. 2007. Pentecostal Witchcraft: Neo-liberal Possession and Demonic Discourse in Ivoirian Pentecostal Churches. *Journal of Religion in Africa* 37(4): 461–490.

Robbins, Joel. 2004. The Globalization of Pentecostal and Charismatic Christianity. *Annual Review of Anthropology* 33: 117–143.

Sanders, Todd. 2001. Save Our Skins: Structural Adjustment, Morality and the Occult in Tanzania. In Moore, Henrietta and Todd Sanders (Eds), *Magical Interpretations, Material Realities: Modernity, Witchcraft and the Occult in Post-colonial Africa*. London: Routledge

Shaw, Rosalind. 1997. The Production of Witchcraft/Witchcraft as Production: Memory, Modernity, and the Slave Trade in Sierra Leone. *American Ethnologist* 24(4): 856–876.

Simensen, Jarle. 2006. Religious NGOs and the Politics of International Aid: The Norwegian Experience. *Forum for Development Studies* 1: 83–104.

Tanner, R. 1970. *The Witch Murders in Sukumaland: A Sociological Commentary*. Uppsala: Scandinavian Institute of African Studies.

Weber, Max. 1904–1905 [2004]. *The Protestant Ethic and the Spirit of Capitalism*. London: Routledge.

Woodberry, Robert. 2006. The Economic Consequences of Pentecostal Belief. *Society* 44(1): 29–35.

Zalanga, Samuel. 2010. Religion, Economic Change and Cultural Development: The Contradictory Role of Pentecostal Christianity in Sub-Saharan Africa. *Journal of Third World Studies* 27(1): 43–62.

4
Pentecostalism and Post-Development: Exploring Religion as a Developmental Ideology in Ghanaian Migrant Communities

Rijk van Dijk

Introduction

Based on post-development theory as developed by Nederveen Pieterse (2000) and Escobar (2007), among others, this chapter explores how and why Pentecostal ideologies and practices foster certain notions of development on their own terms. Pentecostal churches in Ghana can be seen as having introduced these developmental notions to their membership while they promote participation in specific activities and ritual practices that focus on the 'growth' of the individual, the community and the nation (as against the state). Interestingly, these developmental notions and practices have also become relevant for the ways in which Pentecostal churches have become transnational and linked up with Ghanaian migrant communities elsewhere. Much of the ethnography presented in this chapter is from the Ghanaian Pentecostal community in Gaborone, Botswana, where in recent years many Ghanaians have settled and set up small businesses – beauty salons, grocery stores and car repair workshops. Ghanaian Pentecostal churches have also established themselves in Gaborone, catering mainly for these migrants, as well as migrants from countries such as Zambia and Zimbabwe, and a few local Batswana. These churches compete with local Botswana Pentecostal churches, as well as those from Nigeria and elsewhere.

This chapter seeks to demonstrate how in this situation a particular Pentecostal developmental orientation is being pursued that focuses on the market and on fostering entrepreneurship among

Ghanaian migrants. Developing oneself, or one's community, is thereby reinterpreted in terms of pursuing the need to take business initiatives, to become successful in the market and to engage with certain religious practices that are meant to provoke a 'breakthrough' and that foster entrepreneurial skills and competences. Pentecostal prayer meetings, business fellowship meetings or Bible study groups address these issues and make people aware of the developmental power of the faith. By drawing attention to this embedded developmental thinking in Ghanaian Pentecostalism, this chapter addresses the problematic analytical distinction between religion and development, by showing how in a post-developmental perspective the two are becoming deeply intertwined in new and unprecedented ways.

Development, post-development and religion

Post-development theory emerged in the late 1980s and early 1990s in a setting where, in developing countries themselves, disillusionment with development efforts had been growing and where development practice increasingly came to be perceived as a form of Westernisation, inspired by a Western pursuit of middle-class ideals. In the words of Nederveen Pieterse (1998: 360):

> Perplexity and extreme disaffection with business-as-usual and standard development rhetoric and practice ... are keynotes of this position. Development theory and practice are rejected because it is the 'new religion of the West' (Rist 1990), because it is the imposition of science as power (Nandy 1988), giving rise to laboratory states (Vishvanathan 1988), because it does not work (Kothari 1990), because it means cultural westernization and homogenization. (Constantino 1985)

While the post-developmental movement in its agenda of formulating alternatives to development in the 1990s initially found inspiration in Marxism – particularly in the way it perceived Western development efforts as another means of capitalist encroachment on local societies and economies that would turn locals into consumers of the products of the global market – over time the workings of the market as a local form of development have been incorporated into this thinking as well. In this sense the market becomes another example of the way in which local societies may engage in unstructured, unplanned, non-linear, non-dictated processes of progress which may harbour alternative

notions of development (Escobar 1992, Kothari 1990, Matthews 2004). In the works of Crush (1995), Escobar (1992, 1995), Kothari (1990) and Nederveen Pieterse (2000) to name but a few, post-development is seen as a critical social theory that intends to democratise and culturalise development thinking and efforts. It wants to shift 'development' away from its Western origins and power relations and instead pursue a trajectory by which local notions of progress are rendered relevant.

The mounting critique of the Western development paradigm was not only fuelled by publications by these post-development writers in the 1990s, but also found further substantiation in the 1997 World Development Report, which drew attention to the deleterious impact of many development initiatives (Simon 2006). As Sally Matthews (2004) has pointed out, the call for an 'end to development' or for 'alternatives to development' does not mean that post-development thinkers do not want improvements in living standards, better health, less conflict and violence or greater equalities. Being a product of what some have termed 'a crisis in modernity' (Ferguson 1999), the issue is that post-development thinkers want to move away from the 'post-World War Two development project' – the specific model determining what development should be like, often emphasising a process towards the increasing pursuit of Western middle-class and bourgeois ideals. Post-development challenges the underlying universalistic claims of this post-World War development project and looks for other valuable (particularly local and cultural) sources and resources for notions of development. Matthews in particular draws attention to the fact that this seems highly relevant to the African situation, while she at the same time critically remarks that post-development theory strangely neglected Africa, and that African scholars have neglected post-development thinking (Matthews 2004: 374, see also Andreasson 2005).

It is interesting to note that in much of the so-called post-development literature there is little recognition of the importance of religion as a factor in the way in which post-development can be understood. If we agree with Escobar (2007: 24) that post-development is more a critical theory of practice than a concept, and aims at understanding local contestations of a singular, Western hegemonic perception of 'development', there is a need to look at how local movements formulate re-conceptualisations of the interrelation between political economy and culture. In other words, post-development approaches acknowledge that 'development' is both cultural and a product of Western power constellations that local movements can

resist and contest. One of the most recent publications in the field of post-developmental critical thinking, the edited volume by Ziai (2007) entitled *Exploring Post-Development: Theory and Practice, Problems and Perspectives*, devotes attention to the existence of 'social movements' – the grassroots movements that are of interest to post-development theory – yet does not include religious movements in the discussion. Also the pieces published by Nederveen Pieterse (1998, 2000), while discussing post-development as a radical reaction to the dilemmas of development, fail to take into account the extent to which in Africa post-development is increasingly informed by religion and religious actors.[1]

Post-development theorists have been silent about the new religious groups, in Africa and elsewhere, that are actively developing decentred forms and discourses that likewise seem to critically engage with the West, with unilinear models of growth and progress and with modernisation as promised by 'development' (Ferguson 1999). The absence of the religious factor in the development critique is striking given the fact that, as has often been argued, Christianity in the West fostered the development of modernist ideas of progress, social transformation and innovation in the first place. Africa became a continent with a marked history of missionary forms of Christianity introducing notions of what has been aptly described as a 'conversion to modernity' (Meyer 1998, Van der Veer 1996) through schools, hospitals and innovative agricultural technologies. In a dialogical process, this transformation also involved and engaged the praxis and ideology of 'development', in many cases turning missionaries into development workers; a conversion to development in a secularised form, so to speak. The early history of the Dutch volunteer organisation SNV, for example, shows that the idea of bringing development to other parts of the world became not only an ideology, but also part of the personal experience of growth, fulfilment and identity formation of these early volunteer workers (Brinkman 2010).

In recent years, a specific type of charismatic Christianity, often known generically as Pentecostalism, has become tremendously popular in Africa (Gifford 2004, Marshall 1993, Maxwell 1998, Meyer 2004, van Dijk 1998). It has begun to promote ideologies and practices fostering notions of development in its own terms. Pentecostal churches can be seen to introduce these notions to their membership by involving their members in specific activities and ritual practices that focus on the 'growth' of the individual, the community and the nation. This chapter seeks to demonstrate how in these situations a particular Pentecostal developmental orientation is being pursued that is focusing

on personhood, behavioural change, initiative and entrepreneurship, and ultimately, on the market.

Cultural breakthroughs

Since the 1980s Pentecostalism has become a social force of unimaginable power in many African countries, particularly Nigeria, Ghana, Kenya, Zimbabwe and Zambia. Many authors have recently noted the profound social, political and economic influence that Pentecostal groups are wielding over society. Often engaging middle-class intellectuals, these Pentecostal groups have shown to be effective in drawing upon human and intellectual resources that far outstrip those of other bodies in society, such as political parties, labour unions or the mainline missionary and traditional churches. They are capable of establishing their own structures for learning (such as Pentecostal universities), for social care and even for economic production and consumption. The links between Pentecostalism and certain forms of (religious) entrepreneurship are multifaceted, and a literature is beginning to emerge which explores the way in which a new religious market is developing in Africa (Bornstein 2005, Gifford 2007, Maxwell 1998, Pfeiffer 2005, Pype 2009, Smith 2001).

These forms of Pentecostalism critically engage with Western-inspired paradigms of development as commonly adopted by the governments of the countries in which these Pentecostal groups are active. In the Pentecostal circles that I have studied in Malawi, Ghana and Botswana, notions of progress, growth and development abound, yet are differently informed and based on ideas that do not automatically emulate Western conceptions. As such we can ask how their discourse on progress and prosperity is becoming post-developmental *avant la lettre*.

Much of the literature on the economic relations of faith focuses on what has come to be called the prosperity gospel, which seems to be dominating much of what is perceived as 'miracle-oriented' Pentecostalism in Africa today. This particular brand of Pentecostalism has gained a great deal of public attention because of the emphasis placed on 'God's wonder-working power' in providing people with abundant wealth and miracle healing. The Comaroffs (2000, 2001) have interpreted this particular Pentecostal emphasis on the miraculous in terms of a millenarian articulation between religion and the neoliberal capitalist order. They argue that miracle-based Pentecostalism is transforming the classic Protestant Ethic into a new form in the context of, and in response to, new global capitalist formations.

In this chapter I am, however, interested in exploring a more agentive dimension in the way these miracles address situations of misfortune of various kinds – medical, physical, financial, social – perceiving these as one, but not the only, voice through which Pentecostalism speaks to development. In an agentive mode, in Pentecostalism in Ghana I witnessed how the miracles were commonly meant to put the individual firmly on the road towards progress and prosperity by emphasising first and foremost the need for 'breaking' and for 'breakthroughs' (in Ghana known in local parlance as *obubu*). Progress can be attained by a proactive break with the past (Meyer 1998, van Dijk 1997, 1998) for which Pentecostalism in many places in Africa has introduced so-called deliverance rituals and deliverance camps (van Dijk 1997). These rituals are meant to forge a break with the past, a break with traditions and customs and, as such, should cause a 'breakthrough' in personal circumstances on the road to progress and prosperity.

As I have demonstrated elsewhere (van Dijk 1997, 1998, 2007, 2009a), this 'breaking' of the spiritual bonds with the past, with ancestors or ancestral spirits that are perceived as blocking a prosperous future for the individual, should not be understood as a complete Pentecostal rejection of customary or cultural elements of life or social relations. Some traditions and customary practices are maintained in the personal or social lives of Pentecostals as they can be 'Christianised', or 'neutralised', as some would say, and are therefore not considered to jeopardise the faith. This kind of spiritual 'breaking' with the past to enable progress is thereby in fact a practice and ideology of *taking control*; rather than the powers of an (ancestral) past taking control over a person's life, deliverance rituals produce an experience that one is in control of one's life. It raises a particular critical awareness of specific cultural practices in which they may previously have been involved, such as healing by traditional doctors, involvement in certain funeral practices, the pouring of libations to ancestral deities or the taking of ritual baths, to name but a few examples. This critical awareness is often discussed in terms of the ways in which the powers that are embedded in these practices can be 'neutralised' through prayer, the laying on of hands and through deliverance. There is emphasis on taking the initiative, in doing the 'breaking', in 'taking Jesus' (*fa yesu*, in local parlance) and in not being idle or passive. While in a recent discussion of the dictum of 'breaking with the past', Engelke (2010) problematises the extent to which a breaking is 'really' possible (and argues against an interpretation of Pentecostalism as being able to realise a break with the social environment), I instead emphasise that the rhetoric of breaking is

crucial in transforming the subjectivity of the believer and, in particular, in instilling a new level of proactivity. This is crucial in the process of provoking 'breakthroughs' in personal circumstances.

Narratives about the ways in which deliverance helps people overcome hardship to become successful in business, in relationships, in school exams or in finding lost or stolen property abound in local 'testimonies'. This is a narrative genre, well developed in this form of Pentecostalism, which gives people the opportunity and encouragement to talk about how much their lives have improved since they experienced a 'breaking', how many of the problems that they faced have disappeared and how a bright new future now welcomes them. Sometimes these stories are also recorded in glossy magazines, on TV or in radio broadcasts (De Witte 2008, Pype 2009), and thereby tend to provide an almost ubiquitous narrative of personal transformation, development and progress. This rhetoric of breaking with the past has been applied to many aspects of social and personal life. This chapter deals with two areas most salient for Ghanaian Pentecostal churches in Botswana: relationships and sexuality, and economic behaviour.

Relationships, sexuality and AIDS

The ideology of development based on 'breaking' informs the ways in which influential Pentecostal groups seek to produce 'behavioural change' in the area of relationships and sexuality. In places where AIDS is rampant, such as in Zambia, Uganda or Botswana, Pentecostal groups have become highly proactive in promoting a particular moral agenda that concerns relationships and sexuality (e.g. Burchardt 2009, Christiansen 2009, Geissler & Prince 2007, Prince et al. 2009; van Dijk 2007, 2009b). In emphasising premarital abstinence for youth and faithfulness in marriage (yet often rejecting the promotion of the condom), many Pentecostal groups feel they can break with, or critically confront, culturally accepted lifestyles and relationship patterns. In Ghana I also witnessed how from the mid-1990s onwards, issues of 'moral leadership' regarding sexuality became an important topic for Pentecostals. The Pentecostal emphasis on the nuclear family, on tying sexuality to marriage, and ideas of 'Christian courtship' resonated strongly with ideas being promulgated by faith-based organisations (FBOs) in the 1990s, particularly in places where AIDS was becoming an important issue. Ideas of progress and prosperity have become tied to certain moral regimes in the context of AIDS and sexuality.

Interestingly, whereas in most cases the Pentecostal agenda of influencing sexual and intimate behaviour is usually perceived as 'conservative' in nature, in talking to young people in Botswana a different picture emerges. Botswana, being one of the societies hardest hit by the AIDS pandemic in the 1990s, called on the churches to join what was called a 'multisectoral' approach in the fight against the disease (Nkomazana 2007, Togarasei 2009). This meant that churches had to build a leadership trained in addressing issues of sexuality and intimacy, with which many were initially uncomfortable. Breaking with conventions of silence, a kind of 'theology of sexuality' was developed and churches became active in promoting their particular moral agenda through awareness-raising sessions, counselling and so on. Many Pentecostal churches in Botswana were quick to take up the challenge of AIDS, and often worked alongside FBOs such as BOCAIP (the Botswana Christian Aids Intervention Programme) in its activities of rapid testing and premarital and abstinence counselling for youth and, later, the distribution of antiretrovirals.

Ghanaian Pentecostal churches in Botswana, though initially surprised by this need to address these matters and make 'a break with the past' in a terrain that was new to them, joined the effort and began likewise to organise AIDS-awareness days and prayer meetings (van Dijk 2003, 2009b). In that sense they joined what Klaits (2005) has called Botswana's project of 'Post-colonial Civility'.

Some of the young Pentecostal members that I interviewed were very explicit in saying that they liked the openness and frankness of the kind of counselling they received in these circles in premarital- or abstinence-counselling sessions (see also Burchardt 2009). Discussing intimate sexual matters in detail was both new and surprising to them, something they had never experienced before even in the context of family or kin relations, and something they had never expected a church or faith-based organisation to tackle. The most important aspect of this, however, was that these forms of counselling gave them the proactive tools to formulate a position that would allow them legitimately to break away from common cultural patterns of sexual behaviour. The 'abstinence pledges' that young people make in adherence to ideals of Christian courtship (Bochow 2008) allow them to stand up to peer pressure and to critically contest common practices. Christian courtship means that they can arrange the presence of a third party when they want to visit the one they love, so as to ensure that nothing 'indecent' happens. One unmarried couple even explained to me that since their relationship had become 'too hot' when they were courting, they

decided to have a 'cooling-down period' so as not to jeopardise what they were taught in church counselling.

The point is not so much that these young people develop into 'super-Christians' who are only interested in maintaining certain moral standards about sexuality and relationships, but that there is a real sense of how these new practices are important to progress and prosperity in life (Bochow 2008). Contesting customary and cultural values in these matters again relates to a notion of breaking with a cultural past, in this context in view of how to establish a successful relationship. As many of these young people said: 'Ah, these traditional things' – referring to cultural obligations and expectations – 'don't bring us anything good'. Counselling and Christian courtship thus becomes associated with the prospect of a good and successful life, and with progress and prosperity. The right type of relationship will reduce the risk of AIDS and of teenage pregnancy, and increase the likelihood of finishing school, building a home and creating a good life.

While these ideas may seem modern and progressive, the notion of morality and progress that underlies them conflicts with secular developmental notions of family and gender relations in certain respects. Most importantly, these Pentecostal churches maintain a very conservative position with regard to male dominance in the household. In Botswana, the very same Pentecostal groups that are active in promoting relationship counselling and that promote a new and Christianised 'sexual speak' about intimate matters protested vehemently against the government's policy of reducing the inequality between husband and wife with regards to family possessions and inheritance. The so-called Abolition of Marital Power Law that intended to equalise the power of men and women regarding their properties was accepted by parliament despite the fact that many influential Pentecostal groups declared the law 'unholy' and against biblical principles. So while (pre-)marital counselling emphasises a new and unprecedented openness that is beneficial to men and women alike, the Pentecostal notion of the man being the head of the family and the woman being his subservient helper is still an uncontested dogma in Pentecostal ideology.

The emergence of an entire new sector of Pentecostal counselling, Christian courtship and 'sexual speak' has important implications for a post-development analysis of how differently formulated ideas concerning growth, progress and development are instructive in Pentecostally driven behavioural change in Africa. They show, in particular, how religious change can lead to behavioural change in the most intimate of matters. Another area where Pentecostals are particularly effective in

promoting behaviour change is a rather more public and visible arena – that of economic activity. In this area, as will be shown in the following section, Pentecostals stress the need for individuals to set goals, to be oriented towards the fulfilment of a life project and to plan and budget one's personal life accordingly.

Market breakthroughs

Many Pentecostal circles, fellowships and counselling practices exist that devote extensive time and energy to the particular matter of how a modern believer is to be transformed and developed into a proactive and goal-oriented agent, one who is time-conscious and is prepared to cut away from any social obligations that stand in the way of meeting his or her goal. Pentecostal leaders show people how to handle these social dilemmas and how to manage their time effectively. They emphasise planning, self-control and the fine-tuning of time. In these churches, to be a Pentecostal is to be a time manager.

There is usually a superabundance of activities to be organised in Pentecostal circles. In addition to the constant planning and scheduling of a range of weekly activities that take place, such as fellowship meetings, home-cell meetings, deliverance hours, prayer and worship hours, pastoral hours, business breakfast meetings, harvest and rally-times and so on, the believer is told to plan his or her life meticulously. In Accra, Ghana, I witnessed many meetings in which the major topic of discussion and teaching was 'how to plan your life'. Detailed instructions were given about how planning should proceed and how goals should be set for the immediate, the medium term and even the distant future. Topics covered included financial and family budgeting, time-keeping, joint decision-making with spouses, and how enough room should always be reserved for participation in church activities.

As one of the pastors put it, the careful negotiation of time helps to avoid 'idleness, jealousy, spite and bitterness', and is therefore highly relevant for a godly purpose in one's life. It is because of this careful negotiation and planning of time in these Pentecostal circles that I disagree with Guyer's (2007) recent interpretation of what she calls 'punctuated time', whereby Pentecostals are seen as either formulating ideas concerning the immediate present or ideas concerning the escha-tological future, thereby failing to create a notion of time that concerns the immediate future of planning and strategising. These Ghanaian Pentecostals are very much concerned with planning and strategising and acting in the short and medium term.

The anthropology of Pentecostalism has now arrived at a point where it should take this developmental Pentecostal discourse seriously and explore and understand how and why these Pentecostal ideas of life planning and strategising may be relevant and, indeed, may have desired outcomes. It is too superficial a critique, often aired in the public media, to say that Pentecostal churches are into ideas of prosperity and progress only for their own financial and economic interests, affluent though some of these churches indeed have become. Participation in these Pentecostal fellowships, workshops and counselling sessions does indeed lead to changes in the way that members take care of their resources and finances, are 'hardened' to keep obligations towards the extended family at bay and are made aware of how they can protect both their resources and their time against the onslaught of all sorts of obligations and customary practices. I have witnessed the effects of the Pentecostal ideology of progress and of setting goals in individual lives, particularly where it comes to taking economic initiatives in starting a business, becoming an entrepreneur, safeguarding one's money and in exploring new economic opportunities through migration.

While some Pentecostal groups believe that their notions of progress and prosperity involve the production of what they call 'moral leadership', little thinking has developed concerning the need for structural change in societies such as Ghana or Botswana. There is little room to believe that Pentecostal notions of progress and prosperity move beyond a standard middle-class perspective. The ideas of personal growth, of recognising God's purpose for one's life and of breaking with the past do not imply fundamentally different ideas concerning the prevailing power and class relations of society. While Pentecostal leaders in Ghana, such as the well-known Mensa Otabil of the International Central Gospel Church, have been making public statements and have written books about 'God's purpose for the Black Race' (van Dijk 2004), these proclamations are rarely revolutionary in what they entail. Important Pentecostal leaders are often close to ruling or prominent elites and it is thus not surprising that their ideas on progress and prosperity do not call for a radical change of society, the market or governmental practices. Yet, on an individual level, in everyday life, becoming a member of a Pentecostal church and starting to plan and budget your life may be a revolutionary step to take. It can lead to profound changes in economic practices, and it is an open criticism of certain structures in life such as those of the family, kinship, the authority of the older generation and the power of chiefs.

The Pentecostal churches that stress careful time management and planning pay less attention to the kind of miraculous prosperity teaching that has been described by Comaroff and Comaroff (2000, 2001), Gifford (2004), Marshall (1993) and Meyer (1998, 1999, 2004). It has become clear that in discussing Pentecostal ideas of 'breakthroughs', different paradigms exist side-by-side. Whereas in the Ghanaian context some Pentecostal leaders have been promising unimaginable wealth to the faithful, this particular brand of the Pentecostal ideology did not inspire the Pentecostal churches that migrated to Botswana in the 1990s and that linked themselves up with the Ghanaian migrant community there. This community is dominated by small-scale business people – those engaged in trading, shopkeeping, running hair and beauty salons, selling and repairing cars and so on. And here the Pentecostal churches have been promoting an ideology that emphasises business rationalities, and which thus has found appeal with Ghanaians seeking to explore new opportunities in the Botswana neoliberal economy.

The Ghanaian Pentecostal churches in Botswana chose to follow the teachings of leaders such as Mensa Otabil, Enoch Sitima and Dag Heward Mills on how to understand the workings of the market and its dynamics. These leaders have been producing a literature that explores how the gospel and business competences are related and showing how to engage with the market in order to develop a successful enterprise (Gifford 2004: 49, van Dijk 2004, 2009a). Some of the most notable publications include Mensa Otabil's *Buy the Future* and *Four Laws of Productivity*, Dag Heward-Mills' series of booklets entitled *Success and the Ministry* and Michael Ntumy's *Financial Breakthrough: Discovering God's Secrets to Prosperity*. A similar literature has also been produced by Nigerian Pentecostal churches, such as David Oyepedo's *Understanding Financial Prosperity* and *Maximise Your Destiny*.

In this literature Pentecostals are taught how the gospel becomes a resource for the successful planning of one's economic endeavours and therefore one's success in business. Pentecostal messages become prescriptive in view of lines to follow, initiatives to take and resources to utilise. Pastor Michael Ntumy of the Church of Pentecost, for example, writes in his book *Financial Breakthrough: Discovering God's Secrets to Prosperity*:

> Plan a budget: many people are in financial bondage because they fail to plan a budget ... The principle of planning is not only an economic one, it is a very fundamental biblical principle ... God has

given us the power to get wealth. This is the power that ensures us the financial breakthrough. We have this power.

(Ntumy n.d. 59–60, 70)

This approach does not disqualify the prosperity type of gospel and its notions of miraculous wealth, because through divine intervention it is possible that a person may reach a blessed and affluent state of affairs. Ntumy writes:

The safest, easiest, risk-free form of investment which guarantees the multiplication of finances is by investing in the banking institution at a favourable rate of interest. At any given rate of interest, your finances will multiply over a certain period of time. Dr. Bernard Jordan of Zoe Ministries in New York calls this 'The Rule of 72'... [it] simply means that if you divide the rate of interest the bank offers by 72, the result you get equals the approximate number of years it takes for your money to double... Dear Child of God, this is the time to learn these principles of multiplication to maximise our gains for the sake of global evangelisation.

(ibid.: 83–84)

The stressing of skill, competence, preparation and planning places a high level of responsibility on the part of the individual to 'realise God's purpose'; decisions need to be both goal-oriented and to be inspired by biblical revelation and injunctions. Budget-planning, first of all, requires money to be set apart for tithing and offering to the church, as Ntumy (ibid.: 70) writes: 'The agents that trigger-off the financial breakthrough are two: tithing and offering!'

In Bible schools, classes and business fellowship meetings the Pentecostal imperative for members to be efficient and competent is strongly emphasised. As Lauterbach (2010: 270) also argues, the acquiring of skills and competences through such Pentecostal modes of learning applies to young pastors as much as it applies to common members. They are taught emphatically that in all financial planning the first requirement before any other step in the budgeting of business affairs is to ensure that tithing is done. If this condition is not met, any competence in doing business will not take the believer far, since it will lack the presence of benevolent heavenly powers.

In an earlier article on the notion of 'social catapulting' (van Dijk 2009a), I have drawn attention to how in the Gaborone-based Ghanaian business community Pentecostal prayer meetings, women's fellowships

and church services pay much attention to themes such as 'God has a plan for you', 'Dressed for success' or 'Be a risk-taker!' Pentecostal practices, such as weeks of fasting, are perceived as preparing members for taking risks in life in business, and in exploring opportunities elsewhere. In Ghanaian migrant communities in Germany, Nieswand (2010) similarly shows how certain ritual practices and ideological notions, such as fasting and prayer, are considered to give the believer strength to overcome challenges and obstacles.

For Ghanaian migrants who are entering new markets and engaging in new businesses, there is real power in these teachings. During Pentecostal church services testimonies are frequently presented explaining how important it is to be prepared and to acquire the necessary competences. There are lengthy discussions about what it means to plan ahead, to budget and to consider options. These testimonies elaborate on how the person's success was brought about by careful time management beyond the immediate here and now. It is often reported that God gave them a vision for their lives and their businesses. There is a Ghanaian expression: 'If a bird sits too long on a branch of a tree it can expect a stone to be thrown at its head.' This is often quoted in these teachings, emphasising that it is necessary to take risks, to venture into the unknown by travel and exploration and to be prepared to face challenges and to test one's strength in the market.

Members can become marginalised in the community if they are not prepared to be involved in 'risk-taking' in business activities, do not start a business themselves or if their businesses are not very successful (van Dijk 2009a). They may find themselves excluded from leadership positions and other roles that signal prestige. Looking down upon those who apparently had not been able to make it in the booming economy of Gaborone was often combined with a perception that this lack of success must have been the result of not consulting the Pentecostal leadership sufficiently intensively. After all, as Nieswand (2010) also emphasises in the German Ghanaian situation, 'the pastor knows best'. He is not only a 'man of God', but is also expected to be able to offer a great deal of practical, economic or migration-related advice as well.

Pastors commonly write letters of introduction for church members that indicate their wish to travel overseas in order to try their luck, and these letters of introduction enable easy access to the Ghanaian migrant churches in other countries. In Botswana, pastors regularly visit the businesses of their members and offer prayers for the (spiritual) protection and prosperity of the place and the workers. Competition is fierce, and fear exists that envy is particularly common on the part of the 'locals',

leading to anxieties of affliction by occult powers that may damage their business. There is considerable uncertainty about the precise nature of the occult powers in this host society, about where they are located and how they can bring about negative effects on businesses (van Dijk 2003). The teachings they receive during prayer meetings and Bible classes are seen as instructions on how to protect their businesses and avoid running into difficulties with these powers. These teachings emphasise strengthening one's own personal power so that these challenges can be met as a test of the strength of one's faith.

Ghanaian entrepreneurs also invite pastors to come and teach their staff and labourers. In their businesses (e.g. hair salons or car-repair workshops), their staff are often invited to take part in prayer meetings and Bible classes organised by visiting pastors. The pastors teach the workers how godly power and inspiration is needed to face the challenges of the competitive market and to warn them against the shrewdness and cunningness of Satan in deceiving people and in destroying their fortune. The teachings also emphasise obedience to business owners and give entrepreneurs increased moral authority in supervising their staff (often a mixture of Ghanaians, locals and other nationalities).

The pastors compare the situation of running their churches in what they perceive as being the religious market of Gaborone with running a business in an equally competitive business market. In Gaborone there are many Pentecostal churches that compete for a place on the religious market, while at the same time businesses increasingly compete with each other in the economic market. The fierce competition that has emerged for churches and businesses alike in having to fight for a place in either the religious landscape or the economic domain is exacerbated by tougher governmental policies that seek to control access to what Botswana's public domains have to offer (Good 2005, van Dijk 2003).[2]

In these Pentecostal communities there is a tendency to marginalise and to look down upon those who do not adopt the church entrepreneurial ideology, who do not relate to the pastors in the way that will inspire them to take on risks in starting a business and do not seem to have the 'character' (*suban* in Twi) to engage in the competitive domain. Those who are not prepared to become risk-takers are often perceived as people with lesser resources, therefore signalling that 'God has not been at their side'. The lack of success, the lack of opportunities to start a business or to explore possibilities and opportunities elsewhere through travel and through expanding business contacts, is seen as a weakness and a shortcoming in the faith of the individual. Rather than considering the contextual factors that may have hindered this person

from taking initiatives to become an entrepreneur or to travel, these failures are interpreted as being entirely personal. They are thought to show the person's unwillingness to be serious about the meticulous and goal-oriented task of planning one's life and demonstrate a stubbornness in not allowing 'the Holy Spirit to take over' and drive the person forward towards success. It is considered a matter of attitude if such a person does not follow the church's imperatives to engage the challenges of the market, and church members often voice harsh criticism if this lack of character is found among the circles of the church. The questions asked about such a 'stubborn' personality are often particularly addressed towards young men, and there is a lot of disdain for being idle and for not being proactive in pulling resources together. There is little consideration of structural problems and the fact that those without education, those who are stuck in low-paid jobs or those who have just arrived in Botswana may find it extremely difficult to 'jump' into entrepreneurial activity.

The internationally renowned leaders of big Pentecostal churches, such as Mensa Otabil and Dag Heward Mills from Ghana and Enoch Sitima from Botswana, are seen as inspirational role models for Pentecostal success in enterprise. Otabil's Central University in Accra trains students in Theology and Business Administration, such that they can follow in Otabil's footsteps. The affluent lifestyles of these leaders are read as a signal of their godly blessing and give weight to the truth of their words. The fact that they are rich and affluent enables them to make legitimate and apparently truthful claims about the power of the faith and about the power of 'breakthroughs'. Even those who fail to breakthrough into the market and who do not manage to achieve success still believe in the truth of their leader's words. In such cases leaders will tell their audience that more deliverance is required, more dedication to the goals set in one's life, more competence in dealing with the logic of the market.

This reasoning drives home an individualising perspective on success and failure. It creates a new awareness whereby one sees oneself as existing in a market where competition and rivalry exist, both in the visible and the invisible worlds, and where faith is necessary in order to strengthen one's skills and competences. Leaders leave no opportunity unused to stress how they themselves have also been living through all sorts of challenges and that their success never came easy. A market breakthrough as a road to progress and prosperity is thus commonly defined as a personal uphill battle, a battle in which there is actually little to be expected in terms of help or support from the side of

governments or development agencies. Privatisation, in this sense, ties in beautifully with the individualised notion of success and progress that is fostered in these Pentecostal circles.

Conclusion: post-developmental breakthroughs?

While we can only speculate as to why the post-development pursuit of 'alternatives to development' seems to have overlooked religion, there are perhaps some reasons to be found in the specific ways in which Pentecostalism combines notions of cultural progress with economic progress. We have seen how Pentecostalism fosters a particular moral agenda in which the need for a cultural breakthrough is connected to the possibility of having an economic breakthrough. This is in stark contrast to much post-developmental thinking, which tends to look for 'cultural essentials' – 'authentic' cultural patterns or structures – from where cues for alternative ideas of progress and development can be taken (Andreasson 2005, Kiely 1999, Ziai 2007). This may provoke a search for cultural essentials that are not 'touched' by the West, by globalisation or by an encroachment of a neoliberal or capitalist market. In this sense, then, Pentecostalism stands juxtaposed to the post-developmental pursuit, as it proclaims the need for a 'total break with the past'. Pentecostalism in Africa seems little interested in re-rooting its ideas of progress and prosperity in local culture, and can hardly be seen as a custodian of authentic cultural patterns of behaviour. Instead, its notion of development is based on 'neutralising' and Christianising culture, and thereby tailoring it to the needs of the modern believer.

At the same time Pentecostalism also challenges modernist and developmental ideas of the 'disenchantment of the world', as Weber called the progress of increasing rationalisation, bureaucratisation and secularisation (see also Habermas 2002). The Pentecostals are usually highly critical of local cultural traditions precisely because the world is *not* disenchanted and followers should be made aware of the fact that the devil is everywhere and that demons can work through traditional and modern situations alike. To the Pentecostals, modernity and the institutions of government, schools and development it brought are not in crisis for their failure to deliver, but because the evil powers of Satan simply keep on working through them. Hence, the Pentecostal alternative to development does not disqualify the need to make progress in life and to have a breakthrough in circumstances, but instead seeks to create a critical awareness of the moral nature of such development.

In places such as Ghana and Botswana, moreover, Pentecostalism does not speak with a 'singular' voice. The prosperity gospel and the focus on miracles is as much part of Pentecostal reality as its messages concerning market breakthroughs, critical awareness and skills and competences. No Pentecostal message denies miracles and God's wonder-working power. A common denominator, however, remains that in both types of Pentecostalism the believer is not simply viewed as a victim of globalisation, of market forces or of neoliberal structures. In both voices of Pentecostalism an element of agency is instilled in the modern believer, through which the person is empowered to 'take control' of their life. A strong motif in this thinking is the idea of the 'conqueror', whereby true believers are portrayed as conquerors over demonic powers, and as conquerors in the market place. This is enveloped in a rhetoric of becoming armed with 'the armour of God', the 'blood of Jesus' or the 'shield of the Holy Spirit'. In one of the Pentecostal churches in Gaborone I saw small drawings being distributed depicting Roman soldiers wearing spears, shields and helmets as representations of what conquerors look like. This helps to reorient believers to see globalisation and the market as spheres of opportunity rather than as forces of victimhood. The cultural and market breakthroughs that Pentecostalism is preaching in Africa are an alternative to development, and, in a strange way, also an alternative to post-development.

While development theory is engaged in debating issues of post-development, the anthropology of development appears little affected by the paradigmatic shift this debate is signalling. In this chapter I have explored a specific element that appears lacking in current post-development theory – the significance of religion. In terms of the anthropology of development in Africa, there are many reasons to engage with a post-developmental perspective in understanding the significance of religion. Many countries in Africa have been witnessing an unprecedented rise in influential Pentecostal churches that, over the last three decades, have been able to place themselves at the centre of the public domain by presenting a certain developmental discourse in their own terms. While the Pentecostal ideology often claims progress and prosperity in a religiously embedded practice, Pentecostal groups and leaders also specialise in engaging with the market, in becoming religious entrepreneurs and in creating developmental perspectives through a neoliberal approach to the market. On all these accounts, 'development' is reformulated in a Pentecostal rhetoric. It is for this reason that there is a need to sensitise the anthropology of development of these kinds of post-developmental processes, much as they inform – if not

determine – public discourse, and much as they are lodged in powerful religious groups of this particular kind.

Notes

1. Authors such as Rist (1990), Rahnema and Bawtree (1997) and Ferguson (1999) have analysed how within development studies religion is used to formulate a critique about development as being 'a religion of the West' or by remarking how in the non-Western world development has often acquired 'spiritual' dimensions when located in the hands of grassroots organisations. Yet religion as such does not receive further attention in these studies.
2. Botswana is known for its high economic growth rates that began to emerge from the mid-1970s, when De Beers began exploring and merchandising the country's diamonds.

References

Andreasson, Stefan. 2005. Orientalism and African Development Studies: The 'Reductive Repetition' Motif in the Theories of African Underdevelopment. *Third World Quarterly*, 26(6): 971–986.

Bochow, Astrid. 2008. Valentine's Day in Ghana: Youth, Sex and Fear between the Generations. In Alber, Erdmute, Sjaak Van der Geest, and Susan Whyte (Eds), *Generations in Africa*. Hamburg: LIT.

Bornstein, Erica. 2005. *The Spirit of Development. Protestant NGOs, Morality, and Economics in Zimbabwe*. London: Routledge.

Brinkman, Inge and Anne-Lot Hoek. 2010. *Bricks, Mortar and Capacity Building: A Socio-Cultural History of SNV Netherlands Development Organisation*. Leiden: Brill.

Burchardt, Marian. 2009. Subjects of Counselling: Religion, HIV/AIDS, and the Management of Everyday Life in South Africa. In Becker, F. and P Geissler (Eds), *Aids and Religious Practice in Africa*. Leiden: Brill.

Christiansen, Catrine. 2009. The New Wives of Christ: Paradoxes and Potentials in the Remaking of Widow Lives in Uganda. In Becker, Felicitas and Wenzel Geissler (Eds), *Aids and Religious Practice in Africa*. Leiden: Brill.

Comaroff, Jean and John Comaroff. 2001. Millennial Capitalism: First Thoughts on a Second Coming. In Comaroff, Jean and John Comaroff (Eds), *Millennial Capitalism and the Culture of Neoliberalism*. Durham: Duke University Press.

Comaroff, Jean and John Comaroff. 2000. Privatizing the Millennium. New Protestant Ethics and the Spirits of Capitalism in Africa, and Elsewhere. *Afrika Spectrum*, 35(3): 293–312.

Constantino, Renato. 1985. *Synthetic Culture and Development*. Quezon City: Foundation for Nationalist Studies.

Crush, Jonathan. 1995. *Power of Development*. London: Routledge.

De Witte, Marleen. 2008. Spirit Media. Charismatics, Traditionalists and Mediation Practices in Ghana. PhD Dissertation, University of Amsterdam.

Engelke, Matthew. 2010. Past Pentecostalism: Notes on Rupture, Realignment, and Everyday Life in Pentecostal and African Independent Churches. *Africa*, 80(2): 177–199.

Escobar, Arturo. 2007. Post-Development as Concept and Social Practice. In Ziai, Aram (Ed.), *Exploring Post-Development: Theory and Practice, Problems and Perspectives*. London: Routledge.

Escobar, Arturo. 1995. *Encountering Development: The Making and Unmaking of the Third World*. Princeton: Princeton University Press.

Escobar, Arturo. 1992. Reflections on Development: Grassroots Approaches and Alternative Politics in the Third World. *Futures*, 24(5): 411–436.

Ferguson, James. 1999. *Expectations of Modernity: Myths and Meanings of Urban Life on the Zambian Copperbelt*. Berkeley: University of California Press.

Geissler, P. Wenzel and Ruth Prince. 2007. Life Seen: Touch and Vision in the Making of Sex in Western Kenya. *Journal of Eastern African Studies*, 1(1): 123–149.

Gifford, Paul. 2007. Expecting Miracles: The Prosperity Gospel in Africa. *Christian Century*, July 10.

Gifford, Paul. 2004. *Ghana's New Christianity. Pentecostalism in a Globalising African Economy*. London: Hurst.

Good, Kenneth. 2005. Resource Dependency and Its Consequences: The Costs of Botswana's Shining Gems. *Journal of Contemporary African Studies*, 23(1): 27–50.

Guyer, Jane. 2007. Prophecy and the Near Future: Thoughts on Macroeconomic, Evangelical, and Punctuated Time. *American Ethnologist*, 34(3): 409–421.

Habermas, Jürgen. 2002. *Religion and Rationality: Essay on Reason, God, and Modernity*. Cambridge: Massachusetts Institute of Technology Press.

Kiely, Ray. 1999. The Last Refuge of the Noble Savage? A Critical Account of Postdevelopment. *European Journal of Development Research*, 11(1): 30–55.

Klaits, Fred. 2005. Post-colonial Civility. *Journal of Southern African Studies*, 31(3): 649–662.

Kothari, Rajni. 1990. *Rethinking Development: In Search of Humane Alternatives*. London: Aspect Publications.

Lauterbach, Karen. 2010. Becoming a Pastor. Youth and Social Aspirations in Ghana. *Young*, 18(3): 259–278.

Marshall, Ruth. 1993. Power in the Name of Jesus: Social Transformation and Pentecostalism in Western Nigeria 'Revisited'. In Ranger, Terence and Vaughan Olufemi (Eds), *Legitimacy and the State in Twentieth-Century Africa*. London: Macmillan.

Matthews, Sally. 2004. Post-development Theory and the Question of Alternatives: A View from Africa. *Third World Quarterly*, 25(2): 373–384.

Maxwell, David. 1998. Delivered from the Spirit of Poverty? Pentecostalism, Prosperity and Modernity in Zimbabwe. *Journal of Religion in Africa*, 28(3): 350–373.

Meyer, Birgit. 2004. Christianity in Africa: From African Independent to Pentecostal-Charismatic Churches. *Annual Review of Anthropology*, 33: 447–474.

Meyer, Birgit. 1999. Commodities and the Power of Prayer: Pentecostalist Attitudes towards Consumption in Contemporary Ghana. In Meyer, Birgit and Peter Geschiere (Eds), *Globalization and Identity: Dialectics of Flow and Closure*. Oxford: Blackwell.

Meyer, Birgit. 1998. 'Make a Complete Break with the Past'. Time and Modernity in Ghanaian Pentecostalist Discourse. In Werbner, Richard (Ed.), *Memory and the Postcolony*. London: Zed Books.

Nandy, Ashis (Ed.). 1988. *Science, Hegemony and Violence.* New Delhi: Oxford University Press.

Nederveen Pieterse, Jan. 2000. After Post-development. *Third World Quarterly,* 21(2): 175–191.

Nederveen Pieterse, Jan. 1998. My Paradigm or Yours? Alternative Development, Post-Development, Reflexive Development. *Development and Change,* 29: 343–373.

Nieswand, Boris. 2010. Enacted Destiny: West African Charismatic Christians in Berlin and the Immanence of God. *Journal of Religion in Africa,* 40(1): 33–59.

Nkomazana, Fidelis. 2007. Christian Ethics and HIV/AIDS in Botswana. In Amanze, James (Ed.), *Christian Ethics and HIV/AIDS in Africa.* Gaborone: Bay Publishing.

Ntumy, Michael. n.d. *Financial Breakthrough: Discovering God's Secrets to Prosperity.* Accra: Pentecost Press Ltd.

Pfeiffer, James. 2005. Commodity *Fetichismo,* The Holy Spirit, and the turn to Pentecostal and African Independent Churches in Central Mozambique. *Culture, Medicine and Psychiatry,* 29(3): 255–283.

Prince, Ruth, Philippe Denis and Rijk van Dijk. 2009. Engaging Christianities: Negotiating HIV/AIDS, Health, and Social Relations in East and Southern Africa. *Africa Today,* 56(1): v–xviii.

Pype, Katrien. 2009. 'We Need to Open Up The Country': Development and the Christian Key-Scenario in the Social Space of Kinshasa's Teleserials. *Journal of African Media Studies,* 1(1): 101–115.

Rahnema, Majad and Victoria Bawtree (Eds). 1997. *The Post-Development Reader.* Cape Town: David Philip.

Rist, Gilbert. 1990. 'Development' as Part of the Modern Myth. *European Journal of Development Research,* 2(1): 10–21.

Simon, David. 2006. Separated by Common Ground? Bringing (Post)Development and (Post)Colonialism Together. *The Geographical Journal,* 172(1): 10–21.

Smith, Daniel. 2001. 'The Arrow of God': Pentecostalism, Inequality, and the Supernatural in South-Eastern Nigeria. *Africa,* 71(4): 587–613.

Togarasei, Lovemore. 2009. *Draft Rapid Assessment Report for FBOs Strategy.* Unpublished Report, Ministry of Health/University of Gaborone, Botswana.

Van der Veer, Peter (Ed.). 1996. *Conversion to Modernities. The Globalization of Christianity.* London: Routledge.

van Dijk, Rijk. 2009a. Social Catapulting and the Spirit of Entrepreneurialism: Migrants, Private Initiative, and the Pentecostal Ethic in Botswana. In Hüwelmeier, Gertrud and Kristine Krause (Eds), *Traveling Spirits. Migrants, Markets and Mobilities.* New York: Routledge.

van Dijk, Rijk. 2009b. Gloves in Times of AIDS: Pentecostalism, Hair and Social Distancing in Botswana. In Becker, Felicitas, and P. Wenzel Geissler (Eds), *Aids and Religious Practice in Africa.* Leiden: Brill.

van Dijk, Rijk. 2007. The Safe and Suffering Body in Transnational Ghanaian Pentecostalism: Towards an Anthropology of Vulnerable Agency. In De Bruijn, Mirjam, Rijk van Dijk and Jan-Bart Gewald (Eds), *Strength Beyond Structure: Social and Historical Trajectories of Agency in Africa.* Leiden: Brill.

van Dijk, Rijk. 2004. 'Beyond the Rivers of Ethiopia': Pentecostal Pan-Africanism and Ghanaian Identities in the Transnational Domain. In van Binsbergen,

Wim, and Rijk van Dijk (Eds), *Situating Globality: African Agency in the Appropriation of Global Culture.* Leiden: Brill.

van Dijk, Rijk. 2003. Localisation, Ghanaian Pentecostalism and the Stranger's Beauty in Botswana. *Africa*, 73(4): 560–583.

van Dijk, Rijk. 1998. Pentecostalism, Cultural Memory and the State: Contested Representations of Time in Post-colonial Malawi. In Werbner, Richard (Ed.), *Memory and the Postcolony: African Anthropology and the Critique of Power.* London: Zed.

van Dijk, Rijk. 1997. From Camp to Encompassment: Discourses of Transsubjectivity in the Ghanaian Pentecostal Diaspora. *Journal of Religion in Africa*, 27(2): 135–169.

Vishvanathan, Shiv. 1988. On the Annals of the Laboratory State. In Nandy, Ashis (Ed.), *Science, Hegemony and Violence.* New Delhi: Oxford University Press.

Ziai, Aram (Ed.). 2007. *Exploring Post-Development: Theory and Practice, Problems and Perspectives.* London: Routledge.

Part II

Churches and NGOs: Different Routes to Salvation

5
Pentecostal and Development Imaginaries in West Africa

Charles Piot

It would be hard to overestimate the significance of the new Pentecostal churches in the post-Cold War cultural life of Ghana and Togo, especially among the middle classes in the capital cities.[1] In Accra and Lomé alone, there are hundreds of new charismatic churches, some with room to seat thousands of people. On Sundays, the city is dead and the churches, large open-air buildings with booming sound systems, are filled with smartly dressed congregants. Many partake during the week as well – in daily prayer meetings, in Friday 'all-nights', in counselling sessions – and, periodically, in 'conferences' and 'seminars' with visiting pastors, in 'crusades' to heal the sick and win converts, in 'deliverance' sessions to exorcise demons. If you visit the University of Ghana at six in the morning on a school day, you'll find the soccer pitch filled with thousands of students praying and speaking in tongues. Board a plane in Accra or Lagos and you'll bear witness to collective prayers before take-off and landing. Spend New Year's Eve in Lomé and you'll find a larger, more spirited crowd in the churches than at a nightclub or private party. One such New Year's service I attended at the Assemblies of God in 2009–2010 – a service held in the street to accommodate the overflow crowd – started at 10 pm and ended at 3 am, punctuated by a Times Square-like celebration at midnight that featured wild dancing and open-armed exhortation of the Holy Spirit. In the *boites de nuit* themselves, the music is increasingly church disco ('Jesus is the only one, he's my true love'). 'The charismaticisation of Lomé's nightlife?' I suggested to a friend as we walked by a string of nightclubs on the Boulevard Circulaire, all blasting religious pop. 'Yes', she replied, with an approving smile.

This chapter focuses on the recent explosion in charismatic religion, and on the coeval – and, I suggest, co-constituted – development scene,

in Togo and Ghana during the period after the end of the Cold War. This period has been a time of ongoing crisis – a crisis at once political, economic, epistemological. It is a moment when the Cold War monies have dried up, when the state is in retreat from social and developmental fields, and when the colonial and early post-colonial (Cold War) compact between metropole, authoritarian state and chiefs in the villages – the indirect rule system that lasted into the 1990s – is unravelling. It is the churches and the non-governmental organisations (NGOs) that step into the gap left by the retreat of the state, and begin to reorganise the biopolitical field, effectively deciding who lives and who dies (Agamben 1998, 2005).

Despite their differences, both Pentecostal and developmental also exhibit striking similarities – among them, an elicitation of neoliberal subjectivity, a substitution of translocal for local belonging, a turn to affect, a temporality that is punctuated and non-linear, an invocation of a state of crisis, a blaming of the local for the plight of the present. I see these similarities as symptomatic and broadly reflective of the current global moment.

Pentecostalism

Until the mid-1990s, the mainline or mission churches – Catholic and Presbyterian in Togo; Catholic, Presbyterian and Anglican in Ghana – dominated the church scene. Indeed in Togo during the Cold War years, the dictator, Gnassingbé Eyadéma, explicitly forbade any other Christian denominations from establishing themselves.[2] However, with neoliberalisation in the 1990s – including the broadscale liberalising of political, media and religious fields – the dictator's hands became tied and he was powerless to censor religious and cultural fields as before. At this point, a thousand small churches, mostly Pentecostal and charismatic, entered the field and began to attract followers. Some, like Assemblies of God, were virtual carbon copies of those in the US, but most were Ghanaian-Togolese variants of American-style charismatic worship, with distinctive local features added in – more exorcisms, more prayer, more singing and dancing.

While the cities are today knotted with such churches – I know of no neighbourhoods in Lomé or Accra without several, though often more – they abound in the villages as well. There, however, they are smaller, often shoestring operations – 20 worshippers in this Assemblies congregation, 30 in that Church of the Pentecost, 80 in Croix Blanche. Despite smaller numbers, their presence nevertheless fills the airwaves,

for unlike the earlier mission churches they are much less tolerant of village religion and wage spiritual warfare against its 'demons' (spirits and ancestors) whose presence they see as the root of many of Africa's problems today, especially its underdevelopment.

An initial, more sociological, reading of the Pentecostal phenomenon in West Africa is to see the new churches as proxy for an eviscerated post-Cold War state, in part filling the gap left by the state in providing social services (cf. Bornstein 2005, Bornstein & Redfield 2011, Comaroff forthcoming, Marshall 2009, Meyer 2004b). In Ghana, there will soon be more church- than state-owned universities and the ubiquitous orphanages are largely church-funded. In Togo, the new churches are coming to be seen as development agencies, responsible for the building of new clinics and elementary schools, and sponsoring AIDS research and treatment. Significantly, the financial base of the churches is built up less through foreign donations than through tithing within the congregation – a new form of 'taxation'. An interesting squabble took place in summer 2004 in Accra when it was revealed that one of the large Nigerian charismatic churches there, Winner's Chapel, was repatriating tithes raised from its Accra branch to the parent church back home – a not insignificant sum of US$200,000 per month. One of the principal commentaries about the repatriation scheme, commentaries which dominated the public sphere in Accra for several weeks, was to ask what effect such capital flight might have on the economic development of Ghana. 'So now Ghanaians are paying for the development of Nigeria?', one talk-radio call-in listener asked rhetorically.

But the churches do much more for their members than merely provide state functions. They offer a type of total institution or total culture that stands in for the family in otherwise anomic urban conditions (Englund 2007, Meyer 2004b, van Dijk 1997). Many of the churches in Accra and Lomé are organised into 'neighbourhoods' – so that networked members of the church who live near one another can meet during the week for prayer sessions or call one another when in need. Singles and youth groups go on weekend outings at least once per month. As the chapter by van Dijk also illustrates, the church serves as proxy for family and village in regulating marriage, encouraging believers to marry church-endogamously and insisting on premarital chastity. In one church I attended in Accra, several couples were discovered (during the counselling sessions that precede marriage) to have engaged in premarital sex and were paraded before the congregation, before being banished to the back pews for a full year. Extramarital sex

is also considered a serious sin, especially when a woman sleeps with the husband of another.

Most significantly – here still within the ambit of a sociology of the new churches – these communities of believers instil codes of conduct and orientations towards the everyday that provide a virtual blueprint for disciplining the post-Cold War citizen-subject into the neoliberal economy (cf. Comaroff forthcoming). Believers are expected to be hard-working, honest, frugal, sexually chaste, abstemious and – textbook Weber – to see evidence of their faith as success within the new economy. Literacy, too, and middleclassness, is everywhere performed and on display. Thus, church members are urged to take notes on the sermon (in small notebooks tucked into purses and breast pockets) and to write down Bible passages to study and reflect upon during the week, and services are simultaneously translated from the vernacular (*Twi* in Accra, *Mina* in Lomé) into English or French, or vice versa – not only an attempt to draw in multiple constituencies but also to project an educated, cosmopolitan, internationalist image.

Pentecostal narratives

But the new churches are narrative-machines as much as welfare societies and new economy interpellation devices. They generate stories – often fantastic stories – about the world today and the place of West Africa in that world. These are stories that appeal especially to those who are weary of the old narratives that have for too long defined Africa as victim of forces and histories beyond its control. They are also ones that undermine the authority relations of the old regime – of the colonial and dictatorship moment – that sutured a Cold War state to chiefs and elders in the rural areas. I mention here two such narratives, each a tale of rupture – of a 'break with the past' (Engelke 2004, Meyer 1998, 1999a, Robbins 2007, van Dijk 1998, 2001a).

Development and the break with tradition

The first narrative is about development – and its corollary, the disavowal of village religion or tradition. West Africa is underdeveloped, members of the church say, because Satan inhabits the villages. Extirpate the devil and all his manifestations (especially the worship of spirits and ancestors), and West Africa will develop quickly. A pastor, who missionises in the village where I conduct research in northern Togo, gave the following example: Were it not for a sacred forest that climbs the highest ridge in the community (and whose taboos forbid human

intervention – cultivation, house construction – within its parameters), they could build a road that would, as he put it, 'develop the community overnight. It is pagan beliefs like this that are the cause of Africa's poverty today.' When I asked whether it wasn't instead Europe that had 'underdeveloped' and further impoverished Africa (Frank 1971, Rodney 1981), he admitted familiarity with such an explanation ('oh, yes, they taught us that at the university') and acknowledged that that might also be true, but he said that Togolese needed to get their own house in order first and then Europe would make up for past sins.

This 'blame tradition' story was reiterated in a different register by a Togolese schoolteacher from the north. In describing the extravagant spending that went into a recent funeral in which three cows were sacrificed, he upbraided the family for putting their limited means to such ends rather than towards development and material well-being – and blamed 'tradition' for obligating them to do so. 'One cow would have been enough to honour the dead man *and* give everyone a piece of meat. Three was totally unnecessary, and, even worse, much of the meat rotted because there was too much to give away.' His commentary came as a surprise – for despite being Christian he has always been partial to village religion – thus indicating how widespread is the view today that development and tradition are antithetical.

Birgit Meyer (1999a, 1999b, 2004a) has suggested for southern Ghana that the public sphere is now a 'Pentecostalite' one, in which films and soaps routinely index Pentecostal themes and radio talk shows casually reference the Holy Spirit. Here, the Pentecostal demonisation of tradition is written into Nigerian and Ghanaian popular cinema. A theme repeated over and over in these films is that of the urban middle class family with ongoing ties to the village, ties invariably of an occult nature. As the plot unwinds, the family is destroyed by jealousy and village witchcraft (and viewers are implicitly instructed to leave tradition and the old deities behind). The round of Nigerian films airing in Accra in summer 2004 went a step further, transforming these more secular Pentecostal themes into overtly religious ones, with conversion/baptism/rebirth and encounters with the Holy Spirit built right into the narrative itself.

The brilliance of the Pentecostal metaphysic is that it allows believers to have their cake and eat it too: distancing themselves from village religion – and, not coincidentally, from the social obligations that accompany ongoing ties to the village (Meyer 2004b, van Dijk 1998) – while nevertheless remaining thoroughly within its logic and animating categories. Not only do charismatics fully believe in the ongoing

existence and efficacy of the spirits and witches of the village, albeit demonising them, but also they continue to inhabit a village world of opaque signs (that index the machinations of invisible forces) in need of constant hermeneutical attention. Those urban charismatics I know search their everyday worlds as well as their dreams for signs of the workings of malevolent forces, as well as of the Holy Spirit.

Meyer (2002, 2003) reports a fascinating phenomenon among film-watching Ghanaians: that many offered as evidence for the existence of the occult the fact that they had seen such phenomena in popular film itself. Indeed, in the dozens of Nigerian films I watched in Accra theatres in summer 2004, the one moment when people stopped talking and mobile phones went unanswered was the moment when a compact with a spirit or demon was shown or a witch's actions were exposed. The cinematic here serves to visualise and make public that which, in a pre-cinematic world, had remained concealed (for the world of spirits is invisible to the human eye) and could only be accessed through the imagination – thus also, ironically, making the occult seem more 'real'. Moreover, the story that locates Satan in the villages generates a thousand urban legends about the inner workings of the occult in those locales, stories that circulate and feed the imagination and voyeuristic impulses of the urban middle classes, again holding close that world they otherwise strive to keep at a distance.

Here, then, is a textbook example of Foucault's (1980, 1990[1978]) reworking of the repression hypothesis: Pentecostalism's demonising of village religion has done nothing so much as lead to an efflorescence, a promiscuous proliferation, of images of spirits and witches – in the popular imagination, in local films and soaps and in the churches themselves where sermons go into graphic detail about encounters with demonic forces. A sublime irony, however, for much of this occurs in the cities and among those elites intent on distancing themselves from the religion of the villages.

Note, too, the mapping of the West African landscape that accompanies Pentecostal views of the village. In representing West Africa's vast rural spaces as satanic, the Pentecostal constructs a spiritual cartography that opposes village and city as those who are lost to the devil and those saved by Christ. This map cuts long-standing connectivities between rural and urban, replacing them with relays among Pentecostal nodes in Lagos-Lomé-Accra-Abidjan. Moreover, national borders seem to matter little any more, not only because they are transgressed by Christian flows along the coastal corridor but also because mission work into the

satanic rural is no longer strictly contained by the national (as during the early independence period): Assemblies of God in Lomé today sends missionaries to Mali and Niger, into the satanic (also Muslim) north, as well as to rural villages in its home country. This is a mapping that complements that of the NGOs, who see the rural village as a site of poverty in need of 'saving' – focusing, however, on the poverty of the soil rather than of the spirit.

While this 'blame tradition' story echoes earlier modernisation theory narratives about African development and the obstacles posed by 'traditional culture', and while one might thus be tempted to see the latest round of globalisation and its ideologies as little more than a recycling of that earlier (1960s) moment, there are also significant differences. For one, the orientalising impulse has been utterly indigenised and domesticated, and has a mass popular-cultural appeal that it lacked in the earlier moment. For another, the contemporary narrativisation is empowering in a way that the earlier one was not, precisely because it is seen and experienced as self-authored. Moreover, while not easy for the anthropologist to admit, the church's rejection of tradition – of local ritual and cosmology – might also be read as a rejection of the colonial, and, ironically, because done in the name of a religion with Euro-American roots, as an attempt to decolonise the mind. To wit, it was colonialism that 'invented' chiefs and village tradition as technologies of power, projects and technologies that were reissued by post-colonial dictatorships. Charismatics see themselves as attempting to free themselves from the weight of this (to them) oppressive tradition.

One of the most telling aspects of the Pentecostal phenomenon is its refusal of the old structures of authority and mediation. Not only do the new churches see themselves as working outside the chain of colonial/post-colonial authority structures (which connected a metropolitan country to a colonial-and-then-post-colonial state to a hinterland), but also there is a large-scale rejection of the two main colonial ('mainline' or 'mission') churches in Togo and Ghana – the Catholic and the Presbyterian – both because of their association with the older structures of authority *and* because of their liturgical reliance on the mediating power of the church (in administering communion and the sacraments). The Pentecostal is precisely about a more direct/spontaneous connection between believer and deity (Marshall 2009, van Dijk 1998), a non-mediated experience of the Holy Spirit (as exemplified through healing or speaking in tongues). A charismatic friend commented that her confessional moments are now only between herself and God. If she has sinned, she owns up to God alone,

in a moment of prayer in the quiet of her room, asking forgiveness. A West African Protestant reformation this.

In refusing the older authority structures – and the strong identifications with nation and locality that accompanied them – the new religious affiliations are generative of identities that are translocal (here, globally Christian) in nature (cf. Englund 2003, Marshall 2009, Marshall-Fratini 2001, Maxwell 2008, Meyer 1998, 2004b, van Dijk 1998, 2001b). A visiting American pastor, T.L. Osborn, made the point explicit in a sermon in March 2006: 'The born-again Christian has no nation or region that he calls home. He is a member of a single world-wide community, and speaks one language. The different religions and cultures of the world cease to exist for this Christian.' Sunday sermons routinely make the same point, offering accounts of the defeat of tradition/Satan in diverse locales across the world – the Philippines, Mexico, Russia, Kenya, Rwanda – and the entry of remote communities into the global community of Christ. Notice, then, the very different orientation of these churches towards tradition from the earlier colonial mission churches, which worked through the state and which accommodated local belief, even hybridising their own. This earlier 'post-colonial' sensibility – of accommodation and hybridisation – is roundly rejected by the new churches, which seek a transcendence of the local in favour of a Christian global.

But the new charismatic churches also resist contemporary transnational structures of hierarchy/centralisation and influence – acknowledging roots in the US or Nigeria, perhaps, but resisting obeisance – and see themselves as radically autonomous. Why else are there a thousand differently named charismatic-Pentecostal churches in Accra alone, all raising their own money through a system of tithes? 'Our way of worshipping God is being imitated by everyone now, including you in America,' a Lomé charismatic responded when I asked whether she saw her mode of worship as derivative. Indeed, in a striking historical reversal, US pastors are now travelling to Africa to be ordained – because they see African Christianity as a purer form – before returning 'home' to engage in 'mission' work (Jenkins 2002). To repeat, those I know do not see their Christianity as something with origins elsewhere that they have remade or enhanced so much as they have engaged in independent and autonomous cultural/religious authorship. Or better: they see a direct connection between God and West Africa, or God and believer, that requires no other form of mediation.

Caveats are in order here. While much in the Pentecostal moment suggests a positive break with the past – a displacement of the fascist state,

a refusal of patriarchal authority, a move beyond often-stultifying local identifications, an agentive seizing of the current moment – there is nevertheless also a significant way in which many of those identifications are smuggled back in, and indeed in which the necropolitical (Mbembe 2003) might be said to be at the centre of charismatic consciousness. Those imaginaries that describe the work of Satan in the villages, and that seek to extirpate him therefrom, are inordinately violent, as are the commentaries on, and the unblinking endorsements of, US policy in the Middle East, a site of the necropolitical if there ever was one. Moreover, the surveilling tithe-extracting church strikes one as nothing so much as the surveilling, extractive post-colonial state, and libidinal attachments to the church as drawing on and recycling similar attachments to the sovereign dictator. Are these not authoritarian imaginaries, and is this not also the world of the necropolitical?

It is thus tempting to interpret the turn to the Holy Spirit in the 1990s as little more than compensation for loss of the dictator. Indeed, the church has not only taken on state functions (building schools, clinics, orphanages) but also partially fills the space in the public imaginary previously occupied by the sovereign. Moreover, God, church and pastor serve as authority figures in the regulation of everyday life and are celebrated in ways – with singing and dancing – not unlike those previously reserved for the potentate. A connection between the two sovereignty regimes was nowhere drawn so explicitly as in sermons in Lomé at the moment of an electoral crisis in 2005 which compared God's to the state's 'sovereignty', albeit finding the latter wanting. Nevertheless, while borrowing on state imaginaries, charismatic Christianity also transforms them, displacing identification with sovereign and nation onto modes of belonging that are trans-regional and global, and horizontally rather than vertically linked. Moreover, despite the strong authority of God and pastor, the churches encourage broad-based participation and identification across ethnicity (cf. Englund 2007), and divine sovereignty, while transcendent and absolute, is also immanent, global and available to a broad public.

End times, readiness and everyday morality

A second narrative which captures the imagination of West African charismatic communities is that of the End Times – in which those born-again Christians will ascend to heaven to sit beside Christ and those sinners who are 'left behind' will be condemned to a world of war and suffering ruled over by the anti-Christ. Thus, one must do all in one's power to resist the forces of Satan and live the Christian life, in

preparation for the End, an end which may be right around the corner. This is a topic that routinely comes up in sermons: in predictions as to when the Rapture will occur (and in lengthy discussions of false predictions), in exhortations to believers to ready themselves ('if the world ended today, would you be ready?'), in discussions about the anti-Christ (and his many guises and temptations). Again, a narrative of radical rupture – in this latter case, the most extreme of temporal breaks: an end of history as we know it.

While the End Times narrative certainly operates in the most literal of registers, it works in others as well. One is as injunction to live the moral life, thus disciplining the everyday of the believer: Are you living like a Christian? Would you be ready if Christ returned today? Another is as template/exemplar of the way in which rupture and radical indeterminacy define a Pentecostal view of event and history more generally – not only of Christ's appearance at the end of time but also of the quotidian. Thus, those micro-encounters of the everyday – a chance meeting with a stranger, an unexpected phone call, a sudden flash of insight – are potentially pregnant with meaning and might lead to a radical shift in the life of the believer, even changing everything that went before. While a more dramatic version of historical rupture, to be sure, the End Times story is nevertheless no different in kind from those interventions of the Holy Spirit into the everyday. Its narrative prominence in the life of the church thus serves to condition congregants into an openness to a radical/millennialist orientation towards time and the everyday.

Such a non-linear punctuated temporality (Guyer 2007) also resonates with that in other (non-Christian) domains of Togolese and Ghanaian cultural life – in occult imaginaries (whose aim is to account for the unexpected), in development practice (where NGOs appear and disappear without apparent rhyme or reason), in the ubiquitous lotteries (where 'luck' or occult/charismatic manipulation is as important to success as methodical preparation). Immersed in a time and rhetoric of crisis, everyone, it seems, is hedging their bets – on the afterlife, on the lottery, on the miraculous appearance and capture of an NGO – hoping for an intercession that might be life-transforming.

I am suggesting that it is these fantastical narratives – about underdevelopment as sinfulness, about the End Times and the everyday – that animate the imagination and account for the charismatic moment as much as the more prosaic sociological indicators. Moreover, I see the appeal of these narratives as related to peoples' exhaustion with the older (Cold War) narratives – that connected West Africa to the metropole, on the one hand, and celebrated (and

connected the urban middle classes to) tradition and the village, on the other. These new Pentecostal stories – stories of personal and cultural forgetting, and thus stories that are fundamentally anti-hauntological in nature (cf. Baucom 2005, Cole 2001, Connerton 1989, Gilroy 1993, Gordon 1996, Nora 1972, 1989, Shaw 2002, 2007) – are very much about the death of such earlier narratives (and the political-economic conditions that accompanied them) and about the birth of a new (post-Cold War) world. As such they are accounts that empower and attempt to redefine historical agency – as less about a relationship to, or debt with, the past, or to a colonial/post-colonial other in the present, and more about a nostalgia for the future.

Transformations of affect and subjectivity

The charismatic experience also draws on another deep reservoir, on what Deleuze and Guattari (1983, 1988) refer to as 'affect'. Affect is linked, to be sure, to the social and semiotic, but it also escapes and transcends these. It is something other than and beyond meaning alone, and something not simply reducible to psychological state. An affect is a disposition or orientation, something between a feeling and an idea: an experience, an attitude, a sentiment, an intensity. Moreover, in Deleuzian terms (Hardt 1993, 2007, Holland 2002), it is something that 'affects' or changes you, and those around you, something that moves you to action – and, in the charismatic case, something that breaks down boundaries of body-self and subjectivity.

West African charismatic religion strikes me as a brilliant generator of intensities and affects: of joy and happiness, of confidence and pride, of feelings of empowerment and importance (and, in the extreme, of narcissism), of vitality and vitalism, of optimism and hope, of humility, of fearlessness and of intoxicating, even eroticised, attachments to the Holy Trinity (the words of a song popular in 2005: 'Darling Jesus, take me in your arms...').

At a Sunday service I attended in March 2006 at Friends of Christ Church in Lomé, the pastor deviated from the sermon to implore: 'God loves you. Christ loves you. The Holy Spirit loves you. He is happy for you. God is happy for you. You are happy. You will be filled with happiness when you are next to God. You are special. God tells me you are special. Know that you are special. He will help you...' With each injunction, the thousand-strong congregation swelled, voicing its support, releasing ever more enthusiastic cries of approval. Ad-libbing, the pastor then led his followers in a fifteen-minute prayer session during which congregants prayed out loud, each on their own, making requests

of their God, palms open skyward, some gesticulating animatedly in the air, others pounding their sides, some falling to the ground in the aisles, all opening themselves to the power of the Holy Spirit, imploring the Spirit to enter them. 'The power of God is in us. Allelujah', the pastor bellowed as he segued back to his sermon. 'Amen', boomed the congregation.

A schoolteacher and recent charismatic convert put it like this:

The new churches make people feel good about themselves and give them the will-power to take control of their lives. This is especially important in the face of fatalistic attachments to spirits and witches. Here is a simple example. Mahatom [a non-Christian villager] had a pain in his lower stomach, which turned out to be a hernia. He refused to go see a doctor because he thought there was a mystical cause. But after spending months visiting diviners, and still not getting better, we convinced him to go to the hospital and have an operation. Now he is fine. But look at all the time and money he wasted along the way. And remember the time when Palabei was seriously sick and thought he had been bewitched and refused to go to the clinic [because medicine is not efficacious when witchcraft is involved]? Day after day, he went to diviners, looking for a supernatural cause. Finally, near death, we took him to the clinic, where they discovered that he had pneumonia and gave him antibiotics. Within a week he was back to normal and lived twenty more years. His resistance was the fear of the villager in the face of invisible forces. Yes, the Christian believes that witches are real, but he doesn't give them power over him. If he gets sick, he will turn to Jesus right away and ask for help. And he will go to the hospital to get medicine. But this is only a small example of how Christianity empowers. It gives people the feeling that they can take hold of their lives and make them better, something that is lacking in the religion of the villages.

Another put it this way:

When I walk down the street as a Christian, I hold my head high. I know I have something that others don't. I am not wealthy and I am not classed ['classé'], but I have something even better. I have Jesus on my side, and with Jesus anything is possible. Others look at me and wonder where this confidence comes from, because they don't see money or class. But this is what Jesus does for you. Every

day I get out of bed and feel that today will be even better than the day before.

I have accompanied this person to church on many occasions, and am always struck by the pure joy and utter enthralment she seems to experience during the service, especially when praying and singing. 'Once you've felt the power of the Holy Spirit, you are never the same. There is nothing else like it', she exults. Such rapture and embodied affect, in its most noted form 'speaking in tongues', is the figure of immanence itself – of the presence ('in-filling') of the Holy Spirit in the life and body of the believer.

Immanent globality also manifests in a merging of Holy Spirit and commodity form. In that worldly success is taken as a sign of the divine, charismatics celebrate and offer church testimonials not only to healings and the defeat of spiritual adversaries but also to the acquisition of things material (mobile phones, televisions, cars, money). Such testimonials of the coming into commodities offer proof positive of the proximity between believer and Holy Spirit, suggesting that s/he is one of the elect. Note, however, that church members also often refigure commodities in Christian ways – watching strictly Pentecostal programming on television, putting only religious songs on an i-pod, configuring mobile phones with Christian visuals and messages.

These are affects – of joy and pleasure, of confidence and boldness, of worldly accomplishment, of personal empowerment – that certainly sit well with the neoliberal moment and with the current global conjuncture, dominated as it is by the 'immateriality' of labour and the production of affective experience (Clough & Halley 2007, Hardt 2007, Hardt & Negri 2001, 2005). But also, and even more importantly – doubling its effectiveness – the church is producing bold, confident, vital subjects in a post-colonial environment that, like its colonial predecessor, has long thrived on instilling inferiority, humiliation and fear in the populace.

Development

Today, there are over 5000 NGOs and NGO-like Associations in Togo (FONGTO 2006), most created since the early 1990s. Often little more than one- or two-person shell organisations, they appeared during the decade after the end of the Cold War in village and city alike – as if out of nowhere, like mushrooms after a spring rain – to capture international funding at a time when state monies (salaries to civil servants,

development aid to communities) had largely disappeared. Riding the tide of the times, and quickly divining those projects favoured by international donors (micro-finance, children's education, AIDS, orphanages), an array of local actors (from de-salaried state employees to unemployed university students) opened offices to deliver social services to localities throughout the country – and to access scarce personal resources.

Alongside these smaller organisations, a new breed of international mega-NGO also crowded the development field, introducing ambitious country-wide projects, many focused on health and education. One such organisation, BØRNEfonden ('Foundation for Children'), a Danish child sponsorship agency whose aim was to increase school attendance through broad interventions into family life, initiated projects in 27 locales throughout the country. Another, an American NGO with a Foucauldian name, Population Services International (PSI), launched high-visibility projects focusing on HIV, teen pregnancy and malaria. Known for its creative approach, PSI paid motorcycle-taxi drivers to educate clients about the risks of AIDS, held seminars with truck drivers and soldiers about condom use, purchased television ads and giant billboards urging parents to keep their daughters away from older men, and distributed insecticide-treated bed nets (to ward off malarial mosquitoes) to over half a million Togolese families.

Filling the gap left by the retreat of the state in the 1990s, these NGOs have in many ways become the new sovereign, deciding the future of populations today. It is they who decide which projects – what areas of life and development, what aspects of community – will be funded. And it is they who determine which villages and which villagers (men/women? elders/youth?) will be blessed. It is no exaggeration to say that today it is the NGOs who decide who lives and who dies.

It is striking how few contemporary development initiatives are concerned with things material or infrastructural (roads, schools, clinics) – as during the period from the 1970s to the mid-1990s. Today's projects are largely focused on things immaterial – on health and education, on healing bodies and minds, on developing human potential. In addition to the ubiquitous micro-finance initiatives, child sponsorship and orphanage projects abound, as do those focusing on HIV, malaria prevention and child trafficking.

Moreover, in its focus on youth and women (most micro-finance schemes enlist only women), development has largely abandoned elders and men (a move that complements Pentecostalism's rejection of tradition). Many of the new projects are also future-oriented. The head of BØRNEfonden told me in 2006 that he is thinking not just 10 but

20 years down the road. 'Through our sponsorship programmes, we hope to educate children who will transform this country. But I am not looking for results today or even tomorrow. I am prepared to wait for two decades to see the results.'

Child sponsorship: re-parenting Africa

In the village where I work in northern Togo, the largest, most ambitious development scheme of the decade after the end of the Cold War – and one that continues to fill the developmental imagination in the area six years after its departure – was the Danish child sponsorship programme BØRNEfonden. Believing, as one of its promotional flyers states, that 'the development of the community depends on the development of the individual' (BØRNEfonden 2005), BØRNEfonden seeks to address Africa's development crisis by focusing on the education of children – and does so by setting up personalised relations between Scandinavian families and individual children in West African villages. For each sponsored child in one of its target communities, a donor family pays school fees, purchases school uniforms and books, contributes food to the child's family and subsidises regular health check-ups. BØRNEfonden today runs over a hundred village-based projects in four francophone West African countries, and had 27 in Togo alone during the 1990s.[3]

When BØRNEfonden arrived in the area in 1992, locals immediately took to the programme – though, it seemed, less out of a strong desire to see their children educated than to capture scarce resources in a time of crisis. Families flocked to BØRNEfonden's centre in the nearby town of Farendé to put their names on the list, and, because the project stipulated that it would support only one child per family, some attempted to play the system by sending children to live with childless uncles or grandparents. Kabre in the south also sent children back to the north to live with siblings – so that they might partake in the spoils. In the mid-1990s, hundreds of families in the communities of Farendé, Kuwdé and Tchi-Kawa had children in the programme, with school enrolments swelling to new highs.

The quid pro quo was not only that children had to go to school and remain in good standing but also that parents had to write letters to the child's sponsor in northern Europe several times per year. These letters thanked the donor – often a donor couple – for their aid and detailed the progress of 'their' child. One such note:

> I write to inquire about your health and that of your family. My wife and I, and your daughter Essowé, are in good health. Your financial aid has enabled us to change our lives and rise above what we had

before. Thanks to the money you sent, I have started a garden and my wife is selling kerosene in the market. With our earnings we can better feed Essowé.

Essowé has just begun the new school year and feels fortunate to have this opportunity. Her school day begins at 6:30, when she is already in the school yard... Her favourite subject is arithmetic, though she also finds it difficult and spends many hours studying after she comes home at night...

May God bless you for your help and support you in your work.

The return letter described where this Danish couple lived – in a small town two hours from Copenhagen – and said that the man worked for an automobile company. They complimented Essowé for her hard work at school and encouraged the parents in their new-found work initiatives. The letter closed by promising continued support if Essowé continued to perform at school.

This process of letter-writing was the vexed talk of the airwaves when I was in the village of Kuwdé in the late 1990s. For most parents, the writing itself was an excruciating process: penned in French (by someone whose speaking and writing ability was typically little more than elementary school level), the letter was submitted to a staff member in Farendé who subjected it to often-withering critique (of its spelling/grammar/content), after which the parent was sent home to start over. In some cases the parent of the sponsored child trudged up and down the mountain for weeks, 90 minutes each way, writing and rewriting, before the letter was accepted. It was then sent to the capital of Lomé, where it was translated into English by a member of BØRNE-fonden's team of translators – nine full-time employees rendering letters from French to English for Togo's 27 projects – and sent to the sponsoring family in Scandinavia, a process that reversed itself when the family wrote back.

I want to pause for a moment on this letter-writing, which I see as the symbolic heart of BØRNEfonden's project. It is the letter which makes the aid flow, for the letter conveys a sense of direct contact between 'child' and sponsoring 'parent' (despite the presence of multiple intermediaries – the real parent who actually penned the letter, those who critiqued/edited/translated it, the sprawling apparatus of the international organisation). This is the 'affect' that child sponsorship programmes call on and nurture: inciting, indeed hailing, a European not only to invest in the life of an African child – 'their' child – and

thus in Africa's future, but also enabling this European couple to have a personal relationship with that child. The letter speaks from the heart – from one heart to another – expressing both need and gratitude ('your financial help has enabled us to change our lives and rise above the standard we had before. Thanks to the money you sent ... '). Thus, too, it re-inscribes the African subject as aid-dependent, as saved, always saved, by the European – and the African parent as always inadequate and incomplete/impotent (cf. Bornstein & Redfield 2011). Notice that the African parent here has gone the way of the African sovereign, both replaced by new international agencies – new sovereignties – agencies disguised as parents and would-be parents as agencies. Notice, too, what is never expressed but always implied – that this is a case of virtual adoption, with a Danish couple becoming 'parent' to an African child (*'your daughter Essowé'*), a child who nevertheless has parents – but ones who are unable to provide for their children.

But the letter-writing also struck me, whether intentional or not, as very much about the 'disciplining' and humiliation of the peasant. Picture this stream of farmers from mountain villages making their way down rocky paths to Farendé, letters stuffed in the pockets of their tattered overcoats, presenting themselves at the BØRNEfonden office where they are made to wait – often for hours, sometimes all day – before their letter is covered in red ink and they are instructed to return home and start over. The message conveyed through the letter-writing process is about the role of education and the superiority of *'l'homme du papier'* (the person who knows how to write) – the staff member who knows the conventions and protocols of letter-writing, and thus commands the magic that makes the money flow. If this were not about discipline, about conveying the inferiority of the peasant, why make him rewrite again and again when a translator in Lomé will rework and sanitise it for the Danish couple? Moreover, the threads extend outward from a practice like this into the larger social field, a field in which 'tradition' and (non-literate) chiefs are on the way out, being replaced by modernity and (literate) mayors.

Another effect of this project and sign of the times: a parent of a sponsored child told me that he was in more frequent contact with the European couple who supported his child than with kin in southern Togo – that, because of the ongoing economic crisis, the latter no longer sent remittances back home and only infrequently made their annual trips to the north as before, and that he was now more reliant on the European couple for his survival. Again, a shift away from local to translocal dependencies/sovereignties/governmentalities,

with a Danish development agency standing in for family and state – teaching rural peasants how to be proper citizen-subjects.

In 2002, after ten years in Farendé, and needing to cut 9 of its 27 Togo projects, BØRNEfonden closed its doors and moved on, citing staff misconduct and excessive bickering and jealousy among villagers. The office in Farendé and BØRNEfonden's headquarters in Lomé had been flooded with complaints from families who had not been chosen – and with revelations about the scamming that others were engaged in. The village of Tchi-Kawa complained that it was discriminated against by those from Farendé and had been denied promised resources. And, the last straw, the local head of staff in Farendé was accused of building his own bar-boutique with project monies. As a result, BØRNEfonden decided to withdraw from what it saw as a hornet's nest of local in-fighting and invest elsewhere.

And yet, despite this sudden abandonment, and despite the ordeal and humiliation of the letter-writing, people in Farendé and Kuwdé today see BØRNEfonden as the high point of recent development efforts in the area. It brought money and resources to the north, it brought the offspring of diasporics back home, it filled the schools with children and, more generally, it animated the region. Moreover, remarkably to me when I first heard it, locals blame themselves for BØRNEfonden's departure. 'It is because of our jealousy, because we couldn't get along with one another, that they left,' is a refrain I heard again and again. This seems a secular version of the Pentecostal 'blame tradition' narrative – 'we blame ourselves for our backwardness' – and, as in that instance, it seems an attempt to resist victimising narratives that vacate local agency, locating responsibility beyond local control.

Convergences

To be sure, there are differences in aim and impact between development projects like this and the work of the new churches. The one is secular, the other religious; the one attends lightly to the subject, while the other aims for a total transformation of self; the one works through communities, the other aims at a radical separation therefrom. But there are also striking parallels.

Both projects – the developmental and the Pentecostal – extract persons from families and groups, producing individual subjects on a scale that is unprecedented in the contemporary era. The church not only hails a neoliberal subject – hard-working, upwardly mobile, prosperity-seeking – but also urges its denizens to cut ties to tradition (and thus

to family and village). Development projects, no longer place-based or place-reifying, increasingly recruit individuals rather than groups or villages, pulling them out of communities to their training centres and schools – to develop human potential. Development too, through its financialisation (micro-finance) schemes, its incentivised learning and its quid pro quo entrepreneurialism, elicits neoliberal sensibilities and personhood.

Both development and church inaugurate a shift away from local to translocal dependencies and sovereignties. In the case of BØRNE-fonden, a northern European development agency comes to stand in for family and state – not only providing social services but also teaching rural Togolese how to be proper (modern) citizen-subjects. For their part, the churches cultivate Christian subjects in search of transcendent/translocal sovereignties. Moreover, a charismatic Christian's ties are to other converts (rather than to family or village) and to Christian nodes across West Africa and beyond.

Both church and development are today preoccupied with affect and affective relationship. It is embodied (heart-to-heart) relationship which lies at the core of BØRNEfonden's project – and of a thousand development projects across the continent. The charismatic Christian, too, cultivates an unmediated, personalised, affective encounter with the Holy Spirit.

In attacking tradition and gerontocracy in the villages, both development and religion urge a break with the past – and with those temporalities and teleologies that accompanied the Cold War compact between dictator and village chief – aiming to reorient individual, community and nation towards a different future, whether youthful or apocalyptic. Pentecostal time and NGO time, however, are evanescent, punctuated and non-linear (cf. Guyer 2007): NGOs come and go, parachuting in and out, not unlike the Holy Spirit in the life of the believer.

Both Pentecostalism and development inhabit, and indeed cultivate, an ongoing state of crisis. For the Pentecostal, crisis inheres in the dogma that we all live in personal and collective sin, sin that demands intervention and remediation. Development too sees itself jumping from epidemic to epidemic: from the crisis of over-population, to that of HIV, to malaria, to child trafficking. Whether crisis here is 'real' or not – whether it is actual or discursively staged – makes little difference.

Finally, both charismatics and those in development blame the local – Africans/Togolese/Ghanaians – for Africa's failures and plight today.

In both cases, the aim is to resist evacuating local agency and to restore a sense of personal (neoliberal) empowerment and possibility.

Are these convergences between development and Pentecostal imaginaries mere coincidence or happenstance – thus, largely unrelated phenomena inhabiting parallel domains? Alternatively, is one domain influencing the other – has Pentecostal discourse, for instance, colonised development discourse or vice versa? This does seem to be the case, at least in part. For example, Pentecostal attacks on 'tradition' have clearly crept into more secular (development) critiques of the 'wastefulness' of ceremonial excess in the villages or of time taken off from work to attend funerals. Moreover, crisis talk travels easily from one context to the next. But I am more inclined towards another possibility: that both domains are also the product of a larger common field – of new configurations of governance and sovereignty, of immanence and affect – at work in the global today.

Notes

1. While most of my work on the new churches has been in Togo, I spent the summers of 2001 and 2004 in Accra – and there visited churches and interviewed devotees. Despite differences of language and political context (Ghana is West Africa's neoliberal poster-child, and Togo its enfant terrible), the Ghanaian material complements, and remains broadly consistent with, that from Togo, illustrating the presence of a vast field of Pentecostal and charismatic worship that crosses national boundaries throughout the sub-region, especially along the Nigeria–Benin–Togo–Ghana-Côte d'Ivoire coastal corridor.
2. In Ghana, Pentecostal churches were not so much censored during the 1980s as left on the margins by the mainline churches, who maintained strong ties with the state. With the loosening/liberalising of authority relations in the 1990s, membership in the charismatic churches soared to the point where they have today displaced the mainline churches at the centre of Ghanaian cultural-religious life.
3. Continent-wide, child sponsorship has been at the centre of development practice since the early 1990s and today remains one of the more popular development interventions. Among others, World Vision, the second largest development organisation in the world, is a child sponsorship NGO (Bornstein 2005), as is the multi-billion dollar Christian Children's Fund.

References

Agamben, Giorgio. 2005. *State of Exception*. Chicago: University of Chicago Press.
Agamben, Giorgio. 1998. *Homo Sacer: Sovereign Power and Bare Life*. Stanford: Stanford University Press.

Baucom, Ian. 2005. *Specters of the Atlantic: Finance Capital, Slavery and the Philosophy of History*. Durham: Duke University Press.

BØRNEfonden Organizational Flyer. 2005.

Bornstein, Erica. 2005. *The Spirit of Development: Protestant NGOs, Morality, and Economics in Zimbabwe*. Palo Alto: Stanford University Press.

Bornstein, Erica and Peter Redfield. 2011. An Introduction to the Anthropology of Humanitarianism. In Bornstein, Erica and Peter Redfield (Eds), *Forces of Compassion: Humanitarianism Between Ethics and Politics*. Santa Fe: School for Advanced Research Press.

Clough, Patricia and Jean Halley (Eds). 2007. *The Affective Turn: Theorizing the Social*. Durham: Duke University Press.

Cole, Jennifer. 2001. *Forget Colonialism? Sacrifice and the Art of Memory in Madagascar*. Berkeley: University of California Press.

Comaroff, Jean. Forthcoming. The Politics of Conviction: Faith on the Neoliberal Frontier. In Kapferer, Bruce (Ed.), *Vital Matters: Religious Movements, Emergent Socialities and the Post-Nation*.

Connerton, Paul. 1989. *How Societies Remember*. Cambridge: Cambridge University Press.

Deleuze, Gilles and Félix Guattari. 1988. *A Thousand Plateaus: Capitalism and Schizophrenia*. Minneapolis: University of Minnesota Press.

Deleuze, Gilles and Félix Guattari. 1983. *Anti-Oedipus: Capitalism and Schizophrenia*. Minneapolis: University of Minnesota Press.

Engelke, Matthew. 2004. Discontinuity and the Discourse of Conversion. *Journal of Religion in Africa* 34(1–2): 82–109.

Englund, Harri. 2007. Pentecostalism beyond Belief: Trust and Democracy in a Malawian Township. *Africa* 77(4): 477–499.

Englund, Harri. 2003. Christian Independency and Global Membership: Pentecostal Extraversions in Malawi. *Journal of Religion in Africa* 33(1): 83–111.

FONGTO (Fédération des Organisations Non Gouvernmentales Togolais) Publication. 2006. Lomé.

Foucault, Michel. 1990(1978). *The History of Sexuality. Volume I: An Introduction*. New York: Vintage Books.

Foucault, Michel. 1980. *Power/Knowledge: Selected Interviews and Other Writings, 1972–1977*. C. Gordon (Ed.). New York: Pantheon.

Frank, Andre. 1971. *Capitalism and Underdevelopment in Latin America*. New York: Penguin Books.

Gilroy, Paul. 1993. *The Black Atlantic: Modernity and Double Consciousness*. Cambridge: Harvard University Press.

Gordon, Avery. 1996. *Ghostly Matters: Haunting and the Sociological Imagination*. Minneapolis: University of Minnesota Press.

Guyer, Jane. 2007. Prophecy and the Near Future: Thoughts on Macroeconomic, Evangelical, and Punctuated Time. *American Ethnologist* 34(3): 409–421.

Hardt, Michael. 2007. Foreword: What Affects Are Good For. In Clough, Patricia and Jean Halley (Eds), *The Affective Turn: Theorizing the Social*. Durham: Duke University Press.

Hardt, Michael. 1993. *Gilles Deleuze: An Apprenticeship in Philosophy*. Minneapolis: University of Minnesota Press.

Hardt, Michael and Antonio Negri. 2005. *Multitude: War and Democracy in the Age of Empire*. New York: Penguin.

Hardt, Michael and Antonio Negri. 2001. *Empire*. Cambridge: Harvard University Press.

Holland, Eugene. 2002. *Deleuze and Guattari's Anti-Oedipus*. New York: Taylor and Francis.

Jenkins, Philip. 2002. The Next Christianity. *The Atlantic Monthly*, October.

Marshall, Ruth. 2009. *Political Spiritualities: The Pentecostal Revolution in Nigeria*. Chicago: University of Chicago Press.

Marshall-Fratani, Ruth. 2001. Mediating the Global and Local in Nigerian Pentecostalism. In Corten, Andre and Ruth Marshall-Fratani (Eds), *Between Babel and Pentecost: Transnational Pentecostalism in Africa and Latin America*. Bloomington: Indiana University Press.

Maxwell, David. 2008. African Gift of the Spirit: Pentecostalism and the Rise of a Zimbabwean Transnational Religious Movement. *Africa Today* 55(1): 138–141.

Mbembe, Achille. 2003. Necropolitics. *Public Culture* 15(1): 11–40.

Meyer, Birgit. 2004a. 'Praise the Lord...': Popular Cinema and Pentecostalite Style in Ghana's New Public Sphere. *American Ethnologist* 31(1): 92–110.

Meyer, Birgit. 2004b. Christianity in Africa: From African Independent to Pentecostal-Charismatic Churches. *Annual Review of Anthropology* 33: 447–474.

Meyer, Birgit. 2003. Ghanaian Popular Cinema and the Magic in and of Film. In Meyer, Birgit and Peter Pels (Eds), *Magic and Modernity: Interfaces of Revelation and Concealment*. Stanford: Stanford University Press.

Meyer, Birgit. 2002. Occult Forces on Screen: Representation and the Danger of Mimesis in Popular Ghanaian Films. *Etnofoor* 15(1/2): 212–221.

Meyer, Birgit. 1999a. *Translating the Devil: Religion and Modernity among the Ewe of Ghana*. Edinburgh: Edinburgh University Press.

Meyer, Birgit. 1999b. Popular Ghanaian Cinema and 'African Heritage'. *Africa Today* 46(2): 93–117.

Meyer, Birgit. 1998. 'Make a Complete Break with the Past': Memory and Post-Colonial Modernity in Ghanaian Pentecostalist Discourse. *Journal of Religion in Africa* 27(3): 316–349.

Nora, Pierre. 1989. Between Memory and History: Les Lieux de Mémoire. *Representations* 26: 7–24.

Nora, Pierre. 1972. Mémoire Collective. In LeGoff, Jacques, Roger Chartier and Jacaues Revel (Eds), *La Nouvelle Histoire*. Paris: Les Encyclopédies du Savoir Moderne.

Robbins, Joel. 2007. Continuity Thinking and the Problem of Christian Culture: Belief, Time, and the Anthropology of Christianity. *Current Anthropology* 48: 5–38.

Rodney, Walter. 1981. *How Europe Underdeveloped Africa*. Washington, DC: Howard University Press.

Shaw, Rosalind. 2007. Displacing Violence: Making Pentecostal Memory in Postwar Sierra Leone. *Cultural Anthropology* 22(1): 66–93.

Shaw, Rosalind. 2002. *Memories of the Slave Trade: Ritual and Historical Imagination in Sierra Leone*. Chicago: University of Chicago Press.

van Dijk, Rijk. 2001a. Contesting Silence: The Ban on Drumming and the Musical Politics of Pentecostalism in Ghana. *Ghana Studies* 4: 31–64.

van Dijk, Rijk. 2001b. Time and Transcultural Technologies of the Self in the Ghanaian Pentecostal Diaspora. In Corten, Andre and Ruth Marshall-Fratini

(Eds), *Between Babel and Pentecost: Transnational Pentecostalism in Africa and Latin America*. Bloomington: Indiana University Press.

van Dijk, Rijk. 1998. Pentecostalism, Cultural Memory and the State: Contested Representations of Time in Post-colonial Malawi. In Werbner, Richard (Ed.), *Memory and the Postcolony: African Anthropology and the Critique of Power*. London: ZED Books.

van Dijk, Rijk. 1997. From Camp to Encompassment: Discourses of Transubjectivity in the Ghanaian Pentecostal Diaspora. *Journal of Religion in Africa* 27(2): 135–160.

6

Saving Development: Secular NGOs, the Pentecostal Revolution and the Search for a Purified Political Space in the Taita Hills, Kenya

James H. Smith

This chapter examines semiotic and social-political overlaps and differences between Pentecostalism and non-governmental organisations (NGOs) in neoliberal Kenya, focusing on the Taita Hills of southeastern Kenya in the 1990s. I make broad comparisons between NGOs and Pentecostal churches because they each have come to fill the vacuum left behind by a retreating state in the post-structural adjustment, 'neoliberal' era, and they often share much in common with each other. For example, both Pentecostalism and most NGOs aim to reform individual habits and dispositions, usually with a view to making people better citizens and accessing new sources of wealth. After a discussion of the religious history of development discourse and practice in Taita, I examine how NGOs and Pentecostal churches intervened in the structural transformations affecting Kenya and Taita in the 1990s, seeking to create a new social situation and a new kind of human being through the erasure of the past and the disciplining of subjects. I discuss how the methods and concepts employed by NGOs and Pentecostal churches overlap, and argue that they tend to diverge in their attitude towards people, concepts and institutions that are locally associated with the past, especially the autochthonous past. Despite the efforts of Pentecostal churches and NGOs to ground reality in something fixed and unassailable (whether the Divine or civic democracy), their proliferation in a competitive market also contributed to a local perception of undomesticated danger that was acted on in religious terms. In the final section of this chapter, I focus on an example of how, in practice, NGOs

and churches interacted in ways that were unanticipated and generative, and offer some thoughts on the implications of this open-endedness.

Development and religion in Taita

Development in Taita has always been expressed and appropriated through religion, and understood in religious idioms by Taita people (Wataita) themselves, just as religion has been understood as a 'development' project at once economic and spiritual (Smith 2008). Until the 1980s, most Wataita were either Anglican or Catholic (Catholic on one side of the hills and Anglican on the other), and these churches were visibly associated with modernity for Wataita; they provided access to education and other services (including, in some cases, health care). Schooling, in turn, led to employment opportunities and political power, especially for the first generation of schooled Taita. Education came to the Anglican side of the hills before it came to the Catholic side, and the Anglican side has always been thought of as more 'developed', as well as politically connected (e.g. Catholics say that Jomo Kenyatta favoured Taita Anglicans and Anglicans in general). Many people living in the 'Catholic zone' remember the opening of the first Catholic schools, and associate their 'development' as a people with particular Catholic missionaries who 'opened' them up to education, and so enabled them to compete with the Anglicans, who dominated Taita business and politics; even today, the wealthiest Taita families are mostly Anglican, and the wealthiest Catholic families are descended from people who converted to Catholicism early on. The efflorescence of Pentecostal churches in the 1980s and 1990s coincided, historically, with the decline of wage labour and the waning authority and legitimacy of Anglican and Catholic politicians. While in the beginning there were a few discrete Pentecostal churches with ties to America, there have been so many break-away churches and independent prophets over the years that the earlier affiliations are no longer very relevant, as Pentecostalism long ago took on an African life of its own (however, the most well-known Pentecostal church in Taita is the Full Gospel).

Taita people (Wataita) live throughout Kenya, and are especially prominent in the coastal city of Mombasa, but the Taita Hills in southeastern Kenya, near the Tanzanian border, are home to around 300,000 people. This now deforested former rainforest area is comprised of a group of steep hills enclosed within Tsavo National Park, Kenya's largest game park, and home to several international tourist hotels. Prior to colonialism, Tsavo was used by Wataita and other African

peoples as hunting and grazing land, and today the park would be Taita's 'natural' space for expansion and growth. But, instead of being a boon to them, the boundaries of Tsavo are like the walls of a prison, and Wataita often complain that they are incarcerated in the park, which takes up over 60 per cent of the district's land. Not only do Taita people receive no revenue from the funds generated by park entrance fees and tourist hotels, but they are routinely tortured and/or shot for poaching if found within the boundaries of the park. This incarceration of Taita people goes a long way towards explaining Taita understandings and implementations of 'development'; these usually entail expanding or moving beyond the Taita Hills, while continuing to maintain land rights and social connections there (Smith 2008). Negotiating this situation – becoming free from dependence on Taita without becoming 'lost', as Wataita put it, in the city or elsewhere – is central to what 'development' has come to mean.

To cope with this 'modern' (colonial and post-colonial) Taita situation, Taita men have long tried to access the job opportunities that were available to them in urban Mombasa, about 100 miles to the east. Throughout most of the twentieth century, Wataita were in a privileged situation with respect to other coastal people because they had higher levels of education, and their future ethnic competitors (such as the Kikuyu) were living in the African Reserves in Central Kenya and were focusing their activities on Nairobi. Throughout the colonial period and after, schools in Taita were mission schools, so being educated was synonymous with conversion to Christianity (Bravman 1998). Beginning in the early twentieth century, mission families lived in square-housed villages that were separated from non-Christian villages, and were organised in straight lines rather than in round houses organised in concentric circles (Harris 1978, see also Comaroff & Comaroff 1992). The most loyal followers were buried on church property, while non-Christians were buried at home and their heads exhumed and placed in a small cave with the skulls of other members of a small lineage (Harris 1978). From the beginning then, Christianity sought to create a break with the past (Meyer 1998), and in the process connected Wataita to a world marked as foreign – specifically, the Swahili dominated urban centres on the coast.

The most successful families in Taita were those who were able to parlay their religious belonging and education into employment in Mombasa, and these 'developed' Wataita were almost always heavily involved in their church councils back home, and often tried to raise at least one son to be a priest or minister. In the large Catholic community

where I did most of my research in the 1990s (really a collection of several villages), the wives of men with well-paying jobs were all heavily involved in church prayer groups that were organised along village lines, each named after a particular saint. These groups raised money for the church and for development projects that were carried out under the auspices of the church. For most of the twentieth century, health care was also associated with the church, with large churches having their own clinics, in which nurses often incorporated religious elements into the healing (such as the use of rosaries, which many Catholic Wataita considered at least as effective as medicine).

As the mainline churches grew in influence over the course of the twentieth century, almost everyone became Christian, and the wealthiest families continued to secure for themselves positions of prominence in the church council. During the post-colonial period they parlayed these positions of influence into other state-driven development committees, becoming chairmen, treasurers and secretaries of the various councils that defined civic life. Typically, men secured these civic positions, which had status and could be remunerative, upon retirement from their employment in salaried positions (often the civil service or police, and sometimes the coastal tourist industry). Those who were not able to muster the cultural capital or social ties needed to acquire prominent positions in the churches became ritual specialists in the 'other' church that never really went away, despite the best efforts of Catholic priests and Anglican ministers: these were the 'traditional' or non-Christian ritual specialists (who actually usually saw themselves as Christians), who continued to perform healing, rainmaking and protective rituals that Taita people sought out. People contributed to these rites on the side, and they came to be seen as underground 'development projects' in that, through rain or protection from outsiders, they brought prosperity and security to people in the hills; however, they were shunned by 'developed' Christians who forged more familiar practices of 'development' by connecting to the city.

So, throughout the colonial period there was an alternative narrative, and set of institutions, that ran counter to the church, and which drew their authority from an imagined autochthonous source. For its part, the state (or actual state officials) courted and encouraged both the 'Christians' and the 'traditionalists', sometimes requiring that people contribute to a community rainmaking fund (and often taking a cut in the process), while also contributing to the church, speaking at church functions and attending church frequently. Despite this apparent eclecticism, those in positions of power drew explicit boundaries

between Christian and non-Christian ways, and both became widely viewed, and acted upon, as alternative forms of power. Thus, there soon developed a critical counter-narrative about the churches, which held that they weakened traditional Taita power (Smith 2008). During my fieldwork, even prominent Catholics told stories about how past generations of Taita fathers had been seduced, through gifts of luxury goods, into sending their kids to church and school; moreover, education caused students to lose the ability to perform 'traditional' Taita rites, such as *fighi* renewal.[1] For example, Wataita told stories about how they once had magic that rendered entire villages invisible, and this made colonial governance and taxation impossible; but when people converted to Christianity (usually after being offered foreign commodities such as sugar as 'gifts') they suddenly lost this knowledge, and future generations became vulnerable to state control.

Wataita continue to cast the struggle between 'traditional' and 'modern' Taita beliefs and practices in terms of education: they say that schooling and Christianity literally destroyed particular Taita beliefs and practices that had formerly allowed Wataita to enclave themselves from disempowering exogenous forces, like the state and foreign markets. Nevertheless, it is more productive to see these concepts (the non-Christian and the Christian, the 'traditional' and the 'modern') as developing in tandem: schooling and conversion to Christianity prepared Wataita for urban labour markets and opened them up to outside influences, but most were never able to survive completely outside of Taita. *Fighi* and rainmaking rites, and the seniors who presided over them, protected Taita values and space, while making agricultural land productive in the context of Taita's new incarceration in the park. On a more abstract level, Wataia tried to generate development by managing their relationship to what they themselves had come to see as 'the present' and 'the past'.

So, in sum, during the colonial period an idealised and rarely fully realised system developed that was not only a labour system, but a politicised moral value system and worldview, in which the 'traditional' and the 'modern' were at once antagonistic and complementary. Christians sometimes railed against the continued practice of non-Christian rites and practices, but many Wataita moved back and forth between them, partly because each was socially and epistemologically inadequate when taken on its own: for one, most Wataita could not afford to live in the city, and were compelled to live in the countryside and to come to terms with people and places that were historically loaded. They could not simply ignore long-standing grudges and resentments that

played out within families and villages, but were compelled to deal with them, and non-Christian ritual and religious practices offered avenues for this, including divination and reconciliation rituals, which the church saw as satanic, partly because they undermined its authority and control. But, in the 1980s and 1990s, a series of structural transformations changed this tenuous but articulating economic and cultural system, and threw into question its key concepts and constituent parts. In response, Wataita developed critical, even conspiratorial, theories about the tragedy that had befallen modernity's vehicles (schools, churches, roads), and some sought to engage directly with 'the past' (ancestors, traditional ritual, forest spaces), which they viewed as a scarce resource that had been neglected by mainline Christians (Appadurai 1981).

Neoliberalism in Kenya

In the 1990s Kenyan society was changing fundamentally, and this transformation would impact not only the national economy and political system but also on the worldly ambitions and social and religious worldviews of many Kenyans, Wataita included. What happened, in brief, is that the established avenues for achieving what Kenyans had come to call 'development' (or *maendeleo*, in Swahili) were disappearing, and this is partly because international lending institutions pushed their belief in the infallibility of the free market, and their suspicion of state institutions, onto a country whose primary employer had long been the state. In 1993, the Kenyan Minister of Finance initiated what was perhaps the most rapid and total deregulation of an African economy ever seen: Kenya eliminated import licensing and price controls, floated the Kenyan shilling, removed restrictions on the repatriation of profits, dramatically cut public spending and reduced the number of civil servants, and began privatising a broad range of companies. School fees skyrocketed and teachers went months without pay, as public funding disappeared at the same time as education had ceased to prepare students for employment opportunities. Then, in 1997, the year I began conducting fieldwork in Taita, the International Monetary Fund (IMF) withheld a US$220 million aid package, citing widespread corruption at all levels of government (Barkan & Ng'ethe 1998). Aid was not resumed until 2000, and was again withheld the following year, apparently because of delays in privatising the Kenyan telecommunications and power companies. During this time, the period of my dissertation fieldwork, the capital city of Nairobi was literally plunged into darkness,

as electricity went out, roads turned into quagmires and the nation's dependence on foreigners became increasingly obvious and humiliating to all Kenyans.

As a result, all of the practices and institutions that Kenyans had equated with development since colonial times – the necessity of schooling as a *sine qua non* for acquiring employment; conversion to established forms of Christianity historically associated with 'literacy'; migration away from one's rural home in search of work in the city; formal sector employment; and 'development' patronage from powerful politicians – came to be seen as dysfunctional, even dangerous, by many Kenyans. Instead they came to view these institutions, places and power brokers (schools, the state, politicians, the city) as sources of witchcraft (the occult destruction of others for selfish ends), or as having been sabotaged by witchcraft or devil worship. In response, they imagined and set about forging new modes of self-making and social transformation, often seeking recourse in the revolutionary potential of divine power – hence the rapid spread of Pentecostalism throughout the region during this period.

Both Pentecostalism and NGOs responded to the vacuum left by a retreating state, while also responding positively to the new conditions by creating energy directed at innovation, the production of a new world and the overhaul of dead or dying institutions. They also sought to reform individual behaviours, while connecting people with shifting and mobile sources of value, both transcendental and material. Pentecostal churches have been broadly appealing to many social groups, and there are different Pentecostal churches for different social groups (some appealing to the wealthy, who tend to be the descendents of the first generation of converts to either Anglicanism of Catholicism for example, while others appeal more to the poor). And Pentecostal ideology – for example, the idea of being saved, and of publicly confessing one's former sins – has been appropriated by the Anglicans and Catholics who hope that these reforms can stave off the Pentecostal revolution and the exodus of converts. So, while it is probably the case that approximately a quarter of Taita's population belong to a Pentecostal church, everyone has been affected by the ideologies and practices associated with Pentecostalism. In this way, the Pentecostal experience is general and bottom up, and cannot be equated with specific institutions or churches, especially when we take into account the home-based prophets, whom people visit even when they continue to attend Catholic and Anglican churches.

Pentecostalism's revolutionary dialectics

Pentecostal churches overflow their material limits, constituting a loud, undulating movement of people, colours and noise – a fusion of sounds and scents designed to create a new kind of experience, and a new kind of person. 'I was a new man. The old nature had passed away,' a saved Pentecostal Kenyan friend of mine once put it to me, describing his experience of becoming 'born again'. Everything that takes place in the church is oriented towards putting people in contact with a divine power that has the capacity to transform reality forever, and so obliterate the past – in particular, peoples' subjective states and, through them, the nature of shared political and social reality. As a Taita woman once put it to me, 'When everyone is saved there will be no corruption in Kenya, because people will only desire that which is good for everyone, not simply what is good for themselves. The politicians are ruled by things of this earth, and the devil is in charge of things on this earth, but God rules things in heaven.'

Pentecostal prayers forge a direct line of communication with God and, in the process, function by creating, for individuals, a boundary separating the present and a prospective miraculous future from a demonic past that is both personal (one's own troubled past) and social (the past constituted by social relationships and entanglements that are historical, and which drag entire communities down). This 'breaking with the past' (Meyer 1998, see also Marshall 2009) is accomplished, first, through public confession and testimonials, in which people describe the sins they committed and then collectively express grief for their violation of God's will. No matter what they admit to having done, including murder (to which people sometimes do admit), they are forgiven, due in part to the overriding claim that the past, and the person who committed those acts, is in fact dead, and so is irrelevant. Those actions belong to another person, and blaming the convert for them would be like blaming a complete stranger. When converts become saved before the witnesses in a church, they are remade, and unencumbered by the desires that dragged them down in the past; when they leave the church, though, they will be forever haunted by demons, who are angered by the convert's decision to abandon them, diminishing their demonic power on earth.

The Pentecostal approach to the past is generalised and becomes instrumentalised in everyday Pentecostal practice: first, the people one has known in the past are potentially dangerous, having the

capacity to draw one away from the new, individuated subjectivity created through Pentecostal prayer. This prayer protects people from these proximal, historical relationships in a very real, material sense, in that saved people do not, by definition, drink, and in Kenya beer consumption is an important, if financially depleting, social rite, at least for men. Prayer also protects people from the contemporary consequences of the past actions and emotions of others: witchcraft. Because the historical past is demonic in and for itself, Taita Pentecostals will often, after becoming saved, visit the forests, where ancestral spirits that have sovereignty over protective herbs and medicines reside, and exorcise them so as to break Taita people's dependence on their demonic past. Taita who are not saved complain about this, and sometimes seek out defensive remedies to protect autochthonous Taita power, by visiting communities that have not been heavily influenced by Pentecostalism.

In addition to this ritualised 'breaking with the past', the second major Pentecostal ritual technique that places saved people in a new experiential reality is what Achille Mbembe refers to as the language of the 'divine sovereign': the 'gift' of speaking in tongues (Mbembe 2002). The language of the divine is quite literally a gift, in the sense that it is usually conferred onto saved congregants by master virtuosos in a public ceremony. Typically, this spiritual patron hails from another, far-away country (say, e.g. Nigeria) and his or her upwardly mobile foreignness (hailing from a country that Kenyans perceive as being more 'developed') is the social foundation upon which his or her xenoglossic knowledge depends. 'Learning' xenoglossia, though, is not like learning another language, in that the speaker does not actually know the language s/he is speaking, and is not aware of what s/he is communicating: one knows only that it is a language that human beings do not know. The function of this language that one speaks without knowing is to transform the state of the soul by strengthening one's relationship to God, expurgating sin and deflecting demonic influences from the spirit world and from the immediate social environment (e.g. other peoples' witchcraft). What comes out of people's mouths during these moments is dramatic, ecstatic and angry, and the speakers complain of suffering from headaches and great fatigue, which they usually interpret as demons trying to keep them from speaking in this language.

These are some of the revolutionary, socially levelling dimensions of Pentecostalism, then: that it tries to create a new reality by 'breaking with the past' and ritually producing direct communication with God, both through prayers and xenoglossia (which, though it has an ambiguous status as communication, is supposed to confer the power

of God on parishioners). In the process, Pentecostalism also elevates certain categories of people, such as youth and women, to new positions of influence. Salvation is a great equaliser, in that all saved are equally saved and some are recognised as having great power, which can be translated into social and financial influence (though this is not supposed to be the object). These adepts become 'prayer warriors' engaged in the act of praying for others in exchange for tithes paid to the church to which the congregant or parishioner belongs, as well as other gifts and business opportunities along the way. Often the most humble of people, including women and youth, become the most powerful prayer warriors, and are able to parlay this social and spiritual power into founding their own church.

Another democratising feature of Pentecostalism is the ritual of public prayer itself, which is a huge outpouring of emotions (anger, grief, love) and an extremely physical and aural experience that engulfs people in classic collective effervescence. Finally, on an explicitly 'political' level, Pentecostalism undermines the authority of the mainline churches, which have been one of the principal career-building sites for state politicians. Politicians have long donated to churches of historical depth in a specific community – in Taita, the Catholic and Anglican churches – using these churches as platforms to deliver campaign speeches, while contributing to development projects through the church.

On the other hand, the populist, ecstatic and open atmosphere created in Pentecostal churches is orchestrated by spiritual patrons whose churches receive tithes from parishioners – though parishioners may eventually break off and form their own churches, if they can acquire a suitable following. Their tenure in the church, if successful, can provide these converts with spiritual skills (the ability to pray for others, to communicate directly with God, to serve as a medium of God, to see demons and to speak in tongues) that stand them in good stead later on, when they start their own churches. Their time in the church is marked by a process of becoming disciplined by a capricious force (God) that commands the newly saved person to do things that he or she is not expected to understand. For example, there is often a period in which the parishioners become disciples of a particular spiritual patron, and are expected to perform various tasks for him or her in exchange for spiritual and material rewards in an unspecified future.

During my fieldwork in Taita, I used to spend time in the home of a Pentecostal preacher named Eloji. Eloji was born out of wedlock and his father had refused to accept him as his son, and by all accounts treated him badly. Eloji was barely educated, spoke no English and, prior to

becoming a preacher, was penniless; he did not have his own church, and drew his legitimacy from the prophecies he gave in his home, news of which spread by word of mouth. Eloji was renowned throughout the area for his special and direct relationship to God, and people would come to Eloji at his house for miracle-inducing prayers and to hear God speak through him directly. During these times, God, speaking through Eloji, claimed that he was Elijah, God's true servant, and that he was completely immune to all disease. Believers claimed that Eloji cured the sick, created business opportunities, enabled people to marry or give birth, transformed simple foods into exotic and expensive ones (including McDonalds burgers) and transformed physical terrain so that he might create a space to commune with God in secret (inside a boulder or a tree, e.g. which would become an expansive cathedral for the time that Eloji inhabited it). Eloji received money from these prayers in the form of tithes, which he explained were gifts he received in exchange for the greater gift that God had given, or would give, the person for whom he was praying (a job or a business opportunity or a child). If the recipient of prayers did not receive the gift that was expected from prayer, God would inform that person, through Eloji, that s/he had done something wrong: had not waited long enough, or had not paid the tithe in time or had backslided in some way.

Around Eloji there was always a core group of people who would travel with him, from time to time, to pray at different places. The idea here was that there were certain locations where prayer was more effective, and that these changed on a constant basis. Accessing these opportunities as they came up was essential if the prayer warriors, and the people for whom they prayed, were to be successful in their spiritual and worldly endeavours. 'We have to be available to access God's power,' Eloji used to say. 'We do not know where God wants us, and we cannot decide for Him. We must be flexible.'

Clearly, Pentecostalism is paradoxical, and this is part of what makes it so generative and dynamic: it is expressive and performative, yet disciplinary; it is democratic yet disempowering; it is oriented towards creating transparency, yet it proliferates new forms of secrecy. Pentecostalism creates the future anew, yet it draws on cultural elements inherited from the past, such as gift exchange and notions of patron-clientage, without overtly acknowledging that it is doing so. It would be wrong to reduce all of this to something economic or political, but there is an elective affinity between Pentecostalism and some of the larger social transformations taking place on the continent, and in Kenya specifically. Although there are many sociological differences between the mainline

churches and the Pentecostals (somewhat more youth and women in the latter than in the former, in particular), the most notable difference in the social composition of these churches is the types of work in which their members are engaged, or have been engaged in the past. In particular, mainline churchgoers tend to be people who have had formal employment of some kind for most of their lives, or who hail from families that have depended on male migrant labourers. In contrast, Pentecostals tend to be entrepreneurs, though not necessarily successful ones. As one, admittedly biased, young Pentecostal man put it, in English:

> Saved people are looking for something new, a miracle. They are experimental, and they are not so focused on trying to find work somewhere in Mombasa. We know that development can happen wherever we are.

In Taita in the 1990s, state retreat and the rapid proliferation of new churches and NGOs had caused development to become the object of public discussion, with different groups of people arguing about how best to achieve 'it', and who should be in control of it. The figure of the state was increasingly absent, or derided, in these conversations: politicians' promises were seen as empty, and their focus on land and jobs (particularly, on pushing for access to Tsavo National Park) were seen as dead horses. Pentecostals in particular saw the Catholic Church as having a stranglehold on the community, and they associated it with a backward past, and with slavishness in the face of state and other forms of authority. For example, in a conversation after a state-sanctioned assembly (called a *baraza*), in which an employee of the NGO Plan International (discussed later) had lambasted the public because of its submissive attitude before the state, some young men, all of whom were Pentecostals, discussed their efforts to form a youth group to get funding from Plan or another international NGO. They immediately hit a snag when they tried to hold a meeting at the local social hall, which was governed by the Catholic Church council: the council had asked them to pay a fee, and the youth refused, claiming that the social hall had been constructed with funds from Plan and they were the now grown-up child targets of Plan's development interventions in the community (two of these young men had been Plan 'foster children', or the siblings of foster children, a concept discussed later). One young man echoed the NGO employee's comments about flexible entrepreneurialism (she had claimed that Wataita needed to stop

depending on politicians and formal employment, and to seek business opportunities and new emerging markets). This idea of flexible readiness in the face of capricious opportunities articulated easily with Pentecostal ideas about direct communication with God and mobile flexibility in response to His commands. As he put it:

> We have to finally recognise that there is no particular place where we have to be to get development. We have the capacity in ourselves, wherever we are.

Another person responded by talking about how Taita's backwardness had kept them in thrall to the Catholic Church and a clique of elite witches. He used the example of a corrupt priest who had allegedly used the community as leverage to acquire funding from an international NGO:

> This priest has been telling people that if they read the Bible they'll go insane...Two years ago he hired a secretary to draft letters and keep accounts. He warned her when he hired her that, if she told anyone what she saw, he would destroy her with the power of God. You know what he did? He was writing proposals for funding from America, and he got lots of money, but he just kept all that money for himself! This secretary, she helped him write false reports back to the NGO! She knew what she was doing was wrong, but she feared the priest would curse her and she would die. That priest became very rich, and then he left us.

Both NGOs and Pentecostals invoked the figure of new beginnings and tried to discipline people in such a way as to be transformed and in turn go out and transform the world. But there were significant differences as well, and these were not necessarily what one would expect them to be – for example, that NGOs tended to be secular (although some were not), while Pentecostals were focused on the other-worldly. The main difference was concerned with their attitude towards the imagined past, which set into motion unpredictable and surprising events and accommodations.

The spirit of NGOs

When I use the category NGO here, I am employing the term that was in use during my fieldwork in the late 1990s; at this time, it referred

to a range of different organisations, some small and others large, some local and others international, some faith-based and others secular, all of which promised to bring 'development' to Taita: either through a project, through a rotating credit union or by educating people about their civic and political rights and responsibilities. At least one NGO, the Danish International Aid Organisation, Danida, was not technically an NGO, and they left some years ago. Plan International, Aphia, World Vision, Global Education Program, Compassion International and Action Aid have worked in Taita, though Plan left Taita around 2002 and had a more exhaustive and transformative presence than any of the other organisations combined. The smaller NGOs were registered with the government, and could apply for funding from state and international sources. These days, the rules regarding NGOs have changed, and what were in the 1990s called NGOs are now called community-based organisations (CBOs); these CBOs may have several members and be organised on the basis of gender, generation or territory (faith-based CBOs are called FBOs); they apply for money that comes from the World Bank and other international sources, usually through the Kenyan government. According to a civil servant at the District Development Office in Taita in 2010, there are currently about 400 registered CBOs in Taita, 50 registered FBOs and perhaps an additional 700 unregistered CBOs. In addition, there are four or five Kenyan NGOs that apply for money directly from international foundations and organisations.

It is risky to make bald assertions about how Pentecostals differ from or are similar to NGOs, largely because there are so many different kinds of NGOs. Those that are more directly involved in community life, and in disciplining members with respect to business or agricultural practices, share more sympathy with Pentecostalism's emphasis on re-hauling the person through a different kind of conversion – to thriftiness, transparent books and accounts keeping, and business and lending practices that are unsullied by past relationships (such as those based on kinship, which are also a bane for the Pentecostals). Obviously, the faith-based NGOs overlap more explicitly with Pentecostal NGOs, and this becomes obvious in their policies towards things they consider to be of the past, such as 'traditional' healing. But there are many other subtle affinities.

On the surface, the NGOs I knew in Taita had very little to do with Pentecostalism and, aside from a few faith-based NGOs, were predominantly secular in language and orientation. The name of the largest NGO in the area where I conducted research was Plan International, and its name evoked secular rationalism, and had no trace of the ecstatic or

transcendental about it. However, NGOs like Plan share very explicitly in some of the features of Pentecostalism in that they are trying to directly overhaul society to generate 'development', which tends to be conceived as a problem that is not primarily economic, but social and spiritual (Bornstein 2005). Moreover, NGOs endeavour to connect directly with sources of power and patronage, often bypassing or claiming to bypass abusive state authorities, which are depicted as being old and corrupt in the same way that mainline religions (which are closely associated with state authorities, since state elites have long hailed from these churches and use them to extend their influence) are for Pentecostals. Connecting directly with exogenous power requires the disciplining of people's practices, so that they become more cognisant of, and responsive to, local and regional markets, and learn how to orient their productive activities for these markets, which are depicted as shifting and capricious (much in the way that the Pentecostals see prayer as mobile work that requires adaptability and secret knowledge). Like the Pentecostal churches, NGOs tend to cast themselves as socially revolutionary, and many of them (especially the international ones) make a point of hiring and providing assistance to socially disadvantaged groups, especially women and youth (see also Elyachar 2005, Karim 2011). If Pentecostal churches impose discipline through the institution of the tithe, NGOs do so through defined contributions, as people are usually expected to donate a certain amount of money to an NGO development project, be it a micro-finance operation or a project to build schools or water taps.

NGO personnel tend to depict development as the product of personal virtue and the development of certain skills. On the surface this seems very different from the Pentecostals' emphasis on ritual and xenoglossia, but in practice the differences are not actually so great, as NGOs often claim that knowledge of English and bureaucratic procedures will magically bring development in the form of assistance from abroad. People say that NGOs have to be seduced and attracted, and the proposals that youth groups write for NGO support are often described, sometimes in jest, as a kind of prayer that has to be crafted in exactly the right way. In Taita, the youth and women's groups that sought assistance from NGOs inhabited an idea of the person, and of social action, that fit well with Pentecostalism and the neoliberal ideology promoted by NGOs, as well as the decline of the state. They were mostly youth groups, and they were in a perpetual incipient stage: their members spoke in a charismatic way, redolent of the Pentecostal church, and bandied about ideas ranging from writing a Taita dictionary, to cultivating African violets

(another now virtually non-existent resource that is indigenous to the Taita Hills), to developing small-scale tourism, to selling bootlegged videos, to using the Internet to promote awareness about conditions in the hills to the world community. These groups combined a neoliberal concern with law, order and office – uprooted from the state, but in some ways containing the state within itself – with at least a tacit interest in imagined traditional forms of solidarity.

In sum, then, Pentecostal churches and NGOs tend to share a few important things in common. For one, they hold a vanguardist approach to the past, from which they seek to break (cf. Meyer 1998). Second, they view 'development' as at once a moral and economic issue, and work to change people's dispositions so that they are in a better position to access wealth (Bornstein 2005). Third, they attempt to circumvent older institutions and authorities, so as to access power and wealth directly, and this is one of the main ways in which they break with the past (whether by establishing a direct communication with God or by accessing international patrons outside the state). Fourth, they are socially more democratic than older institutions, like the state or the Catholic Church. Fifth, they aim to fulfil specific needs and are intimately involved with their targets; thus, Pentecostal preachers speak directly with congregants about what kind of mobile phone God thinks they should buy, and NGO representatives are also involved in fulfilling basic needs, and often get to know individual families directly. Sixth, they share an ideology of mobility, advising members to be aware of changes taking place in the market or in the world as a whole, so as to be able to access something of value (whether it be God's grace or the grace of the market). Finally, because they often take people's money (a percentage fee), and can come and go quickly and without accountability, Pentecostal churches and NGOs are often seen as risky or untrustworthy 'businesses'.

One of the main differences between many NGOs and Pentecostals was that, despite their shared revolutionary, vanguardist stance in relationship to the past, secular NGOs usually directed their scorn on a more recent set of past institutions and relationships (such as the state and the politics of state patronage), but they often tried to revitalise a more distant past, by recreating what they imagined to be pre-colonial political systems based on a mixture of gerontocracy and electoral democracy. Some NGOs tried to harness and secularise the power of the autochthonous past. Those NGOs often ran into opposition from churches, especially Pentecostal ones, which had quite different ideas about the traditional past. For example, when I was

conducting fieldwork among Luo people in western Kenya in 2003, I spent time with a group of people who had organised an NGO around a python that many believed to be a returned ancestress named Omieri (Smith 2006). The NGO, which was comprised of unemployed, educated, former Luo elites (one had a degree in cultural anthropology), was named after two intersecting nearby rivers, and its personnel's stated mission was to use local resources and history to generate sustainable development for the people of Nyakach, a very poor and isolated district. Their major proposed development project was to acquire funding from the international community and the state to build a snake park to house Omieri and other animals, and to protect this resource from the Kenya Wildlife Service, which had transported the previous incarnations of Omieri to Nairobi, where one had died in the National Museum.

This vernacular, autochthonous development project was directed against a large, state-driven dam project, which promised to add electricity to the national grid (but not the village in which Omieri had appeared), while drying up the local river beds and potentially decimating local wildlife and ecology. While the NGO's outlook was clearly modernist in its approach to wildlife – a fact which upset many people in Wasare, who felt that Omieri's visitation was not something that should be controlled through secular means – their efforts were depicted as atavistic in the national and international press. When the Luo Pentecostal community, as well as the Anglican Church, heard about this community that was treating a python like a person, they publicly threatened to burn it alive. They claimed that Wasare's people were worshipping an incarnation of the devil, and that the village's historical past was itself satanic.

In what follows I use the example of Plan International to show how religious organisations and NGOs interact to produce events and transformations that are often surprising and unanticipated. Despite the similarities of NGOs and Pentecostals, in practice their different orientations to the past can help to produce some profound conflicts. Thus, in the case below, an NGO dedicated to child sponsorship ended up giving power to an established, but broke, local Catholic elite, provoking a challenge from Pentecostal youth, who tried to acquire control by appealing to the NGO's secularism.

Saving children: Plan International, decentralised planning and religious conflict in Taita

There were a host of different NGOs, both local and international, at work in Taita during the 1990s, just as there was a whole world of new,

Pentecostal-style churches. Some of these NGOs were explicitly religious and some were not. Some were human rights organisations aimed at promoting an awareness of the constitution and constitutional reform, while teaching people about the limits of state authority and defining corruption for the populace. Others were 'developmental' and focused on small projects, especially rotating credit unions. Both NGOs and churches proliferated in the context of state decline conditioned in large part by structural adjustment programmes and related state-downsizing. Many of these NGOs were actually providing some of the basic services that the state was no longer capable of providing in the post-structural adjustment period – especially help with school and medical fees. And, to be sure, many churches followed suit. But not all NGOs had a positive impact. Some more closely resembled the Music Man than a coherent articulating system of institutions promoting a particular vision of development in collaboration with, or in opposition to, the state: they set up shop, collected money from people and disappeared, their owner-managers using some of their profits to pay off state officials and police so they could continue their business, sometimes living in the same area in which they had 'stolen' from people (this happened quite a bit with NGOs that would now be called CBOs). But Plan International stayed in Taita for well over a decade, invested heavily in the community and established strong connections with state actors and local citizens. In the end, the organisation significantly reshaped the political and patronage structure of Taita society. In addition to confronting the state apparatus and its patronage system of chiefs and politicians, Plan competed and collaborated with the Catholic Church, one of the major conduits of development in the region.

Plan was originally founded in 1937 to assist child victims of the Spanish Civil War. The very name of the organisation bespeaks its secular, rationalist orientation, and this is compounded by the fact that Plan continues to orient its activities around children. The reason for this, as related to me by Plan officials and Taita people who participated in Plan projects, is complex. On the one hand, the organisation wanted to assist youth because they are 'the future', but on a deeper level, Plan workers hoped that, by framing 'development' around the figure of the child, they would sidestep some of the problems that had plagued 'development' in Taita up to that point: mainly the concept's connection to certain institutional actors (state officials, politicians, the church, established adult men with jobs) that had come to be perceived by NGO officials, and by many Taita people – especially youth – as corrupt and backward. Organising development around the child also meant locating it centrally within the household, and implied, for many

Wataita, a shift from thinking about development as a male-generated activity to thinking about development as female-generated – as matricentric rather than patriarchal. As one man put it to me, 'If we're talking about development beginning with children, what we're really talking about is women, because women give birth to children and raise them.'

Plan sent its employees to households throughout the Taita Hills, enrolling people in their 'foster programme' by convincing them to agree to offer their child for sponsorship by a host family in Europe or the US. The contract was cemented through photographs, which were taken of the children, and then distributed to the sponsoring families abroad. While the funds were intended for the communities in which the child lived, most Wataita interpreted sponsorship as an individualised affair (the sponsoring family would, it was widely thought, receive funds from Plan in exchange for the photos which they had received, and would in turn presumably be selling for profit). Plan's focus on children was widely seen as a positive intervention, but it was also sometimes seen as potentially dangerous, especially in the beginning, when the community was not directly involved in the process. Presumably, Plan employees were selling the photos of children and getting rich in the process (as one man put it to me, 'Plan employees are so fat from selling pictures of our children that their bellies hang to the ground!'), and Taita families were not seeing any of the profits from what Wataita sometimes depicted as something like a global child pornography ring. Moreover, what was to keep US and European sponsors of the foster programme from coming to Taita and claiming the children they had 'adopted'? Rumours circulated that Plan was a satanic organisation – actually, a local branch of the international Satanic church – aimed at expropriating Taita's future by taking away its children. Interestingly, these rumours were promulgated primarily by Pentecostal churches.

The rumours helped to influence and ultimately change the way Plan operated in Taita, spurring on the process of decentralisation which would ultimately put power into the hands of established Catholic families. In the beginning, Plan employees were directly involved in planning and implementing projects, all of which were focused on households and designed to benefit individual homes. They built granaries, water tanks and pit latrines for families that enrolled in the foster programme, in exchange for 10 per cent of the projected anticipated cost from individual households. But Plan was most popular for helping foster families pay for their children's school fees. Over time, there were complaints from the community, and apparently also from higher-ups at the Plan Office in Nairobi, that funds were being misappropriated

(people who had no children in the foster programme received projects). And individuals who had given their photographs were not receiving the money that they had originally anticipated from the sponsors. At this point, Plan institutionalised a system of 'planning units' comprised of elected Taita people. The planning units would decide which households would receive projects from Plan, while Plan officials continued the work of transferring letters back and forth between sponsoring families in the US and Europe and recipient families in Taita. Plan also began to gradually focus on public projects, especially tap water and community livestock projects.

One of the immediate effects of Plan's work is that, as it continued and eventually became more focused on public projects, as opposed to household ones, it came to visibly displace the state, although state institutions (such as the Ministry of Water and the Ministry of Development) collaborated with Plan. State employees also used the opportunities provided by Plan projects to make money for themselves as contractors (according to them, the law required that Plan involve them in project planning procedures, such as creating impact assessments and conducting surveying work prior to laying down water pipes). This partial displacement of the state became visible for everyone when Plan built an office for itself adjoining the chief's office in Mgange. Many Wataita pointed out that this juxtaposition of Plan alongside the state – and its physical eclipsing of the state – brought home to people just how useless the state had become: while the chief was in one office presiding over disputes and receiving bribes, Plan's employees were in an adjacent room working out actual development projects that mattered to people. More importantly, Plan had resources to give: cows, water pipes, money for school fees. All of this flowed through the planning units, and into the community, even if there was a great deal of disagreement and resentment concerning who was benefiting and at whose expense. While they collaborated, state officials complained that Plan was 'changing the power base of the society', by taking power away from politicians and chiefs (even though politicians invariably claimed that it was they who had courted the NGOs, including Plan, and brought them to Taita; sometimes these politicians even claimed that they were the actual sponsors of the projects, rather than the NGOs).

In state-sanctioned public meetings called *barazas*, Plan representatives – and sometimes representatives from other NGOs – took the floor, and often used the opportunity to chastise the public for their obsequiousness in the face of politicians. Women representatives played on local and national gender dynamics, and accused

Taita women of pandering to local politicians and becoming their 'prostitutes' when they sold their votes and loyalty in exchange for the cooking implements and foodstuffs that politicians gave to them during election campaigns. These NGO representatives repeatedly mocked the paternalistic form of the *baraza*, including the structure of chief-orchestrated call, response and applause/ululation, often upstaging the authority of chiefs. And they urged women and youth to get involved in small businesses, and to open themselves up to new opportunities and new locations for doing business, rather than depending on politicians and wage labour in urban centres. And, of course, they spoke out against the evils of witchcraft, arguing repeatedly that jealousy of one's neighbour – which sometimes culminated in witchcraft accusations or actual witchcraft attacks – kept Wataita from collaborating in business ventures and investing in income-generating opportunities (for fear of inspiring the wrath of witches), and so inhibited the generation of a locally sustainable development.

The progressive, at times almost revolutionary, cadence of NGO rhetoric, and their attempt to overhaul old, oppressive structures, definitely dovetailed with Pentecostalism and appealed to actual Pentecostals. But Pentecostals complained that, despite the best efforts of NGOs, the elite Catholic 'witches' who sat on the church councils continued to commandeer local development projects for their own benefit through the planning units, while resisting any efforts by the public to know what they were doing. Ironically, when Plan opened their process to locally elected officials two things occurred: On the one hand, local concern that Plan was a potentially dangerous organisation intent on taking away Taita's children, perhaps in keeping with some global satanic plot, dissipated completely. On the other hand, instead of democratising and levelling Taita society, as Plan seemed to want to do (and as the Pentecostals wanted Plan to want to do), Plan ended up handing over control to established local elites: senior men with strong links to the Catholic Church. Now, it is true that these planning unit representatives were voted into positions of authority by the community, but they also used their connections in the Catholic Church, and Plan representatives had made statements in public which suggested that they wanted to work with recognised local leaders – in this particular community, that meant people with long-standing connections to the church.

Plan had tried to create something new by revitalising something they imagined to be old (an imagined indigenous political system based on councils of elders that had existed prior to the incursion of the colonial

state, supplemented by electoral democracy), but from the perspective of many youth all they had done was to recapitulate the power of the Catholic Church in everyday life. Many Wataita in the area began to complain that the planning units were corrupt – specifically that people had used their position in the planning units to get resources for themselves, and to use these resources to extend their own kin networks and to repay debts accrued through bridewealth and other exchanges. For example, in one instance, Plan gave cows to the committee, who ended up distributing these cows to themselves and their close kin; when the cows quickly died, they received more cows from Plan and distributed them in the same way.

Some young men from the neighbourhood, all of whom were Pentecostal, began visiting the local Plan representative in her house and complaining about corruption in the planning units. Doris, the Kenyan Plan representative, had much to complain about herself, since she was spending all of her time writing letters back to the sponsor families in the US, and in the process was being blamed by many people for allegedly stealing the gifts that everyone imagined the Americans and Europeans were sending from abroad. 'There are no gifts! Everything gets filtered through the main Plan office in Nairobi. There are just letters, only!' Doris insisted, exasperated. She explained that the planning units were supposed to be writing the letters anyway, but the old men were not skilled sufficiently in English to the point of being able to translate them.

Gradually, a plan was hatched between Doris and the local Pentecostal youth who, everyone agreed, would be in a better position to serve as secretaries for the planning units. At the same time, the Plan office in Nairobi had started a new project designed to bring water to all homes in Mgange, and to ensure that the water from the spring at Ndolwa did not stop at the central tap in the market, but flowed downstream, below the market, where people lived. This was widely seen as a democratising effort that would displace power from senior, Catholic elites who were also the town's shop owners; these shop owners had allegedly entered into an arrangement with the chief, whose office was nearby, to stop the flow of water through taps downstream and to use it instead for their bar, butchery and *matatu*-washing businesses.

Doris called for new elections, in which certain male Pentecostal youth were elected to make changes in the planning units, and these youth began attending meetings alongside their Catholic seniors. The seniors had welcomed their involvement originally, partly because they believed that these youth were going to help in keeping minutes and

eventually in translating the letters between sponsor and target families. But it became clear during the first meeting that the youth saw their mandate as having to do with books and accounts keeping; and it is true that Doris had mentioned book-keeping during the *baraza* in which it was announced that the seniors would be getting help from Taita youth, who happened also to be Pentecostal. Straight away, the young men and one young woman demanded to look at the old men's books, because they believed that the latter had been skimming some of the money that had been contributed by the community for the water project and other large projects. The seniors seemed offended and refused, and over the course of several months Pentecostal youth argued with Catholic seniors in these meetings, the latter refusing to show the youth their books or producing random scraps of paper that did not make any sense to anyone. The Pentecostals called them illiterate and old-fashioned, and the seniors reminded the youth of their relationship to the Catholic Church and of the long history of the Catholic Church in the development of Taita. The church had turned a once savage and backward place into a land of light and education. In turn, the youth responded with a secular argument redolent of Plan's mission statement, but delivered in the revolutionary spirit of Pentecostalism: They claimed that development was for the living, for everyday, not just for church days, and that it was meant to be for everyone, regardless of their relationship to God.

The youths' focus on accounting was not only about ascertaining what the seniors had done with the money they collected from the community. It was, more fundamentally, about reforming people's habits and way of thinking by making them committed to transparency, legibility and accountability through literacy. In this way, the Pentecostal youth saw their actions as revolutionary, and as a recapitulation of the original promise of missionisation dating back to the early twentieth century, with its focus on literacy and universalism. But in the end, these meetings did not go very far. Seniors and youth reached an impasse and the youth abandoned the meeting, and the planning units, to their seniors. Plan soon left the community, and the planning units were renamed Community-Based Organisations, and continued extending and maintaining the water pipes and initiating other development projects with the 10 per cent they had collected from households over the years (cf. Jones, this volume). The youth formed their own organisation, and wrote business proposals to NGOs for funding in the hope of upstaging or marginalising their seniors by securing a more powerful foreign donor, in much the same way as they sought out a more direct connection to divine power in their Pentecostal practice. The

Pentecostal youth had tried to save the NGO Plan International (and themselves), but Plan's decentralisation programme had augmented the political power of the Catholics. Now religious politics, and the generational politics of the household, were playing out visibly in public life, with each constituent group seeking a direct connection to foreign patrons (INGOs).

Conclusion

In this chapter, I began by showing how the project of development in Taita, dating back to the colonial period, has always been perceived as a religious affair, and that state actors and patrons have always also been religious actors. At the same time, an idea of autochthonous development emerged in a dialectic with Christian understandings, and was at once antagonistic and complementary, always linked to an urban wage labour migration system that was partially necessitated by Wataita's enforced incarceration in the hills. In the 1990s, structural adjustment programmes and neoliberal transformations threw modernity's vehicles and 'development as usual' into question, since people could not continue to survive and succeed in the ways to which they had become accustomed. These changes also revitalised discussion and thought concerning the value of the autochthonous, or pre-colonial, past: Was it truly satanic as Christians had long claimed, or was it of value, as actual Christian practice had often affirmed?

Pentecostalism and NGOs rapidly took off in this context of state transformation and retreat, providing both material services and a moral imperative to start anew, while simultaneously working to reform and discipline individual subjectivities and, through them, society. Pentecostal churches and NGOs share a great deal in common, both structurally and culturally, as described above. Where they differ is not necessarily in their attitude towards the divine (their secularism or their religiosity, for example), but in their attitude towards imaginary past places, activities and beliefs. If Pentecostals demonised the past, NGOs often developed a complex, collaborative relationship with their idea of the past – trying to resurrect it while also managing it, in the process trying to make it secular and democratic. And, when NGOs and Pentecostal churches collaborated or came into conflict, the content of the disagreement often concerned their respective attitudes towards an imagined past.

In addition, Pentecostal churches and NGOs became staging platforms for larger social conflicts that were fuelled, in part, by the

economic and political transformations taking place in Taita and Kenyan society. Seniors and youth, as well as men and women, debated and came into conflict through these institutions, each trying to secure funding and positions of authority by connecting to international patrons (a secularised divine power redolent of Pentecostal practice), while articulating their claims in religious idioms. In this way, the politics of the domestic sphere became public politics at the same time as the language of public politics infiltrated domestic relationships in peoples' homes.

Note

1. *Fighi* are medicinal shrines that protect Taita neighbourhoods, and Taita as a whole, from malicious foreign people and influences, especially those forces that threaten patriarchal power (such as Masaai cattle raiders, Kikuyu businessmen and non-Taita politicians).

References

Appadurai, Arjun. 1981. The Past as a Scarce Resource. *Man N.S*, 16(2): 201–219.
Barkan, Joel and N. Ng'ethe. 1998. Kenya Tries Again. *Journal of Democracy*, 9(2): 32–48.
Bornstein, Erica. 2005. *The Spirit of Development: Protestant NGOs, Morality, and Economics in Zimbabwe*. Palo Alto: Stanford University Press.
Bravman, Bill. 1998. *Making Ethnic Ways: Communities and their Transformations in Taita, Kenya, 1800–1952*. Portmouth: Heinemann.
Comaroff, John and Jean Comaroff. 1992. *Ethnography and the Historical Imagination*. Boulder: Westview Press.
Elyachar, Julia. 2005. *Markets of Dispossession: NGOs, Economic Development, and the State in Cairo*. Durham: Duke University Press.
Harris, Grace. 1978. *Casting Out Anger: Religion among the Taita of Kenya*. New York: Waveland Press.
Karim, Lamia. 2011. *Micro-Finance and Its Discontents: Women in Debt in Bangladesh*. Minnesota: University of Minnesota Press.
Marshall, Ruth. 2009. *Political Spiritualities: The Pentecostal Revolution in Nigeria*. Chicago: University of Chicago Press.
Mbembe, Achille. 2002. African Modes of Self-Writing. *Public Culture*, 14(1): 239–273.
Meyer, Birgit. 1998. 'Make a Complete Break with the Past': Memory and Post-Colonial Modernity in Ghanaian Pentecostalist Discourse. *Journal of Religion in Africa*, 28(3): 316–349.
Smith, James. 2008. *Bewitching Development: Witchcraft and the Reinvention of Development in Neoliberal Kenya*. Chicago: University of Chicago Press.
Smith, James. 2006. Snake-Driven Development. *Ethnography*, 7(4): 423–459.

7
Development and the Rural Entrepreneur: Pentecostals, NGOs and the Market in the Gamo Highlands, Ethiopia

Dena Freeman

Introduction

Since the late 1980s structural adjustment programmes and neoliberal economic policies have been implemented across Africa, largely at the behest of the World Bank and the International Monetary Fund (IMF). These policies include financial liberalisation, export-oriented industrial policy, the promotion of private sector development and a major cutting back in state spending (Bond & Dor 2003: 1). The neoliberal project in Ethiopia began in 1992, after the fall of the Marxist government of the Derg (1974–1991) and with the new government of the Ethiopian Peoples Revolutionary Democratic Front (EPRDF) privatising the economy, devaluing the currency and abolishing state monopolies and price controls (Demissie 2008). With major cuts in state spending, particularly in social welfare, there has been a huge growth in third sector organisations which have expanded to fill this gap. Most of these organisations fall into one of two groups: secular development non-governmental organisations (NGOs) and Pentecostal churches.[1]

While at first blush development NGOs and Pentecostal churches may seem like very different kinds of organisation, on closer inspection it emerges that they have much in common. Both have come to the fore in the same neoliberal context and both work to improve social welfare. They are also both agents of change, bringing new ideas, outlooks and social models, as they work to transform Ethiopian society. The ideas and outlooks that they bring are in fact remarkably similar, and fit so well with the prevailing neoliberal context that it is possible to see both of them as (possibly unwitting) agents of the neoliberal

agenda (Comaroff & Comaroff 2001, Hearn 2007, Klees 2002, Manji & O'Coill 2002). Both of them have a part of play in the conversion to capitalism that the neoliberal agenda requires (cf. Hefner 1993).

Thus in contemporary Ethiopia, particularly in rural communities in the South and the West, Pentecostal churches and development NGOs are the new agents of social transformation. The aim of this chapter is to compare and contrast the workings and the impact of these two types of organisation, both global in their connections and salvationist in their vision, as they work to change selves and societies in rural Ethiopia. The first section sets out Ethiopia's new neoliberal approach to development and the ideology of transformation that underpins these policies and the work of many of the NGOs. The second section offers a brief history of Pentecostalism in Ethiopia and discusses the seemingly rather different ideology of transformation that underpins the Pentecostalist project. The final section then provides a detailed ethnographic analysis of what happens when a development NGO and a Pentecostal church both begin to work in a previously rather traditional village in southern Ethiopia. As will become clear throughout, this chapter is also concerned with the longstanding debate between Marxist and Weberian theories of change, and the relative importance of economic ('base') factors and religious ('superstructure') factors in driving social transformation from pre-capitalist to capitalist social forms.

Secular development actors: NGOs and the state

The EPRDF set out its vision of development in its Sustainable Development and Poverty Reduction Program of 2002. Their aim is to bring about economic growth and poverty reduction in a context of macroeconomic stability. The programme clearly commits itself to the neoliberal economic vision of building a free market economy and aiming for significant growth in gross domestic product (GDP). The Government of Ethiopia aims to do this through an approach called Agricultural Development Led Industrialisation (ADLI), which seeks to bring 'development' out to rural agricultural areas, rather than focusing on manufacturing and industry and thus keeping 'development' in towns. The overriding focus is on the commercialisation of agriculture, strengthening the private sector and achieving rapid growth in market exports. The programme sets out two possible futures for today's primarily subsistence farmers – they either become workers in large commercial farms and plantations, or they become small-scale entrepreneurs growing cash crops for the local or export market (FDRE 2002). Put another

way, they will be pushed into a capitalist mode of production and must be transformed into either proletariat or entrepreneurs.

NGOs are an integral part of this development programme. Since the 1990s the numbers of both national and international NGOs in Ethiopia has skyrocketed. Until then the size and strength of the NGO sector in Ethiopia was small compared with that in other African countries and consisted only of some 50–60 NGOs, most of them international, mainly carrying out relief and humanitarian work after the famines of 1973 and 1984 (Clark 2000: 4). With the change of government in the early 1990s, international NGOs flooded in and there was also a huge growth in local NGOs. By 2000 there were 368 NGOs registered in the country (122 of them international) and by 2007 this had grown to nearly 2000 (234 international) (Rahmato et al. 2008: 12).

Most NGOs work in rural areas and until recently many of them have focused on the provision of basic services, such as schools, clinics and potable water. However since the early 2000s there has been a noticeable shift towards projects focusing on market-driven economic development, in line with the ADLI approach. The vanguard area for today's pioneering NGOs is projects engaged in private sector development, value chain development and pro-poor market development. The focus is overwhelmingly on production for the market and the transformation of Ethiopian smallholders into rural entrepreneurs. This neoliberal ideology is prevalent across the vast majority of international development NGOs working in Ethiopia today. Here are just a few examples:

FARM-Africa, a well-respected British NGO that has worked in Ethiopia since 1988, has a number of projects that involve sending 'business mentors' to work with rural communities so that they can turn traditional activities into income-generating enterprises and help 'communities gear up to work as business partners to the private sector, and to run their own enterprise initiatives' (FARM-Africa et al. 2005: 27).

CARE, a large American NGO, is currently leading a consortium of NGO partners to implement a high-profile USAID-funded project called Linking Poor Rural Households to Micro-finance and Markets in Ethiopia. As the name suggests, the major aim of this project is to turn smallholder farmers into rural entrepreneurs by providing them with access to credit so that they can buy agricultural inputs and grow cash crops, and then link them up to private sector businesses who will buy, and usually export, their product (Burns et al. 2010).

SNV, The Netherlands Development Cooperation, has recently completed a five-year programme called Business Organisations and their

Access to Markets (BOAM). This programme 'aims to contribute to sustainable poverty reduction in rural Ethiopia through value chain development...by developing business services to farmers and entrepreneurs along the whole value chain' (www.business-ethiopia. com). The head of the BOAM programme, a Dutchman with an MBA and a background in business development and financial administration, explained to me how the value chain approach marked a radical shift in development interventions:

> It's a different model of development. We used to focus on push-side, on production. Demand-side is new. What we did before was not sustainable. We increased production, but not based on market demands. We want farmers to be pulled into value chains by the opportunities provided by the market. That's the new change coming up in development thinking. And value chains are a tool to achieve that.

All of these NGOs, and many others like them, are intent on transforming smallholder farmers into entrepreneurs. They clearly believe that the way to do this is by changing economic structures – facilitating access to agricultural inputs, brokering market linkages, providing access to credit and so on. There is no thought given to the social and personal transformation that must take place for a smallholder farmer, entangled in close-knit family and community relations, redistributive economic systems and traditional politico-ritual structures, to emerge as an individualist, strategic, profit-maximising agent. As we will see below, it is the Pentecostal churches that often bring about this kind of personal transformation.

Converting to capitalism: Pentecostal churches in Ethiopia

Ethiopia's encounter with Christianity has been very different from that of most other countries in Africa. Orthodox Christianity came to the northern highlands in the fourth century and has been the official religion of the Abyssinian Empire since that time. When the northern Abyssinians conquered the people in the South and formed the Ethiopian state in the closing years of the nineteenth century, Ethiopian Orthodox Christianity became the state religion and was introduced to the largely animist peoples of the South and West (while the East was predominantly Muslim). Many people took on some of the new

Orthodox practices and combined them with their traditional animist beliefs in a syncretic mixture which left the animist practices very little changed (Eshete 2009, Freeman 2002a: 34)

Having escaped colonialism, Ethiopians were never subjected to the 'civilising missions' of European colonial powers. Foreign missionaries have been working in Ethiopia only since the 1930s, and they have always been treated with suspicion by those in power. Their activities have been somewhat constrained and their work limited to certain geographical locations.

Nonetheless, foreign Christianity, particularly various denominations of Protestant Christianity, was taken up by a minority of people in Addis Abeba and in many towns of southern and western Ethiopia over the course of the twentieth century. The mission churches of the 1930s were taken over by home-grown Ethiopian evangelists in the 1950s and 1960s and many were transformed into locally run Ethiopian churches. The two largest Protestant churches are the Kale Heywet Church, which emerged from the fundamentalist Sudan Interior Mission (SIM), and the Ethiopian Evangelical Church of Mekane Yesus, which has its origins in the Lutheran Swedish Evangelical Mission (Donham 1999, Eshete 2009, Fargher 1996).

Pentecostal missionaries first arrived in Addis Abeba in the 1950s, and during the 1960s a charismatic revival took place that soon spread throughout most of the existing Protestant churches and led to the formation of several new, indigenous Pentecostal churches (Eshete 2009, Haustein 2009). The first and largest of these new Pentecostal churches was the Mulu Wengel Church. Despite their more conservative origins, all of the other Protestant churches eventually became charismatic by the 1980s, and today's believers consider them to be basically the same and move between them with surprising speed. The Pentecostal and charismatic churches of today have adapted the Protestant Christian message to the Ethiopian context, enlivened it with spirit-filled ecstatic devotions and preach a mild version of the Prosperity Gospel.

These churches strive to bring about a total and totalising transformation of their members. Their starting point is the 'spiritual transformation of the whole person', or as we might see it, the transformation of the self. Not only do they take on Jesus Christ as their saviour, they learn to see themselves in a whole different way, as people who will go to heaven or hell, who can be infused with the Holy Spirit if they will only open their hearts, and as people who can make choices about their actions, their relationships and their future. They are encouraged

to make a break with the past, to start over, to become reborn (cf. Meyer 1998). Having made such a break, they are then encouraged to build a new life, in a new way. Spiritual transformation is thus just the first step in a broader process widely known as 'transformational development', through which believers are encouraged to build new relations, new communities and new economies.

The concept of transformational development, or 'holistic ministry', has spread widely through the Protestant and Pentecostal world and puts an emphasis on 'serving the whole person' and addressing what are perceived as social, physical and spiritual needs. One key text states it thus:

> I use the term *transformational development* to reflect the concern for seeking positive change in the whole of human life, materially, socially and spiritually. The adjective *transformational* is used to remind us that human progress is not inevitable, it takes work... True human development involves choices... This requires that we say no to some things in order to say yes to what really matters. Transformation implies changing our choices.
>
> (Myers 1999: 3, italics in original)

This concept of transformational development is used in all the Protestant and Pentecostal organisations that I spoke with in Ethiopia. It is about development as much as it is about spiritual growth. In fact it is an ideology of development that is radically different from that used by secular development organisations, starting from the spiritual and then moving out to the social and the material. The head of SIM, an American man who had been living in Addis Abeba for the past eight years, went as far as to say:

> The Christian approach, transformational development, is an anti-materialist approach to development. It is a repudiation of Marx, who saw human beings as material beings only... We start with spiritual development and then social and physical development follow.

The Pentecostal transformation of the self is thus closely related to an ongoing process of social and economic transformation. It is not limited to a supposedly private sphere of 'religion', but encompasses and influences attitudes to all areas of life (cf. Comaroff, this volume). In fact, by starting with the self, rather than with economic practices as the NGOs do, the Pentecostal project of transformation goes straight to the heart

of farmers and their communities, and offers to transform them from the inside out.

So we can see that the development NGOs and the Pentecostal churches have very different ideologies of transformation. While the former focus on material and economic matters, such as agricultural techniques, access to credit and market linkages, the latter focus on changing consciousness, bringing new ideas and attitudes to transform subjectivities so that people will make new choices, choose new activities and form new relations. It is rather as if each had taken opposing sides in the theoretical debate between Marxian and Weberian theories of change, with the NGOs siding with Marx and the Pentecostals with Weber.

It also appears, surely, that between them they offer the two sides of the transformation coin. Either type of organisation on their own will not be able to bring about a major social transformation. Indeed the anthropological literature is full of examples of development projects that did not work because the proposed changes clashed with local people's ideas, values and social forms. Likewise it includes many examples of peoples that converted to Pentecostal Christianity, but continued to live as subsistence farmers in broadly traditional communities. The scenario that the rest of this chapter explores is what happens when development NGOs and Pentecostal churches work in the same community? When both sides of the transformation coin are offered, what kind of social transformation takes place? We will explore these questions in the village of Masho, in the Gamo Highlands of southwest Ethiopia, where this conjunction of agents of transformation occurred in the early years of the twenty first century.

Religion and development in the Gamo Highlands

The Gamo Highlands are a relatively remote part of southern Ethiopia. While the major roads and towns are located in the lowlands, Gamo communities live high up in the mountains. Up until very recently road access to Chencha, the largest town, was difficult, and even now the vast majority of Gamo communities can only be reached by foot. Because of this lack of accessibility, the Gamo Highlands were not targeted by development NGOs until the late 1990s and development activities have spread out from Chencha town only slowly since then.

People in the Gamo Highlands cultivate barley and wheat, along with potatoes, cabbage and *enset* (the so-called false banana plant), and most households keep one or two head of cattle and use the manure for

fertiliser. Until 1998 theirs was predominantly a subsistence economy, and during the twentieth century it was going through a process of agricultural decline as the population increased, landholdings decreased and the soil became increasingly degraded. Subsisting from agriculture was becoming more and more difficult. Some men were also engaged in weaving, sometimes migrating to towns and cities and sometimes staying at home.

Market exchange is most certainly not new to the highlands and networks of markets have dotted the area for many decades, while trade routes have connected southern Ethiopia to the Gulf of Aden port of Zeila and onto the countries of the Mediterranean and Arabia since at least the first century AD (Abir 1970: 119, Bahru 1991: 8). During the twentieth century the local markets have thrived on a lively trade in agricultural crops from different altitudes. These days you can also find notepads, pens, padlocks and clothes in these markets, but there are relatively few other consumer items. Most villages have a central marketplace with markets held once or twice per week. Large markets may be attended by some 500 people, while even small markets are likely to get 100–200 visitors.

Men have been involved in production for the market since the early to mid part of the twentieth century, when people from this area took up weaving and became some of the most accomplished weavers in the country, producing the white cloth shawls that are Ethiopian traditional dress. The first community to take up weaving was Dorze, and the technique spread to Masho only in the 1950s or 1960s. Around this time people also started small-scale trading, carrying small items from the local towns for sale in the rural markets. However, both petty trading and weaving are labour intensive and time-consuming, and neither generate very much profit. A very few people have been able to generate enough wealth to accumulate capital and invest in further business operations from such activities. And these people have long since removed themselves from their village and relocated to Addis Abeba or other towns. Even in the mid-1990s there were very few opportunities for wage labour and most families depended on agriculture, or a mixture of agriculture and weaving, and struggled to get beyond a subsistence level. Thus while people have been involved in production for the market for at least 50 years, they have not been engaged in a local capitalist economic system, as no one has been able to accumulate capital and invest in future business activities in the village. As in many other parts of the world, market exchange has been able to exist at the edges of an essentially pre-capitalist economy (Humphrey & Hugh-Jones 1992).

Since Ethiopia was never colonised, the people of the Gamo Highlands never had to contend with European colonial capitalism. They were never forced into wage labour or cash crop production, they were never resettled or the subjects of colonial economic development planning, and although reduced to clientage status by northern Ethiopian conquerors during the early twentieth century, and organised into cooperatives by the Marxist government of the Derg during the 1970s, they never lost control of their subsistence production. The history of their encounter with market capitalism, and as we shall see later, with Christianity, is thus significantly different from that of many small-scale farmers elsewhere in Africa.

The traditional Gamo moral economy is essentially a form of 'redistributive feasting' whereby men, along with their wives or mothers, seek to amass surplus wealth in order to take prestigious titles, such as *halak'a*, by sponsoring huge feasts at which the community and, more particularly, the elders, eat (Freeman 2000, 2002a, Halperin & Olmstead 1976, Sperber 1973). Through these *halak'a* initiations, wealth is circulated and redistributed in particular ways throughout the community to ensure that fertility, wellbeing and ongoing wealth is bestowed by the spirits. At the same time it ensures that no one is able to accumulate too much wealth, as those with a surplus are always encouraged to become *halak'a* or take one of the even more senior titles. This type of moral economy, where surplus wealth is used to build relationships and buy status, is common throughout southern Ethiopia and has been aptly described as one based on 'production for connectedness' (Hamer 2002: 613).

While the initiatory system has changed and evolved over the past few hundred years (Freeman 2002a), and was significantly disrupted during the time of the Marxist government between 1974 and 1991 when people were initiated in small, secret ceremonies, at no time during the twentieth century have Gamo men not become initiated. The highlands have thus witnessed a high degree of continuity in both subsistence production and moral and ritual life during the twentieth century. The moral and economic system has incrementally evolved and adapted to new circumstances as, for example, landholdings have become smaller and younger men began to access wealth through weaving. Nevertheless, at no point have the changes been so great that subsistence production was radically changed or the initiations ceased to function. In the mid-1990s, when I was conducting my first period of fieldwork, people were throwing feasts and becoming *halak'a* in great numbers (Freeman 2002a, 2002b). This, then, is the background

context in which to consider the arrival of the Pentecostal church and an international development NGO.

The Pentecostal transformation of self in Masho

The SIM mission, and later the Kale Heywet Church, first set up in Chencha in the 1950s. While initially treated with severe hostility, they succeeded in making a few converts in Chencha town. Their efforts to find followers in the surrounding rural areas were, however, far less successful. Nonetheless, by the early 1970s they had managed to create a small group of some seven or eight believers in Masho who would hold prayer meetings in people's homes. For reasons that do not concern us here, this small group soon switched allegiance and sought support from the Mulu Wengel Church, which some of them had encountered while working in regional towns as weavers. However, throughout the 1970s, 1980s and 1990s, this fledgling church grew only extremely slowly. During my first period of fieldwork between 1995 and 1997, the Pentecostals were only a small minority in Masho, accounting for about 10 per cent of the community. For the most part, people were uninterested in this 'foreign' religion and its strange practices.

Most of the earliest people to convert were in some way marginal to mainstream community life. Many of the initial converts were people who were among the first to get involved in weaving and trading in the 1960s. Very much a minority occupation at this time, these weavers and traders were some of the first to leave the highlands and live for periods of time in local and regional towns, and many of them became exposed to Pentecostalism there and brought their ideas back with them. Others were outsiders in Masho, people who had settled there from other Gamo communities, while others were young men whose fathers had died and who suddenly found themselves bearing the responsibility of family productive and ritual matters. Others still were members of the despised outcaste group of blacksmiths and tanners (Freeman 2003).

The few people that did convert during this early period removed themselves from many traditional practices, particularly the *halak'a* initiations, and many of them underwent a profound personal transformation. Let me give the example of Wendu,[2] who was one of the early Pentecostals, joining the fledgling church in the mid-1970s at the age of about 18. Before joining, Wendu grew up in a traditional household and farmed the land with other household men. He did not go to school and describes himself at that time as 'a real farmer'. His cousin had joined the Mulu Wengel Church while weaving in Wolaita, a town

some 100 km to the north, and on his return to Masho he tried hard to convert Wendu. But Wendu was totally uninterested and ridiculed his stories of a God that lived in the sky and could make your life better. Then one night he had a frightening dream in which he saw a big, white man floating in the air with a book in his hand. The man said, 'should I kill you? Or will you believe?' Terrified, Wendu said that he would believe, and the next day he made his first visit to the little church.

Once he had recovered his composure, Wendu realised that he liked what he was hearing at the church. He recounts:

> They told me not to lie, to work hard, to get involved in trade, not to wear dirty clothes, not to drink araki. I liked these ideas.

Almost immediately the church elders encouraged him to go to school so that he would be able to read the Bible. And so, at about 18, Wendu started to go to the newly opened local school. His family refused to provide him with school books and the other necessities, so, at the suggestion of the preacher, Wendu started to weave local mats and hats and sell them in the market in order to put himself through school. With the encouragement of the church elders he felt a new sense of purpose and started working and studying with diligence. As well as secular education and literacy skills, the early converts became immersed in hours of religious education and Bible study. The preacher set up study groups and, week by week, introduced them to core Pentecostal Christian concepts, slowly building up a different view of the world, a different kind of morality and a different vision of community. Wendu, along with the other students, learned new spiritual concepts such as the Holy Spirit, sin and hell and also learned new values such as individualism, entrepreneurship and productivity. Through these small group sessions, full of radical ideas and powerful group bonding, Wendu learned a new way of looking at the world. The process changed him in quite fundamental ways. He says:

> When I first started going to church and learning, my thinking began to change. Before I didn't really think very much. As I started to learn, my thinking became wider...It changed me. I thought more about my life, about what I want, about what is good and what is bad, about how to live. Before I just lived. I didn't think about it very much.

From that time onwards he shunned all traditional practices, refused to become *halak'a*, stopped drinking alcohol and refused to eat meat from

animals that had been slaughtered in offerings to the spirits. During traditional mourning ceremonies, Wendu would sit on the side with the few other Pentecostals and refuse to join other community members who marched round the mourning field brandishing spears and chanting war songs. While partaking in communal work groups, Wendu would sit separately with the Pentecostals at breaks and refuse to drink the traditional beer, instead being served milk (Freeman 2002a: 57–59). These acts of separation and the refusal to follow the tradition often led him into conflict with his father, Shano. Time and time again Shano, as well as other community members, tried to convince him to leave the church, but Wendu never budged.

After six years Wendu had to leave school and return to farming due to family events, but he was now one of the few literate people in Masho. This put him in high demand in other areas, as he was frequently asked by community members to write letters and read documents for them. It also paved the way for his entry into local politics, as he was soon chosen first as secretary and then as chairman of the local Peasant Association.

Through his education, Bible study and growing experience in local politics, Wendu's world began to open up in new directions. He started attending church programmes and conferences in nearby areas beyond the Gamo Highlands, such as in Wolaita and Sidama. In these conferences he came into contact with people from all over Ethiopia and with new ideas and ways of living. The church teachers and elders encouraged him to be open to new things and to try to find ways to be self-sufficient and not dependent on his father. He told me:

> In the past if you were poor you looked to rich people to help you. If you were young, you looked to your father to help you. There was no other way. The church elders showed me that there was another way, that there were different possibilities. They showed me that by weaving, by trading, by making things to sell in the market, it was possible to find your own way, to be independent.

He began to develop a very entrepreneurial attitude and in the late 1980s he attempted to set up a bakery in Masho's marketplace. He wanted to bake white bread like he had seen in Chencha town and which people preferred to the rough brown bread that was then available in Masho. He spent over two years going from one government office to the next, trying to fill in all the forms and get permission and credit for this business endeavour. However, the Marxist regime at the time did not encourage

entrepreneurial activity and he faced obstacle after obstacle. After two years of trying to get the necessary permissions and loans he eventually gave up and returned to farming.

For many years Wendu was thus rather frustrated. He had been transformed by his engagement with the church and fervently sought to better his life, but try as he might, he saw no way to do so. In the early 1990s a development NGO in Wolaita asked the local government in Chencha to select four men from the district (*woreda*) to attend a training course on timber craft skills. With his skills, enthusiasm and connections, Wendu managed to get himself selected as one of the four, and he went to Wolaita for six months' training. He learnt well and when he came back he opened a workshop and started producing flat planks of timber and then making them into chairs, tables and beds. I gratefully bought a bed from him when I arrived in the field in 1995, but during my two-year stay there I saw him struggle to find a market for his products: few people at that time could afford to buy new-style furniture. He did not have the means to move to Chencha, where there would be a better market, and it was difficult for him to compete with town craftsmen if he had to pay people to carry his finished products to town. For a few years he managed to earn enough income to pay someone else to farm the family land in his place and to make a small surplus that he managed to keep out of traditional exchange rituals and away from his father. He was one of the first people to own a radio, and unlike many others at the time, he always wore shoes. He started to send one of his older children to school, but the rest remained at home, helping with farming and herding the family cattle. For the most part his limited wealth did not make any serious difference to his life, and after a few years the market for his products dried up completely and he again returned to farming.

This was the situation of many of the Pentecostals at that time – young men with new worldviews and enough education to be literate in Amharic, who often took leadership positions in local Peasant Associations and other government-initiated schemes, but who, for the most part, continued to work as subsistence farmers or weavers and struggled to free themselves from the control of their traditional fathers. The Pentecostal church changed selves but it did not change the prevailing economic or structural situation. As such it created a group of transformed young people, who then found that they had to fit back into the local society and live, more or less, as they had before because there was nowhere else to go and nothing else to do. In this instance, changing ideas, values and subjectivities did not lead to major social

transformation or to the development of a more capitalist economic system, but rather to transformed desires and increasing frustration at the inability to satisfy them.

The development NGO and the expansion of the market

This all changed after the neoliberal turn in the 1990s, and in particular in 1998 when World Vision, an international development NGO,[3] opened up an office in Chencha town and selected Masho as one of its target communities. In line with ADLI and the new government's view of the entrepreneurial farmer, World Vision looked for a cash crop that they could develop in the Gamo Highlands.

They found the apple. As it happens, apples were first brought to the area by SIM missionaries in the 1950s. Local people had never seen apples before and had no interest in eating them. After the missionaries left the area the trees stood there for about 40 years, largely ignored by everyone, until the early 1990s when Caleb, the son of one of the early church leaders and a development worker for the church, had the idea of developing apples as a cash crop and selling the fruit to foreigners living in Addis Abeba. Caleb had just returned from studying horticulture in the UK and was full of new ideas and initiatives. He brought some new apple varieties from the UK and started a nursery to produce apple seedlings. He experimented with different varieties and propagation techniques and eventually decided on a few varieties that would grow best in the local conditions. Over the next few years he trained about 50 farmers, mainly Protestants who lived near the church in Chencha, and provided them with apple seedlings.[4] A few years later, in 1997, when the trees started bearing fruit, he organised the few apple farmers into a cooperative and began to try to find a market.

So when World Vision arrived in 1998, they did not have to look far for a cash crop idea. They immediately saw the apple as the solution to the area's economic problems. They looked for people to train in apple production and propagation techniques in their target communities, including Masho. Of course, the young Pentecostal men jumped at the chance. I do not believe that the fact that World Vision is a Christian NGO is relevant here. These young people were looking for new ideas, new livelihoods and new ways of living and would thus have been open to a project such as the apple project irrespective of which NGO brought it. They were primed and ready and enthusiastic to try something that seemed to offer a promising new type of market-driven livelihood. And with their literacy skills and positions of influence in the local Peasant

Association, they were able to get themselves selected as the first target farmers. In the neighbourhood of Masho where I lived, for example, six of the original seven farmers to receive apple seedlings from World Vision were Pentecostals. Wendu, of course, was one of them.

The existence of this group of transformed young people was, I believe, a significant factor in the subsequent success of the apple development project. Without them it is quite possible that this project, like many other development projects in Africa, would have failed. The conservative mindset of the traditional peasant farmer is well known and the anthropological literature is full of examples of development projects that utterly failed to have any positive impact because local people were not interested in exploring new techniques, taking risks or changing the status quo. And yet here in Masho, because of the previous work of the Pentecostal church, there existed a group of young, educated men who were eager to learn new ideas and new techniques. Moreover, their Pentecostal values of hard work, self-discipline and independence fitted almost seamlessly with the capitalist values underlying the apple project, where hard work, self-discipline and independence would be crucial to succeeding as an apple entrepreneur. The early cohorts of apple farmers learned quickly, worked hard and were soon propagating apple seedlings in large numbers.

Starting in 1998, some seven years before the value chain revolution would hit development thinking in Ethiopia, this project was typically production focused. Other than a general notion of selling to foreigners in Addis Abeba, there was no firm idea of how to market all the apples that would soon be produced. But since apple seedlings take some three to five years to grow into trees and bear fruit, it seemed that there would be time to work this out. As it happened, the year when the World Vision project started was more or less exactly the time when the seedlings planted by the Kale Heywet project in Chencha were beginning to bear fruit and news of the apple project was spreading around the country. People came to Chencha to buy apples, and more surprisingly to buy seedlings to take home and plant. Somehow, the notion that the apple trade would be the next big thing in Ethiopia caught on, and there was a huge interest to join in. Many NGOs working in other parts of the country came to Chencha to buy large quantities of seedlings. Thus for a few years, between approximately 2003 and 2009, there was much more interest in the seedlings than the fruit, and since the price was much higher, local farmers were quick to respond to this surprising turn to affairs. Whereas the apples would sell at that time for about 12 birr per kg (a little over US$1), one apple seedling would sell for

nearly 50 birr (about US$5). Propagating and selling seedlings became a way to get rich fast. So by the time the first few cohorts of farmers in Masho were producing new seedlings, there was a growing and lucrative market developing in the area. And selling 20 seedlings could earn you around US$100 – an extremely large amount of money in this area.

Over the next few years those farmers who were in the early cohorts of the World Vision project and were growing apple seedlings began to make a lot of money. Most of these people, as I have discussed, were long-term Pentecostals, those that were part of the 10 per cent minority in the mid-1990s. The market was booming and apples seemed to offer a very lucrative income. The most enterprising individuals, and those with the most seedlings, made a lot of money very quickly. By providing new economic opportunities, the NGO project filled in the missing gap for the Pentecostals and finally brought about a massive social transformation in their lives.

The Pentecostal entrepreneurs did not need any further training to start to behave like capitalists. They invested their profits into more seedlings, infrastructure or equipment to start small businesses. Wendu invested his profits in land and also built two small hotels, one in Chencha and one in Masho market place. Alemayehu, another success-ful apple entrepreneur, invested his profits into a grinding mill and now runs a booming business, while Eyob invested his profits in a truck, which generates him a nice rental income. These budding capitalists are getting rich and investing in the future. But what about everyone else?

Conversion by market forces

After the first few years, when the wealth potential of the apple busi-ness had become clear, traditional, non-Pentecostal men started to join in too, receiving apple seedlings from World Vision and learning the new propagation techniques. Even though World Vision disbursed fewer seedlings per person as the years went on, and therefore these farmers received less than their more entrepreneurial neighbours, they were still able to earn considerable amounts of money in a relatively short period of time. However, as soon as they generated a surplus they found that kin and community started to demand a share of their wealth, most particularly through demands for them to become *halak'a*.

In this situation, and seeing how their Pentecostal neighbours were able to keep their own money and spend it as they pleased, many peo-ple decided to join the church. The numbers are staggering. While only 10 per cent of Masho were Pentecostals in 1997, some 70 per cent were

in 2007. The conversion was sudden and dramatic and coincided exactly with the apple boom. This might sound like an overly utilitarian understanding of the attractions of Pentecostalism, but the timing cannot be a coincidence. New, recent converts talk currently about the difference between being Pentecostal and traditional in largely economic terms. For example, Adane, a young man who converted to Pentecostalism in 2005, told me that:

> Becoming *halak'a* is not good. It makes you poor. You have to spend all you're your money to become *halak'a*. People sell their land and their cattle and then they have nothing. Look at Zito's family, his father sold their land to become *halak'a* and they all drank beer [at the initiation feasts] and now they are poor. I prefer to go to the church and use my money to grow up my children and live well.

Those, like Wendu, who have been in the church for many years talk quite differently about their faith. And it is to be expected that as the new recruits go through the process of Bible study and Pentecostal education, many of them will also go through a deeper process of personal transformation and come to understand their new faith at different levels. For the time being though, many of them seem to understand the material benefits that it brings and sense the consonance it has with their new capitalist mode of production.

In the last few years even more people have joined the church. For many it now appears as a way to get rich, and even those struggling in the middle and lower echelons of the new Masho society are coming to the church in the hope that it will change their lives and their fortunes. As one very poor woman, Getenesh, explained to me when I asked her why she had recently joined:

> People say that they sing and get rich. I don't really understand how. Maybe God will help me if I sing too.

Capitalism, inequality and the development of (proto-)class society

So the people and community of Masho have gone through a massive social, economic and spiritual transformation in the past ten years. In 1997 most people were subsistence farmers or weavers and followed the traditional way of life. In 2007 most people are cash crop producers and Pentecostal Christians. Masho in 1997 was largely

a traditional economy, while in 2007 it is increasingly a capitalist economy, integrated into the national economy of Ethiopia.

These changes are palpably felt in day-to-day activities, and life in Masho in 2007 has a very different feel to that in 1997. In the earlier period people engaged in their daily activities at a relaxed pace and frequently down-tooled and went to their neighbours to drink coffee – a lengthy process also involving the consumption of roasted barley, the burning of incense and the enjoyable exchange of gossip and jokes. People often worked together in traditional or new-style work groups and visitors were always popping in and out of each other's households to borrow knives and axes, visit the sick or simply to sit and chat. By 2007 much of this behaviour had disappeared. Invitations for coffee were far less frequent with people complaining that they were busy and did not have time for such idle affairs. Inter-household visiting had also significantly dropped and people told me that they were scared of being accused of plotting to steal their neighbour's apple seedlings, and thus preferred to stay away. Levels of theft had indeed skyrocketed and many households had built more sturdy fences and now kept guard dogs. In these small ways, the fabric of the community was beginning to thin and a new ethic of individualism could palpably be sensed in the flow of daily life.

As the new apple elite gets rich, the degree of inequality in Masho is also increasing rapidly. World Vision has given apple seedlings to some 60 per cent of Masho households since 1998. Those farmers that started growing apples at the beginning typically received more seedlings from the NGO and now, having been propagating them for years, have many more seedlings and apple trees than the others. Those that joined the apple business later can still do well, but those families that still do not own any apple seedlings are largely watching the economic boom from the sidelines. While their neighbours get rich, build houses with corrugated roofs, wear nice clothes and send their children to school, they become relatively poorer, remain in their bamboo houses and ragged clothes and cannot afford to send their children to school.

Some quantitative data from one neighbourhood of Masho will help illustrate some of the changes. This neighbourhood consists of 64 households, 67 per cent of which are growing apples. Table 7.1 shows the number of households that have many, some, few or no apple seedlings.

It is clear that a class structure is beginning to develop. The elite 22 per cent are predominantly the original target farmers from the first two to three years, and they are predominantly the long-term Pentecostals. They are investing their profits into land, infrastructure

Table 7.1 Apple seedlings per household

No. of seedlings	Households	%
Many	14	22
Intermediate	6	9
Few	23	36
None	21	33

and new businesses. They are the new wealthy capitalist class who have accumulated capital, invested it wisely and are building for the future.

The story for the rather larger lower class – those 69 per cent who have few or no apple seedlings – looks less rosy. Those with no apple seedlings at all are unable to partake in the economic boom, and are being left behind. As prices rise but their income does not, they are less and less able to buy from the market and many of them are falling deeper into poverty. Some receive food aid from the government, while others manage to struggle though. Many come to beg for food from the apple elite or to ask for occasional paid work on their farms. At present they are refraining from asking for ongoing employment with the apple elite, as this still seems akin to slavery to them. But their transformation into the future rural proletariat has surely begun.

Conclusion

This chapter has provided a detailed exposition of the recent processes of transformation that have taken place in the village of Masho, since a Pentecostal church and a development NGO began their activities. It has shown the interconnected and recursive way that the transformations brought about by these two organisations interacted with each other through people's lives in order to bring about a very major social, economic and spiritual transformation.

We have seen that for many people it was initially a change in material conditions – the opportunities for weaving and travelling – that led to the first conversions to Pentecostalism, as a Marxian approach would suggest, and then that the profound personal transformations brought about by the church led to the formation of a group of young, literate, entrepreneurial men keen to explore new ideas and create new lifestyles, but who at the time had no material way to do so. We have seen that it was an NGO that finally provided new economic opportunities and that these young Pentecostals became the first people

to get involved with the project and experiment with new production practices and new markets. The fact that these young Pentecostals had previously freed themselves from the obligations of the traditional redistributive economy, given up alcohol and taken on a Protestant work ethic led many of them to be successful in the new apple business and to accumulate capital and invest it in land, infrastructure or new business enterprises, very much in line with the Weberian thesis. We have also seen how, when traditional men joined in the apple business, they overwhelmingly converted to Pentecostalism in order to be able to retain their profits and not have to redistribute them around the community. And we have seen a nascent class society developing, with a fledgling capitalist entrepreneurial class and a poor proletariat working-class-in-the-making.

Finally, we have seen how in order for major social transformation to take place, the kind of transformation that is generally referred to as 'development', there have to be changes in material and economic conditions, in social relationships and in subjectivity, a position strikingly close to the Christian theory of 'transformational development'. At present, however, there is not one type of organisation that enables changes in all three realms. Development NGOs focus on material and economic conditions, while Pentecostal churches focus on relationships and subjectivity. Perhaps this is one of the reasons why development has been so unsuccessful in Africa, and perhaps the increasing conjunction of these two unlikely partners will lead to more success in the future.

Notes

1. This paper is based on 21 months' field research in the Gamo Highlands of Ethiopia between 1995 and 1997, plus subsequent visits in 2005, 2006, 2007, 2009 and 2011, as well as research with several international development NGOs in Ethiopia between 2005 and 2011, and interviews with Pentecostal Church leaders in Addis Abeba in 2009. I am truly grateful for the continued warmth and hospitality shown to me by the Masho community over the years. The initial research was generously funded by the Leverhulme Trust, the ESRC and a grant from the London School of Economics. Later periods of fieldwork were funded by a Research Grant from the Hebrew University of Jerusalem. I was a Visiting Fellow at the Institute of Ethiopian Studies at Addis Abeba University (1995–1997 and 2005–2006) and I am most grateful for their continued support for my research.
2. All names have been changed.
3. World Vision is a Christian NGO, but I do not think that its religious identity is important in what happened in Masho. This is because (1) development NGOs in Ethiopia are forbidden from evangelising; (2) many field staff of secular NGOs are personally Pentecostal Christians; and (3) similar projects

have been implemented by secular NGOs in other parts of Ethiopia, thus the nature of the project does not derive from a particular Christian outlook. For a detailed ethnography of World Vision's work elsewhere in Africa, see Bornstein (2005).
4. Apple trees are actually reproduced by grafting. However, for simplicity I will refer throughout to young apple trees as seedlings, even though this is technically incorrect.

References

Abir, M. 1970. Southern Ethiopia. In Gray, Richard and David Birmingham (Eds), *Pre-Colonial African Trade: Essays on Trade in Central and Eastern Africa before 1900*. Oxford: Oxford University Press.
Bahru Zewde. 1991. *A History of Modern Ethiopia, 1855–1974*. Oxford: James Currey.
Bond, Patrick and George Dor. 2003. Neoliberalism and Poverty Reduction Strategies in Africa. Discussion paper at the Regional Network for Equity in Health in Southern Africa.
Bornstein, E. 2005. *The Spirit of Development: Protestant NGOs, Morality, and Economics in Zimbabwe*. Palo Alto: Stanford University Press.
Burns, John, Solomon Bogale and Gezu Bekele. 2010. Linking Poor Rural Households to Micro-finance and Markets in Ethiopia: Baseline and Mid-term Assessment of the PSNP Plus Project in Doba. Addis Abeba: Tufts University.
Clark, Jeffrey. 2000. *Civil Society, NGOs and Development in Ethiopia*. Washington, DC: The World Bank.
Comaroff, Jean and John Comaroff (Eds). 2001. *Millenial Capitalism and the Culture of Neoliberalism*. Durham: Duke University Press.
Demissie, Fassil. 2008. Situated Neoliberalism and Urban Crisis in Addis Abeba, Ethiopia. *African Identities*, 6: 505–527.
Donham, Donald. 1999. *Marxist Modern: An Ethnographic History of the Ethiopian Revolution*. Berkeley: University of California Press.
Eshete, Tibebe. 2009. *The Evangelical Movement in Ethiopia: Resistance and Resilience*. Waco: Baylor University Press.
Fargher, Brian. 1996. *The Origins of the New Churches Movement in Southern Ethiopia, 1927–1944*. Leiden: Brill.
FARM-Africa and SOS Sahel Ethiopia. 2005. Bale Eco-Region Sustainable Management Programme.
FDRE (Federal Democratic Republic of Ethiopia). 2002. Ethiopia: Sustainable Development and Poverty Reduction Program. Ethiopia: Ministry of Finance and Economic Development.
Freeman, Dena. 2003. Gamo. In Freeman, Dena and Alula Pankhurst (Eds), *Peripheral People: The Excluded Minorities of Ethiopia*. London: Hurst.
Freeman, Dena. 2002a. *Initiating Change in Highland Ethiopia: Causes and Consequences of Cultural Transformation*. Cambridge: Cambridge University Press.
Freeman, Dena. 2002b. From Warrior to Wife: Cultural Transformation in the Gamo Highlands of Ethiopia. *Journal of the Royal Anthropological Institute* (N.S.), 8: 34–44.
Freeman, Dena. 2000. The Generation of Difference: Initiations in Gamo, Sidamo and Boran (Oromo). *Northeast African Studies*, 7(3): 35–57.

Halperin, Rhoda and Judith Olmstead. 1976. To Catch a Feastgiver: Redistribution among the Dorze of Ethiopia. *Africa*, 46: 146–166.

Hamer, John. 2002. The Religious Conversion Process among the Sidāma of North-East Africa. *Africa: Journal of the International African Institute*, 72(4): 598–627.

Haustein, Jorg. 2009. Writing Religious History: The Historiography of Ethiopian Pentecostalism. PhD thesis, University of Heidelberg.

Hearn, Julie. 2007. African NGOs: The New Compradors? *Development and Change*, 38(6): 1095–1110.

Hefner, Robert. 1993. *Conversion to Christianity: Historical and Anthropological Perspectives on a Great Transformation*. Berkeley: University of California Press.

Humphrey, Caroline and Stephen Hugh-Jones. 1992. *Barter, Exchange and Value: An Anthropological Approach*. Cambridge: Cambridge University Press.

Klees, Steven. 2002. NGOs: Progressive Force or Neoliberal Tool? *Current Issues in Comparative Education*, 1(1): 49–54.

Manji, Firoze and Carl O'Coill. 2002. The Missionary Position: NGOs and Development in Africa. *International Affairs*, 78(3): 567–583.

Meyer, Birgit. 1998. Make a Complete Break with the Past. Memory and Post-Colonial Modernity in Ghanaian Pentecostalist Discourse. *Journal of Religion in Africa*, 28(3): 316–349.

Myers, Bryant. 1999. *Walking with the Poor: Principles and Practices of Transformational Development*. New York: Orbis Books.

Rahmato, Dessalegn, Bantirgu Akalewold and Yoseph Endeshaw. 2008. CSOs/NGOs in Ethiopia: Partners in Development and Good Governance. Report for the Ad Hoc CSO/NGO Task Force, Addis Abeba.

Sperber, Dan. 1973. Paradoxes of Seniority among the Dorze. In Marcus, Harold (Ed.), *Proceedings of the First United States Conference on Ethiopian Studies*. African Studies Center, Michigan State University.

8

Pentecostalism, Development NGOs and Meaning in Eastern Uganda

Ben Jones

Last year I returned to the village of Oledai, where I had conducted fieldwork ten years ago. Oledai is located in Ngora sub-county in Kumi district in eastern Uganda, in a region known as Teso. I went to visit pastor George William Anguria, leader of the local Pentecostal congregation for the past 15 years, whom I had interviewed during my earlier stay, and we discussed the progress of his church. Ten years ago the church was a grass-thatched structure that could hold about 200 people. A decade on, the church now had brick walls, an iron roof and the floor space was about four times that of the original. It was still far from complete: The floor was unsealed and the walls were not plastered, but it showed the durability of the church and the robustness of Pentecostalism, a relatively new faith in Teso. The church had its range of weekly activities. On Tuesdays there were fasting prayers for all church members, the youth met on Wednesdays, the women on Fridays and students on Saturdays. The Sunday service was preceded by a meeting of 'prayer warriors' and followed by choir practice. In addition, throughout the week there were a number of 'cell' meetings held by smaller groups of Pentecostals who lived close to each other. Pastor Anguria discussed the problems faced by his congregation, but he also reflected on the successes.[1]

Later on during the same visit to Teso I went to look at a development project, the Katine Community Partnerships Programme (KCPP) in the north of the region. The KCPP is an integrated rural development project in Katine sub-county, about 40 miles north of Oledai. The project, which ran from 2007 to 2011, is sponsored by the UK's *Guardian* newspaper and Barclays Bank and is implemented by the NGO AMREF (African Medical Research Foundation). There are five strands to the

project – health, water and sanitation, education, livelihoods and empowerment – all of which involve new committees and community management structures. My visit was towards the end of the second year and I was interested to see how things were going. During a conversation with a parish councillor, we got on to the subject of the village health teams. These were set up to 'provide basic home-based care and mobilise communities for health action'; AMREF was working with them to make them active and improve their work. The councillor commented that these structures had been there for some time and that another NGO had worked with village health teams in the past, trying to do the same sorts of things. By the time AMREF had started working with village health teams they were again inactive. It was a typical story of development work in the region. The community structures supported by NGOs – such as village health teams – were active only for as long as the NGO was active, but did not do much when the NGOs were not around.

This chapter is a reflection on the above. Pentecostal churches manage to persist in rural Teso, while the committees and community management structures introduced by NGOs are more episodic and ephemeral. The Pentecostal Assemblies of God (PAG) Church in Oledai has become an integral, physical part of the village, a feature as fixed as the longer-established Catholic and Anglican churches. The work of the KCPP belongs to a history of projects, coming and going.

As in much of sub-Saharan Africa, Pentecostal churches have become part of the human and physical infrastructure of villages in Teso only in the past 20 years. The church in Oledai, established in 1994, deals with a range of concerns, both spiritual and practical. Anguria and his congregation belong to the dominant denomination in the region, the Pentecostal Assemblies of God (PAG), which is a relatively conservative branch of first-wave Pentecostalism. Those who become 'born again' in the PAG emphasise personal transformation and becoming a better person, to be achieved through leading a more religious life and through demonstrating salvation in practical ways, such as helping other members of the church. Individual church members in Oledai speak of gifts of healing and new forms of sociality. The form of Pentecostalism observed in Oledai, it should be noted, is in marked contrast to those types that concern themselves with prosperity and material wealth. In David Maxwell's division of African Pentecostalism – between the prosperity-focused Pentecostalism of African cities and the healing-focused churches of rural areas – Oledai belongs very much to the latter category (Maxwell 2006b).

At the same time, the past 25 years has seen a big influx of international NGOs into Teso. Uganda has been something of a 'donor darling', receiving big inflows of bilateral development assistance. Donors such as the UK's Department for International Development and/or Denmark's DANIDA fund NGOs to carry out large-scale development work. Major programmes such as the US$233 million World Bank-funded Northern Uganda Social Action Fund (NUSAF) formed part of this shift towards community-based approaches to development. In the language of the World Bank, the fund 'aims to empower communities in Northern Uganda by enhancing their capacity to systematically identify, prioritise, and plan for their needs and implement sustainable development initiatives' (Manor 2007: 264).

Development projects are typically organised around ideas of sustainability and economic and social development. The building of schools and health centres, construction of boreholes and distribution of new livestock are supported by new committees. The village health teams mentioned earlier are an example of this, but the KCPP also worked with 11 other new committees or community management structures at the village or parish level: Farmer Groups, Rural Innovation Groups, Marketing Associations, Information Education Communication Working Groups, Hygiene Working Groups, Operation and Maintenance Groups (boreholes), Community Medicine Distributors, Water Source Committees, Livelihood Stakeholder Forums, Community Resource Centre Management Committee and Katine Joint Farmers Association.

I list the groups like this because it gives some indication of the volume of the structures introduced by NGOs. The KCPP was only one among many projects at work in Katine sub-county. (A report from 2008 noted four other NGOs working in the livelihoods sector alone.) The logic is that once the funded part of the project comes to an end there are enough community structures and committees in place to make the project sustainable. Oledai, which was not the particular target of a development project during my earlier research, had also been on the receiving end of projects at certain moments over the previous two decades – which I discuss later in the chapter.

In thinking about the development of the PAG church in Oledai, and the more episodic or ephemeral work of NGOs, I make two observations. The first concerns what it means to become 'born again' in the particular context of rural Teso. As Joel Robbins argues, Christian discourse and practice is concerned with transformation and rupture (Robbins 2007). The Pentecostal belief of becoming 'born again' through baptism in the Holy Spirit presents a particularly strong example of rupture, or

what Birgit Meyer terms the Pentecostal preoccupation with 'making a complete break with the past' (1998). 'Born again' Christians show their inner conversion through outward signs, such as giving up alcohol or refusing to join in 'traditional' practices. In this their work had a profound meaning. And in Oledai this break with the past was particularly meaningful because of the experience of a violent insurgency that lasted from 1986 to 1993. The insurgency is remembered as a time of social, spiritual and moral collapse. Established norms, relationships and obligations were no longer possible, or were overturned by the actions of rebels. Helping a neighbour was not possible at that time, and people spoke of life retreating inwards. Rebels often attacked people from within the community, particularly local 'politicians' – chiefs, elders and leaders from the Catholic and Anglican churches. Against this recent history of violence, the Pentecostal message of breaking with the past is particularly powerful, and their success relates in part to their spiritual or moral value.

The work of NGOs, by contrast, did not connect into this recent history of violence. Though the liberal vocabulary of rights, participation and empowerment represents an ideology of sorts, it was a language that was less meaningful than the idea of being 'born again' or breaking with the past in the context of post-insurgency Teso. In interviews there was a fairly insistent concern with showing how life in Oledai had moved on. This could be shown through the work of institutions that included not only the PAG church, but also the village court, organisations based on clan or family obligations and the historic mission – Anglican and Catholic – churches. By contrast, discussions of development projects produced fairly stilted responses. Their work was unrelated to the sorts of rupture or breaking that defined the work of these other community-level institutions. Put simply, the work of NGOs failed to elaborate meaning.

At the same time, I make a further point in this chapter about the way the PAG church in Oledai *seemed* natural. Though Pentecostal discourse emphasises rupture, the 15-year-old church was a mundane feature of the village. The Pentecostal church was regarded as an integral part of the local landscape. In the interview with pastor Anguria he reflected on the extent to which his church had contributed to spiritual growth of the village. The PAG church in Oledai had contributed to a revival in other churches, with groups of Catholics and Anglicans borrowing Pentecostal practices, such as the night vigils or 'prayer warrior' groups. At the same time, the daily struggle to get the church built meant working with local government and customary courts; church members were

prominent on these other institutions. The church *seemed* as if it was something that the village could not do without.

There is a paradox here. The PAG church signified rupture while also seeming permanent. 'Born again' Christianity in Oledai offered a way of breaking with the violence of the recent past. Church members were clear about this. At the same time the church seemed like a natural part of the village, something that would continue over the longer term. This apparent contradiction between a meaning based on rupture and a seeming that was fixed and permanent appears to explain the durability of the PAG church. It was a complicated set of relationships signifying both continuity *and* change. This relationship between meaning and seeming was beyond the work of the NGOs. The community management structures and committees set up by NGOs had an artificiality to them. They seemed episodic and meant less.

A recent history of violence

Teso is a relatively poor region. Its four component districts are near the bottom of the table in development reports on Uganda. The Uganda Human Development Report of 2001 (UNDP 2001) lists the Teso districts of Kumi and Soroti as the the 41st and 45th poorest, respectively, out of 51 districts. People in Oledai make a living through cultivating foodstuffs – cassava, groundnuts, millet, sorghum and sweet potatoes. Life is categorised around a modest hierarchy of activities. Day-labouring for a neighbour, farming one's land or, in the case of women, brewing and selling beer, offer the most regular sources of income for the majority. A much smaller number of people earn money from working in the schools or through casual work in the trading centres. An even smaller number receive money or support in kind from relatives in the towns, though the habit of sending money back home or bringing gifts to the family is not a particularly important part of life in Oledai. In a sub-parish of about 150 households, the most important institutions are burial societies, churches, the primary school, the village court and organisations based on the household or the *ateker* (clan).

This present-day poverty contrasts sharply with the history of the region. Teso was for most of the colonial and post-colonial period a relatively prosperous part of Uganda. The Iteso, the dominant ethnic group, were a semi-pastoralist and acephalous or 'chiefless' society. They were made to settle down by the British to cultivate cotton as a cash crop (Lawrance 1957, Vincent 1982). Cotton and the broader incorporation

of Iteso society into colonial Uganda required the imposition of a number of hierarchical structures – chiefs, schools, mission churches, local government offices – which persisted through the various post-colonial regimes. In line with colonial thinking about martial 'tribes', the Iteso were over-represented in the army and the police force in the governments of Milton Obote and Idi Amin (Omara-Otunnu 1987: 35–36). Profits from cotton production were invested into acquiring large stocks of cattle, which retained their cultural value despite the transition to cash-cropping. It was not unusual to find 'big men' in Teso villages with two or three hundred head of cattle as late as the early 1980s. In many respects Teso falls outside the standard narrative of Uganda. The 1970s – the years of Idi Amin, typically seen as the nadir of Uganda's post-colonial experience – were relatively peaceful in Teso, but in 1986 – the moment of Uganda's 'official' recovery – things started to go wrong (Karlström 2004: 597).

The National Resistance Army (NRA) of Yoweri Museveni seized power in January 1986. Museveni, who would later achieve a reputation as a 'donor darling' committed to the development of Uganda, was in 1986 a military man who had acceded to the position of head of state after a long and bloody guerrilla war against the governments of Milton Obote and Tito and Basilio Okello. When his NRA took power in January 1986, people living in the Teso region found themselves in a difficult position. Many had served in the army or the police force of the defeated government, and were worried that they would be targeted by those who had taken power. At the same time, the return home of many of these former military and security personnel destabilised the region (Henriques 2002: 212–213).

At the same time, Karamojong warriors from the northeast began to loot cattle from the Iteso – estimates put the number taken at about 500,000 (Henriques 2002: 18), and this destroyed the region's wealth. Not only were cattle stolen, but ploughs, hand hoes, stores of grain and flour were looted or sacked. Many blamed the new government of Yoweri Museveni and the NRA, which had disbanded local-level security structures. There is also strong evidence that the army was complicit in the raiding. Opposition to the new government found a ready leadership in the military and political figures that had been displaced by the new government (de Berry 2000: 67). Rebel leaders argued that they could restore law and order, and, given the cattle raiding and insecurity in the region, their arguments found a receptive audience (Ocitti 2000: 342). Popularly called the Force Obote Back Army (FOBA), the rebels drew on popular opposition to Museveni.

Support for the insurgency began to fall off as soon as the insurgency started. The continuous cycle of raiding included not just Karamojong warriors, but also bands of 'rebels'. The loss of cattle had a particularly strong effect on young men who had expected to inherit cattle from the older generation as part of the route into manhood. With cattle gone, many younger men saw becoming a rebel as a more feasible way to achieve adult status as a man. There were also those prepared to use the cover of the insurgency for personal gain, and the insurgency quickly fragmented into a confusing array of groups and alliances:

> *Pascal*: What came at that time was the revenging of conflicts. Over land and women...one man could run to the rebels with a story, and the rebels would come and settle that dispute with a gun. You asked me what rebels did for this place. They got revenge on their own disputes.

Any veneer of military management from the leader-in-exile, Peter Otai, or the nominal commanders of FOBA or the Uganda People's Army (UPA), did not relate to the lived experience of the insurgency. Within Oledai, people recalled at least four different rebel groups working in the area.

As the insurgency dragged on the violence turned inwards and became localised. Rebels from within a particular community attacked their own leaders and clan elders. Much of the violence related to disputes over land, which had become more valuable with the loss of cattle. At the same time, rebels would consult a witchdoctor, or *emuron*, offering prophecies and protection. Some of the major figures in the insurgency were surrounded by rumours of witchcraft and magic, such as 'Hitler' Eragu. Rebel killings were carried out in intentionally sacrilegious ways, without ceremony, often away from home. One of the most notorious ways of killing, 'digging potatoes' (*aibok acok*), involved the victim being taken from his house to a field, to dig the hole that would later serve as his grave. The victim was taken to the swamps or killed by the roadside; and it was made clear to the family that they were not to collect the body for burial. A Pentecostal Christian from Oledai recalled her own experience on hearing of the death of her father:

> *Immaculate*: The rebels would not allow me to mourn, even though I went back to my home area. If they found someone like me mourning you would be forced to sing or dance, to make light of it. You are forced to act happy. If a person had been killed by them and they did

not give you permission to bury, and you then go ahead and bury you will be beaten. You had to wait for their permission. If you wanted to mourn you would have to go to the grave at night, when they are not around.

The particular and profane nature of the violence could be seen, on one level, as a reaction to the hierarchies of colonial and post-colonial government: the killings were a clear demonstration of the limits to the political authority of older men. But for many the violence was mostly understood in spiritual and moral terms. The insurgency was a time of crisis and impoverishment, and it is against this experience that the work of the Pentecostal Assemblies of God is understood. In a survey carried out in Oledai in 2002, I found people's wealth only a sixth of what it had been the year before the insurgency's start, down from an average of US$1867 per household to just US$379 (Jones 2009: 57).

This sense of collapse was further underlined by the experience of internment. In early 1991 the government set up a number of camps to round up the rural population. These camps were placed on the outskirts of towns and were a way of emptying the countryside of people and cutting off support, either voluntary or coerced, for the rebels. Estimates put the number of people interned at over 100,000 (de Berry 2000: 72, Henriques 2002: 223–224), and an Amnesty International report estimated the number of dead at around 10,000 (Amnesty International 1992: 7). If these figures are to be believed, then roughly a twelfth of the interned population died in the camps – a remarkable figure given that the camps were not for humanitarian relief, but rather part of a planned policy of cutting off rebels from their rural support base. Unlike the killing of 'big men', which was targeted and somewhat predictable, death in the camps was the result of poor sanitation, poor food and lack of medicine. Social rather than political categories suffered, with the young, the old and the infirm the first to die. Most of the people who died were buried in communal pits on the edge of the camp. These pit burials, away from home and without proper funeral rites, caused considerable distress: people tried to avoid them if they could. Some paid money to camp guards to leave for a day, so that they could take the body home for burial. Those who could not afford to pay soldiers, or who felt it too risky to return, left a mark on the body of the deceased so that they could retrieve the corpse once the camps disbanded.

For many the experience of insurgency and internment was transformative:

Betty: It was the PAG that led so many people into salvation. They stayed in the camps, and their church was founded in the camps. They would pray and preach and the church grew big. I remember when we went to get the body of our deceased grandmother. I saw how they were in the camps. I found the Pentecostals preaching.

Kevin Ward makes a general observation about stories of a revival of religious commitment in some of the camps in the Teso region, and the social and psychological dynamics of the insurgency that did much to make the message of Pentecostal Christianity persuasive (Ward 1995: 102). The millennial elements of Pentecostalism, the belief that the 'born again' Christian should prepare for the life to come, and that the world itself might come to an end, made sense to many at that time.[2]

An argument, repeated through this chapter, is the close and critical relationship between this recent history of violence and the value people attached to their Pentecostal faith. In talking with people in Oledai there was a profound desire to express that things had moved on. People talked about trying to live a better life, one that was governed by rules and accepted social behaviour. The work of burial societies, for example, focused on providing an orderly, well-appointed funeral that required the contributions of many people. There was a prevailing concern with restoring an idea of community and with propriety, the sense that there was a proper way of doing things to which it was important to adhere. This gave value to the work of Pentecostal churches, which placed considerable emphasis on new forms of sociality and rules and regulations. It also made Pentecostalism an integral part of the local landscape.

In this, Joel Robbins' (2007) argument about the importance of rupture in Christian discourse and thinking has relevance. Robbins observes the extent to which Christianity focuses on 'radical change' and that this 'provides for the possibility, indeed the salvational necessity, of the creation of ruptures between the, past, the present, and the future' (2007: 10–11). In Oledai this emphasis on radical change pervaded the way life was organised, both within and outside church. These changes could be seen not only in lives of Pentecostal Christians, but also in the work of other churches – Anglican and Catholic, the village court and in burial societies. The historic mission churches, for example, had groups of charismatic Christians, who prayed in ways similar to Pentecostals. Judgements in the village court tended to punish younger men and restored a sense of order and hierarchy. Newly established burial societies were places where rupture and transformation could be publicly demonstrated. The way in which I was told that 'only those who go to

church get prayed for when they die', that 'rules at burial are important now' and that 'the dead are now buried in a proper way' underscored the desire for a break with the past.

Pentecostalism after violence

Perhaps the most talked-about change in Oledai over the past 20 years was the increasing importance of a certain sense of proper behaviour in the conduct of public life. The religious, political and moral debates that circulated in Oledai emphasised notions of morality and propriety. There was an understanding that there was a correct way of doing things, which needed to be demonstrated through public displays in formal settings: in church, at court or during a burial service. The value attached to having a decent burial, to attending church or to demonstrating other outward signs of religiosity was incredibly important. Certainly when compared with what has been written of the region in earlier ethnographic work, there would seem to be a considerable shift towards attaching more meaning and value to religiously inflected notions of proper behaviour (cf. Lawrance 1957, Vincent 1968).

In this landscape, Pentecostalism had an obvious and evolving appeal. Pentecostalism's theology emphasises the power of personal transformation through the gifts of the Holy Spirit (Laurent 2001, Maxwell 2006a, Meyer 2004a, van Dijk 1998), and when compared with the historic mission churches working in eastern Uganda – Roman Catholic and Church of Uganda (Anglican) – Pentecostal churches have a much stronger focus on the individual, on the gifts of the Holy Spirit and the possibility of divine healing. Membership in the PAG church in Oledai was, in many ways, a demonstrative affair with church members showing their faith through abiding by a fairly long list of rules and prohibitions. There were enforced prohibitions on drinking alcohol, polygamy, cigarettes and 'marrying out', to give but a few examples.

Nevertheless, this need to show change within the church was paralleled by changes elsewhere. The significance of charismatic forms of worship in the Catholic and Anglican churches was another way of showing how things had moved on (Jones 2007). There were also ways of showing change in non-religious organisations. In the village court, for example, there was a preoccupation with whether the young man involved in the case had been wilful or disrespectful. If such a charge could be made the case would go against him, even if the particulars of the case suggested innocence. This was because the actions of the young man reminded people of the fact that much of the violence during the

insurgency was initiated by youths. As such, court cases, where decisions were strongly biased against younger men, suggested that the power of youths was diminished. It was another way of showing a break with the past.

Pentecostal discourse and practice also contributed to the way Catholic and Anglican congregations had reorganised themselves in the years after the insurgency. Charismatic Catholics, who have been an established presence in Oledai since the mid-1990s, adopted similar notions of personal transformation, adherence to rules and a strong emphasis on a life guided by faith. Most Pentecostals who were interviewed on the subject saw little difference between what it was to be a charismatic and a member of the PAG church:

> *Emmimah Loyce*: The Catholics also have their 'saved' people. They are called charismatics...They all do good work, just like the Pentecostal churches. They do not differ from us. We are together with them in what they do. They also do not drink *ajon* [millet beer].

A charismatic Catholic in Oledai accepted prohibitions on alcohol and smoking, and took the same position on questions such as polygamy and adultery. Charismatics had a similar sort of week to Pentecostals, meeting together to renew their faith and holding separate prayer meetings before the Sunday service. They had a reputation for being respectable and for self-discipline, and were more likely to be critical of church leaders than other members of the congregation. In their way they were another visible demonstration that things had moved on since the insurgency.

The distinctiveness that came with being charismatic signified a more moderate change than becoming a Pentecostal. Those who were not charismatic, but who arrived early for the Sunday service, were welcome to join the assembled charismatics and share in their prayers. It was not uncommon to find a charismatic wife living with a husband who was only an occasional church-goer. And charismatic Catholics – like Pentecostals – saw no obvious contradiction between their personal faith and the desire to take on leadership roles in governmental or customary institutions. Mary, a Catholic and a charismatic in Oledai, was a committee member of the burial society for her clan (*ateker*); Angela, a similarly devout Anglican, was a committee member of the Parent-Teachers Association of the local primary school. Rather, the point to be made is that these individuals belonged to a broader landscape where change rather than continuity was emphasised.

More generally, it was possible to see something of what Meyer (2004b) terms a 'Pentecostalite' public culture, where the sorts of expressive forms of Christianity – the night vigils, prayer warriors, healing ceremonies – valued by Pentecostals affected the work of other institutions.[3] Pentecostalism was part of a context where Christian concerns with rupture and transformation had particular meaning and value.

NGOs after violence

The growth of Pentecostalism in Teso was accompanied by a different, and largely unrelated, development. Starting in the late 1980s the Ugandan government, in partnership with Western development agencies, started funding community development projects in a major way. As the NUSAF report mentioned earlier suggests, these community projects were meant to help people 'implement sustainable development initiatives'. It was part of a broader agenda that combined neoliberal ideas about self-governance and a smaller state with communitarian beliefs about the value of participation and community empowerment.

In the case of Oledai, the experience of NGOs was more one of the remembered past than the ongoing present. There were no major development projects during the 18 months of research I conducted between 2001 and 2003, or in 2010. What was found were the ghosts of former projects. In 2001 I observed the rusted road signs directing the visitor to initiatives that no longer worked. During interviews, village leaders produced faded documents from past projects or described 'trainings' or 'sensitisations' experienced earlier. One-time 'beneficiaries' discussed previous encounters with NGOs, or referred to the life and death of earlier interventions:

Me: What was the programme for helping widows?
Charles: That has gone. Right now there is nothing. That programme was stopped because it had finished.

When I essayed discussions about NGOs I received fairly stilted responses. Questions about past projects or a proposed development initiative would produce matter-of-fact descriptions, which in no way compared to the interest shown in discussions on people's religious lives or the work of churches. The following is an example of the brief conversational encounter with the work of NGOs in Oledai:

Me: I thought SOCADIDO [an NGO] had done something here?

Anna: Maybe you are talking about that money they said was to be given to the widows and women. They do give out goats and some women get money. Maybe that is the money you are speaking of, for that is the only money I am aware of.

Me: Is that project still in this place?

Anna: People had money and goats. But it seems like it has stopped now in this place.

Anna refers to a project set up by the Soroti Catholic Diocese Integrated Development Organisation (SOCADIDO) to involve women, mostly widows, in groups. As the name suggests, the work of SOCADIDO was to be integrated into the community over the longer term. The groups Anna mentioned involved a common pool of money donated by the NGO for business activities, or an improved breed of goat that would move around the group. Anna described a fairly typical experience of development 'stopping', even though the claim of the particular NGO involved in the scheme is that its work is successful and sustainable. This is not to say that the project did not have an 'impact', rather that its impact was fairly time-bound in that it depended on the active presence of the NGO.

The KCPP, mentioned at the start of the chapter, was designed around ideas of community participation and sustainability. The committees and structures listed earlier were at the heart of the project, which was scheduled to run from October 2007 to October 2011. The community structures and committees put in place were meant to help people manage their affairs, while also offering a forum to work with or challenge the district government. These structures were also meant to keep the work of the project going after 2011. In line with contemporary development thinking, the KCPP supported committees and community management approaches, with the expectation that the district government would 'incorporate continued project work into their budgetary plans' once the NGO left (KCPP 2008).

By the second year of the KCPP, the NGO had to offer financial incentives to keep attendance up. Village health team members received bicycles and gumboots, and per diems for attending trainings. When the project management decided to stop paying allowances in 2009 the health team members stopped working. At one level this could be viewed as a consequence of poor planning, or a lack of 'capacity' at the local level. But it could also be argued that the real problem with

these structures (the 11 committees listed at the start) was that they lacked meaning. The village health teams, for example, were seen as something to do with NGOs and government, a technical structure that had a largely instrumental function.

In thinking about the lack of meaning in NGO work, it is also worth observing that many of the NGOs working in the Teso region were faith-based organisations. SOCADIDO was under the Catholic Diocese of Soroti. There was Vision Terudo (a Church of Uganda organisation); the Kumi Diocese Planning Secretariat (the development arm of the Church of Uganda); and the PAG Development Secretariat, which was meant to organise and administer projects through the PAG church. The funding for these structures came from a mixture of Christian and secular international NGOs, including Tear Fund (evangelical Christian), Christian Engineers in Development, Cordaid (the Dutch Catholic development agency) and Save the Children. There was little difference between the work of faith-based organisations and that of secular NGOs.

Mary Douglas makes an argument that links the above, on the importance of meaning, with the next section on seeming (the way the PAG church in Oledai seemed natural). Douglas suggests that institutions – such as a Pentecostal church or community committee – have to 'borrow' from outside themselves if they are to be legitimate and self-sustaining:

> There needs to be an analogy by which the formal structure of a crucial set of social relations is found in the physical world, or the supernatural world, or eternity, anywhere so long as it is not seen as a *socially contrived* arrangement. When the idea is applied back and forth from one set of social relations to another and from these back to nature, its recurring formal structure becomes easily recognisable and endowed with self-validating truth.
>
> (1987: 48, my emphasis)

As Douglas suggests, institutions need to be more than a 'socially contrived arrangement' if they are to last.

Douglas's conception of 'analogy' is also useful. It explains the durability of the PAG church in Oledai, whose work was related to notions of rupture, transformation and a recent history of violence. It also explains why donor-driven attempts at building community institutions dissolve and decay once the NGO leaves. Without a connection to something 'outside themselves', institutional innovations such as village health teams appear to be socially contrived, making it difficult for people

to invest time and energy in them. Though it may seem a somewhat facile observation, the PAG church in Oledai had a naturalness to it; it *seemed* like an integral part of the landscape, even though it was something relatively new. In becoming embedded in the village, the church became a complex, lived-in arrangement that related to what was around the place. The second part of this chapter concerns the extent to which the PAG church in Oledai had become a natural part of the village.

The PAG church as part of the village

The persistence of the Pentecostal church in Oledai was possible not only because of the rupture represented by Pentecostalism, but also because the church itself did not seem socially contrived. Though Pentecostalism was, on the surface of things, a radically different sort of Christianity, it had been an unremarkable part of the local landscape. In 2001, the grass-thatched church in which Pentecostals prayed had been part of the village for more than a decade, and by 2009 that grass-thatched structure had become something made of bricks with an iron roof. Church-goers included some of the more prominent members of the village, including the vice-chairman of the village council. At the same time, the mainstream Catholic and Anglican congregations, which were at one time hostile to Pentecostalism – not least because the Pentecostal church poached some of their more diligent members – had made their peace. In certain instances, leaders in the historic mission churches actually appeared to welcome the spiritual revival brought about by the PAG church, while members of the Catholic and Anglican churches had instituted charismatic groups, appropriating many of the practices found in the PAG church.

In other words, though Pentecostalism was, at the level of discourse, a distinctive creed, with an emphasis on salvation through conversion, much of the logic and structure of the church as a social organisation borrowed from what already existed. The particular structure of the church committee, the schedule of Sunday services and weekly meetings, the collection and handling of funds and the types of punishments meted out all borrowed from other institutional forms in the village. Many of the more mundane practices that sustained the church were appropriations from other local organisations. Even though Pentecostal Christians wanted to claim that their church stood in opposition to the norms and conventions governing the lives of unsaved villagers, as a form of organisation the church borrowed from what

was already there. There is an often ad hoc or approximative process through which new forms of social organisation develop (Douglas 1987: 46–47).

In a way, then, the Pentecostal church did much of the organising itself. It borrowed structures and practices from other parts of the sub-parish (cf. Cleaver 2002). This did not necessarily require conscious 'crafting' on the part of individual actors: Those who joined the church knew what a church was and had some sense of how it was to be organised. The schedule of Sunday services and weekly activities listed at the start of the chapter mirrored the weekly schedule of Anglican and Catholic congregations. At a more mundane level the collection and handling of funds was similar to the way other things were organised in the village. The leadership was elected in a familiar way, and key positions were dominated by people of a certain age and with a certain curriculum vitae (see below). There was a certain idea of what a committee was supposed to be, how minutes should be kept, how the account book should be presented. The PAG church in Oledai took much of its logic and structure from what was already there.

Perhaps the most straightforward way of demonstrating the incorporation of the church into the wider landscape is to look at villagers who were prominent members of the PAG church in 2002. Table 8.1 tells us, in tabular form, that church members sat on other committees in the village. Being Pentecostal did not mean being precluded from other

Table 8.1   Committee positions of Pentecostal Christians in Oledai

Church member	Church committee	Other village committees
Lawrence	Leaders committee, Youth committee,	Member of Ichaak clan elders' committee
John Francis	Youth committee, Evangelists' committee	Vice-chairman of the sub-parish council
Helen	Youth committee, Evangelists' committee	Member of women's committee, Ichaak clan burial society
Joyce	Choir committee	Ikures clan women's secretary; married to treasurer of sub-parish council and of the Ikures clan committee
William	Mobilisers' committee	Married to women's secretary of the sub-parish council

parts of village life, and many of the more prominent members of the church occupied a number of positions elsewhere.

The elders' committee of Ichaak clan, of which Lawrence was a member, for example, deals with land disputes, conflicts between different households and helps with marriage negotiations. The committee met regularly, in response to these demands. The secretary kept a notebook that listed the minutes from each meeting, as well as the agreement reached. If a particular issue could not be resolved the decision would be forwarded to the village council chairman, whose committee would decide on the issue. Or take John Francis, who was youth leader in the PAG church and also vice-chairman of the village council. The village council, when meeting as a court, had a book in which the details of the meeting were kept; judgements reached would be stamped by the council chairman. In other words these different institutions also shared in similar sorts of practices, and this seems to make a difference in explaining the naturalness of the PAG church. New ways of organising, such as a Pentecostal church, are partly the result of what Cleaver terms *institutional bricolage* (Cleaver 2002).

One example of the way the Pentecostal church mirrored developments elsewhere was the slow work of turning Anguria's grass-thatched church in Oledai into a brick and iron structure. This resembled, fairly closely, the slow transformation of a Catholic outstation on the other side of the village. When I first arrived in Oledai in 2001 this outstation was using school buildings for the Sunday service or held prayers in the open air. By the time I returned to Oledai in 2009, some eight years later, the Catholic outstation was well on the way to becoming a permanent structure. There was an iron-sheeted building that was slowly being finished. A later fundraiser for the church on 8 August 2010 detailed a day of activities involving local dignitaries and set about raising the 13.5 million Ugandan shillings (US$6000) for the completion of the church building. The day involved a morning Mass, a welcoming of the guests, an auction and lunch for the guests. The point to make here is not simply that the building work was gradual, but also the way that the building of this church made the work of the PAG church more natural and similar.

In this way the PAG church could both signify rupture while also seeming natural. Change and transformation contained were at the heart of how Pentecostal Christians understood their faith. At the same time there was a naturalness to the church that related to the embeddedness of church structures and activities within the landscape of the village.

NGOs on the outside

The work of NGOs belonged to a different category. While village leaders sat on the committees or community structures set up by development projects, these efforts had not kept going once the funding stopped. This was explained as a consequence of the funding stopping, or people losing interest. The story of the village health teams introduced at the start of the chapter, where one NGO was reviving a structure that another NGO had tried to work with in the past, was fairly typical. Structures that were meant to ensure sustainability fell into disrepair once the funded part of the project came to a conclusion. As Mary Douglas suggests, this was because the institutional arrangements did not appear natural. The work of NGOs was seen as being 'socially contrived'. While a village health team met a 'developmental' need, the work of these teams was, perhaps, too instrumental and too closely allied to the agenda of outside agencies.

This also explains the stiltedness with which people discussed the work of development agencies and NGOs. The language and logic of NGOs was at some distance from the moral, spiritual and political concerns that shaped other local-level institutions. Whereas an interview on what it meant to be 'born again', or on a particular court case, could develop considerable interest and comment, discussions about the work of NGOs or the role of the committees and community structures were dry and matter-of-fact. People discussed who benefited and who did not and seemed to have little interest or input into the structures put in place by NGOs.

In Oledai the consequences of this were apparent in the way past interventions resulted not in anything particularly lasting, but rather in a set of expectations that projects were ephemeral and time-bound. In terms of the institutional structures put in place, none of the water-user committees, micro-credit schemes or women's groups set up in the past were active. And while the decade following the insurgency's end in 1993 had witnessed a number of projects focused on post-conflict reconstruction, their work had come and gone. The 'reporter projects', for example, that organised ex-rebels (those who had 'reported' to the government during a period of amnesty) into groups to manage land as a shared enterprise were meant to be self-sustaining. Ex-rebels were given hoes, ploughs, cattle and seed to manage the enterprise, but these were quickly reorganised. Assets were divided and used by each 'reporter' separately.

A brief discussion of a school sponsorship programme produced similarly disinterested comments. While parents were concerned that only children from wealthier homes had benefited, rather than the orphans who were meant to be the recipients, the general message was that that was how things were:

> *Me*: Parents have complained about that, that some of the money has been diverted. Is that true?
>
> *Silver*: Yes, but it is from the leaders who were given to distribute those things to the children. When they are sent things they just select the children. For sure there are some children who have no parents, but they do not get any help. It is *that* man who has given us so much trouble [he points to the home of Anthony].
>
> *Me*: What causes that?
>
> *Silver*: I cannot tell. It is like he first starts with his own home and all his children get helped by Terudo [a CBO]. They are given a uniform. They are helped first before he helps the other children.

In terms of the value attached to the child sponsorship programme discussed by Silver, there was a fairly brief account of what the project did and why it was failing. Silver did not have much more to say on the issue of child sponsorship. It was a programme limited to the school that did not connect into the wider local landscape. More importantly, there was the understanding that the sponsorship scheme was ephemeral and would not last. This explains, perhaps, why those parts of an interview that focused on the work of NGOs lacked the depth or length that a discussion about other local institutions would produce. Conversations about burial societies, clan committees and the village court – as well as the PAG church in Oledai – generated much more involved and interested responses.

Conclusion

The Pentecostal church in Oledai meant something. It signified rupture and radical change. In the context of a village emerging from a recent history of violence, Pentecostalism represented a very different sort of Christianity – that separated the present from the past. It had a distinct theology, which church members were keen to articulate, emphasising the power of personal transformation through the gifts of the Holy Spirit (see Laurent 2001, Maxwell 2006a, Meyer 2004a, van Dijk 1998). The

sorts of killings and brutality experienced during the Teso insurgency (1986–1993) had a profound effect, and the desire to break with the past, an essential part of Pentecostal Christianity, was profound. Joining the church was a way of signalling that the violence of the recent past was separate from the present.

This need to show rupture or change, so strong in Pentecostal Christianity in Oledai, was also paralleled by changes elsewhere in the village. The significance of charismatic forms of worship in the Catholic Church, for example, was another way of showing how things had moved on. The pattern of a court case, where decisions were strongly biased against younger men, suggested a restoration of pre-insurgency patterns of political authority. The orderliness and sociality of a funeral organised by a burial contrasted with the lonely and sacrilegious killings of the insurgency years. There was, across the range of existing institutions, an insistent desire to make a break with the past, and Pentecostal churches were part of this landscape. The Christian discourse of rupture and transformation was central to life in Oledai.

Against this story it is possible to observe the apparent meaningless of NGO work. The committees and community structures established when development projects arrived in the village did not keep going when the NGO left. The work of community development has mostly technical functions and represents an ideological agenda – of rights, empowerment or participation – that had little purchase. In a fundamental way the work of NGOs lacked meaning. Projects were designed around legible goals, focused on a particular 'need' – health, clean water, empowerment – and tied to an outside funder. This made it difficult for people to engage with the community-level structures put in place – village health teams, water-user committees, women's groups. Without some sort of meaning in relation to the wider landscape, the work of NGOs remained extrinsic and ephemeral.

The PAG church had come to seem like a natural part of the village. It was very far from being considered as a 'socially contrived' arrangement, in the way that a village health team or SOCADIDO women's group appeared. In building the PAG church in Oledai, there were parallels to the construction of a permanent Catholic Church on the other side of the village. In a more general way the church mirrored the work of other local institutions, and was embedded within the local landscape. The organisational elements of his church borrowed from other institutions, while those who occupied positions of importance within the church also sat on other local committees. The PAG church was structured by the institutional landscape – the patterns of thoughts,

the borrowed practices and the analogies people make. There was a naturalness to this that contrasted with the artificiality of NGO institutions. The way the PAG church signified continuity and change, rupture and permanence, suggests how much further it had progressed in becoming part of life in Oledai.

Notes

1. The fieldwork that provides the basis for the chapter, carried out in Uganda from October 2001 to March 2003, was funded by a doctoral grant from the Economic and Social Research Council (ref. R42200034219). Follow-up fieldwork was carried out in 2008 and 2009 with funding from the Danish Research Council for the Social Sciences (ref. 95-0300-03024-05) and the Overseas Development Group at the University of East Anglia.
2. The growth of these churches was for practical, as well as spiritual, reasons. I was told that those who joined the church were less likely to be conscripted into rebel groups, and less likely to be harassed by government soldiers. The differentness of Pentecostalism placed the church membership outside the social and political conflicts that drove the rebellion.
3. In 2002 Pentecostal membership In Oledai was recorded at about 15 per cent of the adult population, but if charismatic Catholics and other 'born again' villagers are added to this then the figure rises to about 25 per cent.

References

Amnesty International. 1992. *Uganda: The Failure to Safeguard Human Rights.* London: Amnesty International Publications.

Cleaver, Frances. 2002. Reinventing Institutions: Bricolage and the Social Embeddedness of Natural Resource Management. *European Journal of Development Research,* 14(2): 11–30.

de Berry, Joanna. 2000. 'Life After Loss': An Anthropological Study of Post-War Recovery, Teso, East Uganda, with Special Reference to Young People. PhD Dissertation, Department of Anthropology, London School of Economics.

Douglas, Mary. 1987. *How Institutions Think.* London: Routledge.

Henriques, Peter. 2002. Peace without Reconciliation: War, Peace and Experience among the Iteso of Uganda. PhD Dissertation, Department of Anthropology, University of Copenhagen.

Jones, Ben. 2009. *Beyond the State in Rural Uganda.* Edinburgh: Edinburgh University Press.

Jones, Ben. 2007. The Teso Insurgency Remembered: Churches, Burials and Propriety. *Africa,* 77(4): 500–516.

Karlström, Mikael. 2004. Modernity and Its Aspirants: Moral Community and Developmental Eutopianism in Buganda. *Current Anthropology,* 45(5): 595–619.

KCPP (Katine Community Partnerships Project). 2008. Six Months Progress Report: October 2007 to March 2008. Prepared by Oscar Okech, AMREF Uganda.

Laurent, Pierre-Joseph. 2001. Transnationalism and Local Transformations: The Example of the Church of Assemblies of God of Burkina Faso. In Corten, Andre and Ruth Marshall-Fratani (Eds), *Between Babel and Pentecost: Transnational Pentecostalism in Africa and Latin America*. Bloomington: Indiana University Press.

Lawrance, J. 1957. *The Iteso: Fifty Years of Change in a Nilo-Hamitic Tribe of Uganda*. London: Oxford University Press.

Manor, James. 2007. *Aid That Works: Successful Development in Fragile States*. Washington, DC: World Bank.

Maxwell, David. 2006a. *African Gifts of the Spirit: Pentecostalism and the Rise of a Zimbabwean Transnational Religious Movement*. Oxford: James Currey.

Maxwell, David. 2006b. Post-Colonial Christianity in Africa. In McCleod, Hugh (Ed.), *The Cambridge History of Christianity, Vol. 9: World Christianities c.1914–c.2000*. Cambridge: Cambridge University Press.

Meyer, Birgit. 2004a. Christianity in Africa: From African Independent to Pentecostal-Charismatic Churches. *Annual Review of Anthropology*, 33: 447–474.

Meyer, Birgit. 2004b. 'Praise the Lord.' Popular Cinema and Pentecostalite Style in Ghana's New Public Sphere. *American Ethnologist*, 31(1): 1–19.

Meyer, Birgit. 1998. 'Make a Complete Break with the Past': Memory and Post-Colonial Modernity in Ghanaian Pentecostalist Discourse. *Journal of Religion in Africa*, 28(3): 316–349.

Ocitti, Jim. 2000. *Political Evolution and Democratic Practice in Uganda, 1952–1996*. Lewiston: Mellen Press.

Omara-Otunnu, Amii. 1987. *Politics and the Military in Uganda, 1890–1985*. Basingstoke: Palgrave Macmillan.

Robbins, Joel. 2007. Continuity Thinking and the Problem of Christian Culture: Belief, Time, and the Anthropology of Christianity. *Current Anthropology*, 48(1): 5–38.

United Nations Development Programme. 2001. *Uganda Human Development Report*. Kampala: UNDP.

van Dijk, Rijk. 1998. Fundamentalism, Cultural Memory and the State: Contested Representations of Time in Post-Colonial Malawi. In Werbner, Richard (Ed.), *Memory and the Postcolony: African Anthropology and the Critique of Power*. London: Zed Books.

Vincent, Joan. 1982. *Teso in Transformation: The Political Economy of Peasant and Class in Eastern Africa*. Berkeley: University of California Press.

Vincent, Joan. 1968. *African Elite: The 'Big Men' of a Small Town*. New York: Columbia University Press.

Ward, Kevin. 1995. The Church of Uganda amidst Conflict: The Interplay between Church and Politics in Uganda since 1962. In Hansen, Holger and Michael Twaddle (Eds), *Religion and Politics in East Africa: The Period since Independence*. Oxford: James Currey.

9
Agents of Gendered Change: Empowerment, Salvation and Gendered Transformation in Urban Kenya

Damaris Parsitau

Introduction

Since the 1980s gender issues have increasingly gained public attention in Kenya. Two very different types of organisation have been central in the struggles to transform gender relations and lead to increased equality and empowerment for women: women-focused non-governmental organisations (NGOs) and women-led Pentecostal and charismatic churches. NGOs have engaged in extensive campaigns to promote socio-economic development, democracy and human rights throughout Kenya. Today there are literally thousands of NGOs operating in Kenya, many focusing on gender issues and seeking to bring about a transformation in women's roles in society. Some of the areas in which they work include girls' education, women's reproductive health, women's economic empowerment and gender equity in legal and policy matters. At the same time a new wave of women-led Pentecostal and charismatic churches has also been seeking gendered social transformation. Focusing on the gospel message of salvation and redemption, they seek to bring about a transformation in women's lives by empowering them both spiritually and materially. Alongside a raft of skills and enterprise training, these churches also seek to build women's confidence, enhance their self-esteem and build networks of fellowship and support. The purpose of this chapter is to compare and contrast these two rather different non-state actors and to consider how, and with what success, they bring about gendered transformation.

Following this short introduction, the chapter first gives some background about the situation of women in Kenya and traces the rise

of the women's movement from the 1980s onwards. It then discusses two women-focused NGOs – Maendeleo Ya Wanawake Organization (MYWO) and the Federation of Women Lawyers (FIDA-Kenya) – and two women-led neo-charismatic churches – the Ladies Homecare Spiritual Fellowship (LHSF) and the Single Ladies Interdenominational Ministry (SLIM) – and considers how these different organisations conceptualise women's problems, engage with women and seek to bring about gendered transformation.

Women in Kenyan society

Kenya is a largely patriarchal society where the status of women is relatively low, with great inequality and inequity prevailing in many aspects of Kenyan society. The pervasive patriarchal ideology is evident in both the domestic and public spheres. Women remain marginalised and discriminated against in all aspects of their lives. This patriarchal culture ensures that women do not play critical roles politically. Until very recently there were hardly any women appointed to public office, either in government or in the private sector.

Women also face tremendous systemic obstacles that prevent them from full enjoyment of their rights and privileges. The situation is reinforced by laws and policies as well as prevailing socio-cultural factors. Some identifiable challenges that women face in Kenya include rape, incest, wife inheritance and other forms of violence against women such as female genital mutilation and early marriages. Others include reproductive health issues and diseases such as HIV/AIDS, lack of access to education, fair representation in politics and public life, advocacy and policy and legal issues.

It was in this context that the women's movement in Kenya began in earnest in the 1980s and gained momentum in the 1990s, when the turn towards multi-party politics opened up a more democratic space that provided more opportunity for women to speak out. Since then women have pioneered in gender activism, gender sensitisation, capacity building, lobbying on gender and human rights issues, and mobilising Kenyan women to take up various political leadership positions. Women started to demand increased voice and representation in national politics and broader society, and many committed themselves to raising the consciousness of their fellow women, especially at the grassroots level, to understand their rights as citizens (Nzomo 1993: 143). Recently, women have even begun to form their own political parties, largely because existing parties in the multi-party context have not adequately

addressed women's concerns. Nonetheless, as one commentator has concluded, 'this pioneer spirit has...failed in achieving effective political participation or the taking up of leadership positions' (Kamau 2010). Even today there are only 22 women legislators in parliament (about 10 per cent of the total), 7 women serving in cabinet and 6 female assistant ministers. And while women constitute over 30 per cent of those employed in the public sector, only about 25 per cent of them are at a decision-making level (Kamau 2010).

The transition from one-party rule to multi-party democracy and the new neoliberal openness of the early 1990s has also led to a growth in a wide variety of civil society organisations, many of which took up women's issues. Among these were both NGOs that focused on women and a number of women-led Pentecostal churches that focused on the salvation of poor and marginal women. In this chapter I seek to explore the different ways in which these two types of women-focused organisation conceptualise the problems that face Kenyan women, and also to compare the different approaches that they use as they seek to overcome them.

Women-focused NGOs

Today Kenya is home to a sea of civil society organisations, NGOs, faith-based organisations and other bodies working on development issues such as governance, human rights, gender issues and health. Around 5000 NGOs were registered in Kenya between 1990 and 2007 (Gifford 2009: 160, Hearne 2003, Parsitau 2009), and several hundred of these specifically focus on issues of concern to women. Some of the most outstanding include the Federation of Women Lawyers (FIDA-Kenya), Forum for African Women Educationists (FAWE), the League of Kenyan Women Voters (LKWV), Maendeleo Ya Wanawake Organizations (MYWO), Mothers in Action, National Council of Women of Kenya (NCWK), the Kenya Network of Women Living with AIDS (KENWA) and the National Committee for the Advancement of Women's Rights. These women-focused NGOs have emerged to address the myriad of challenges and concerns affecting women in Kenya and have agitated for the inclusion of women in the social, economic and legal reforms that are taking place in the country. As a result there has been a significant increase in the number of women assuming leadership positions in public and civic life (Nzomo 1993: 143).

While many women's NGOs focus on health and economic empowerment, a number of them have expanded their focus from social

and economic issues at the local level to political and legal concerns at the national level. Today there is a widespread expansion of gender development activities to include women's political representation and policy advocacy. Yet despite all these efforts, women in Kenya still remain grossly underrepresented in policy and decision-making bodies and organisations in legislative, public and private sectors. Still today, women's representation in Parliament is very low, even by East African standards. Women make up only 10 per cent of Kenya's parliament, while women account for some 30 per cent of parliamentarians in neighbouring Uganda and Tanzania, and over 50 per cent in Rwanda.

In the next section, I focus on the activities and programmes of two prominent women-focused NGOs – Maendeleo Ya Wanawake Organisations (MYWO) and the Federation of Women Lawyers (FIDA-Kenya).

Maendeleo Ya Wanawake

Maendeleo Ya Wanawake (MYWO) ('Development of Women') is one of the largest women's NGOs in Kenya today. While tracing its origins back to an organisation started by the wives of colonial administrators in the 1950s with the aim of improving women's welfare and increasing their involvement in rural development (Gecaga 2001, Kiragu 2006), it has transformed and flourished since independence and today consists of a nationwide network of over 600,000 women's groups, with some 4.5 million women members. These networks of women's groups have become entrenched in Kenyan society and the vast majority of women, whether rural or urban, educated or uneducated, belong to at least one or two of these groups.

Like many women's NGOs, MYWO engages mainly in promoting education for women and girls and in enabling small-scale developmental activities for women, focusing on income generation, welfare concerns and home-making skills. One area that it has championed in particular is the liberation of women from what they see as the worse forms of traditional culture, particularly female genital mutilation (FGM), early marriage and forced marriage. Female initiation rites, including FGM, are important in many communities in Kenya and, despite being banned by the government, they continue in many places. Seeing that simply banning the practices was ineffective, MYWO came up with an innovative approach aimed at transforming, rather than stopping, these female initiations. In discussion with local communities, MWYO has invented alternative rites of passage for rural, particularly pastoralist, women that recognise the social, cultural and religious significance of

the rites but dispense with the painful and controversial mutilation of the female genitalia. Many communities, such as the Pokot, Samburu, Maasai, Kisii and Meru, have embraced these alternative rites, and this has translated into better opportunities for young girls who can now go to school without being initiated and married off before their teenage years. The case of Pauline, a young Maasai woman that I met at a MWYO ceremony, is typical. She finished her primary school education when she was 15 and was eager to continue her education at high school. However, her father had other plans for her and, unbeknown to her, had arranged for her to undergo female circumcision and then get married to a man that Pauline hardly knew. When she found out, Pauline ran away to a rescue centre sponsored by MYWO. Centre staff and counsellors liaised with Pauline's parents and tried to convince them that FGM would seriously harm their daughter and that the alternative rites of passage could adequately serve to mark her transition to womanhood. Eventually they agreed, and Pauline went through the alternative rites and returned to her family.

Federation of Women Lawyers

The Federation of Women Lawyers (FIDA-Kenya) is a non-profit, non-partisan and non-governmental membership organisation of women lawyers and women law students in Kenya. This leading women's organisation was established in July 1985 after the third United Nations World Conference on women, which was held in Nairobi. FIDA-Kenya focuses on national-level political, legal and structural issues affecting Kenyan women, rather than on local level issues and women's micro-economic development. FIDA-Kenya was formed to ensure that women can access justice at all times, to advocate for reform of laws and policies with regards to women's rights and to provide information and enhance public awareness on gender issues and women's rights issues. It provides legal aid to thousands of women and it also engages in advocacy, litigation, lobbying, public awareness, training and education.

When FIDA was first set up initial reactions from Kenyan men were very hostile. The male-dominated culture and media portrayed the organisation as one led by 'a group of divorced women' who were out to 'spoil good Kenyan women'. Despite this initial negative perception from Kenyan men, FIDA-Kenya has fought hard to shed this negative label and has struggled to make Kenyan women aware of their legal, political, social and human rights. FIDA-Kenya carries out numerous trainings for women of all ages and backgrounds, in both urban and rural areas. It seeks to improve women's knowledge about

property rights, inheritance rights and divorce law so that women will be able to demand what is entitled to them during family and community conflicts. The organisation has also raised objections to gender-based violence and has produced extensive reports that have placed the issue firmly on the public agenda. Throughout the post-election violence that rocked the country after the disputed 2007 general election, FIDA-Kenya highlighted its impact on women and children and helped thousands of women in need. In 2009 it organised the first-ever gender festival, an open forum for women to discuss a range of issues, including gender-based violence and issues of family protection. It has ably and articulately raised awareness concerning many issues and challenges facing women in the country, and has also been involved in the formulation of policy for the advancement of women's issues, such as the National Policy on Gender and Development and the Sex Offence Bill.

At the international level, FIDA-Kenya is recognised foremost as an African actor in the area of women's empowerment. It enjoys special consultative status with the African Commission and with the United Nations Economic and Social Council, and observer status with the African Commission on Human Rights. FIDA uses these local and international spaces to bring pressure to bear on Kenyan policy makers in order to improve conditions for women. For example, FIDA has played critical roles throughout the constitution reform process and in the subsequent debates and discourses to improve gender equity in the new constitution that came into effect in August 2010. Although much remains to be done, it is hoped that the passage of a new constitution will help Kenyan women achieve more steps towards their rights in the Kenyan society.

These two women-focused NGOs, and others like them, thus seek to improve the lives and conditions of women in Kenya. While there are numerous differences in scale, outlook and approach, some broad generalisations can nonetheless be made. First, women-focused NGOs tend to focus on the practical. They are interested in economic development, legal structures and bodily integrity. Their concerns are here and now, in the material, matter of fact. Second, their approach can be characterised as 'minimising harm'. They seek to protect women from the various harmful forces and actors that would otherwise hurt them, whether by appropriating their property or hurting their bodies. These women-focused NGOs, and others like them, mainly seek to make a tough life a little easier. Let us now contrast this with the approach of the new women-led Pentecostal churches.

Pentecostal and charismatic churches

Parallel to the growth in NGOs since the 1990s has been the astounding growth of Pentecostal and charismatic Christianity. While most Kenyans have long identified as Christian (Ochieng 2010), particularly Anglican, Presbyterian and Roman Catholic, there has been a rapid rise in Pentecostal and charismatic church movements that cut across social, ethnic and gender divides in both urban and rural areas of the country (Parsitau 2007, 2009). It is now estimated that about 14 per cent of the population are members of Pentecostal or charismatic churches (Kalu 2008: 5) and that seven in ten Protestants are Pentecostal, and about a third of all Catholics can be classified as charismatic (Pew Forum on Religion and Public Life 2006). At the present time, then, Pentecostal and charismatic Christianity represents the most dynamic, powerful and publicly visible form of religious renewal in Kenya and has become a powerful socio-political and religious force (Parsitau 2007). In many parts of the world it has been suggested that the movement has transformative effects on women, particularly those in search of equality. How, then, do these Kenyan churches deal with women and women's issues?

Gendered charisma: the feminisation of Kenyan Pentecostalism

Browning and Hollingworth (2010) have aptly pointed out the gender paradox at the heart of global Pentecostalism, whereby it is 'at once liberating and disempowering for women'. While on the one hand many Pentecostal churches affirm the equality of all human beings and seek to liberate women from traditional cultural structures, they also uphold the sanctity of the patriarchal family and refuse to let women take leadership positions in the church. This characterisation is true of much of Kenyan Pentecostalism, although recent struggles to reformulate the role of the Pentecostal woman are currently leading to some radical new developments, such as female-headed churches and all-women prayer fellowships, as I shall discuss later.

Most Pentecostal churches are male-dominated organisations. The Deliverance Church, one of the largest Pentecostal churches in Kenya, with over 1000 congregations spread all over the country, is a typical example. All of its local, regional and international congregations, except one, are led by men. The Deliverance Church Council, the highest decision-making body of the church, is entirely male. While pastors' wives may serve as co-pastors, their role is ambiguous and has little potential for real leadership. Indeed, most of these women have

full-time jobs outside of the church. In general, women are excluded from leadership positions and many women that I interviewed reported that men make all of the central decisions in the church and that women have very little voice in church matters. Nancy Gitau, for example, used to be a member of the Deliverance Church. She told me how she found the church to be 'totally dominated by men' and was frustrated that they 'refused to accord women leadership roles despite the fact that women are equally endowed with charismatic gifts that enable them to preach just like men'. Eventually she left the Deliverance Church and founded her own ministry, Deborah Arise Africa. In traditional Pentecostal churches such as the Deliverance Church, women's roles are supposed to be in the domestic sphere and they are expected to follow 'God's natural order' by acting as helpers rather than leaders. As one pastor put it, 'men are the head and women are the neck'. Men are also the head of the household and women are expected to submit both to God and to their husbands.

Despite this exclusion from leadership positions, women are extremely active in Pentecostal churches and carry significant responsibilities. They are frequently involved in evangelism, singing, ushering, collecting offerings, social welfare, protocol and church maintenance. For many women, engagement in these activities offers opportunities to learn new skills and to develop their potential. Many become enthusiastic public speakers and build their confidence. Their frustration is then perhaps all the greater when, after this empowerment, they find themselves excluded from the most important positions of church leadership.

While this situation is common in many regular Pentecostal churches, there are a few exceptions that give greater responsibilities to women and further their empowerment to more encompassing levels. Some churches, such as the Redeemed Gospel Church, have even agreed to ordain women pastors, and their Bishop, Arthur Kitonga, has ordained several prominent female clergy. This, in turn, has led to some interesting new developments in Kenyan Pentecostalism, as many of these female pastors have since left their original churches and founded their own churches and congregations. Thus today one of the most striking features of the Kenyan Pentecostal scene is its increasingly feminised face. There is now a proliferation of ordained female clergy, many of whom are founders, presidents, bishops, evangelists, healers or prophetesses in new churches. Examples include Bishop Margaret Wanjiru of Jesus Is Alive Ministries (JIAM); Evangelist Teresia Wairimu of Faith Evangelistic Ministries (FEM); Rev. Elizabeth Wahome of Single

Ladies Interdenominational Ministries (SLIM); Rev. Judy Mbugua of Ladies Homecare Spiritual Fellowship (LHSF); and Rev. Grace Kariuki of Amazing Grace Ministries International. Other examples include the Ladies of Excellence Ministries led and founded by Rev. Lucy Muriu of Maximum Miracle Centers (MMC); Faith Harvest Church Family founded by pastor Zipporah Kimani; Deborah Arise Africa founded by Rev. Nancy Gitau; Evangelist Alice Mugure of Zion Prayer Mountain and the Kenya House of Prayer; Charismata Ministries founded by Evangelist Mama Mwai; Rivers of Joy Faith Christian Church founded by Rev. Esther Maingi; and The Will of God Ministry founded by Apostle Mary Wangui. Such developments parallel similar movements across the continent, where women-led Pentecostal churches have also emerged, for example, in Nigeria, Ivory Coast and Ghana (Olupuna 2002, Walker 1979).

In all these churches and ministries, women have assumed leadership positions to a degree that has not (yet) been replicated in mainstream Pentecostal churches or in public life in Kenya in general (Mwaura 2005, Parsitau & Mwaura 2010). These women are not only assuming prominence locally, but also internationally, as many of their ministries have expanded transnationally, with branches in various other African countries (Parsitau & Mwaura 2010). Moreover, previously marginalised, 'non-typical' women, such as those who are single, divorced or widowed, have also assumed leadership roles in these new churches and fellowships (Mwaura 2005, Parsitau & Mwaura 2010, Parsitau 2010, 2011).

In what follows I will present two case studies of new women-led churches – LHSF and SLIM – and show how they seek to improve women's lives and to bring about gendered social transformation.

Ladies Homecare Spiritual Fellowship

The Ladies Homecare Spiritual Fellowship (LHSF) was founded by the Rev. Judy Mbugua in 1985 as an interdenominational Christian fellowship for ladies, with a mission to raise strong women who are committed to praying for the salvation of their families. Rev. Mbugua explained to me that the fellowship seeks to equip women with the spiritual and practical resources to raise strong and healthy families and, in so doing, to contribute to building a strong nation. This mission is clearly rather conservative and, although it seeks to empower women, it does not challenge the conventional wisdom that their place is first and foremost in the home, helping their husbands and raising their children.

Rev. Mbugua is an accomplished woman. Her life story, as recounted to me in 2009, sheds light on her path to becoming one of the first female Pentecostal leaders. She was born to wealthy and educated parents in 1947 in Limuru, Kenya, and grew up in the Presbyterian church of East Africa. Although she grew up in a wealthy home, she dropped out of school before she had completed her primary school education and married Richard Mbugua while still a teenager. Ill-equipped to shoulder marital and parental responsibilities, she struggled in her new role as a wife and mother. It was at this challenging time in her life that she attended a Pentecostal church crusade. The preacher spoke about spiritual death, and this resonated with Judy, who was feeling exhausted and spiritually drained. She began to crave the spiritual renewal and transformation that the preacher talked about, and soon after, at the age of 20, was 'born again'. This radical spiritual transformation, she says, turned her life around. It gave her hope and strength to cope with her role as a young wife and mother and to envision a positive future for herself. A few years later she went back to school and then trained as a secretary at a government secretarial college. She succeeded in finding employment and steadily worked her way up the ranks to become a top government secretary. She joined the Nairobi Pentecostal Church Valley Road, an affluent and well-known Pentecostal church in Nairobi. It was here that she learned the art of public speaking and discovered a talent for preaching and ministering. As she became more involved with church activities her confidence increased and she began to also learn key leadership and management skills.

However, for much of this time Judy's husband was away working and she felt lonely. She also found that she did not fit in to any of the typical categories of people often referred to in the church services. The pastor would often call out to couples, single parents and widows to be prayed for, and Judy could not stand up and receive the blessing because she did not fit in any of those categories. She became concerned that women whose husbands were not 'born again' were being left out by the pastors. It was at this point, in 1985, that she decided to bring these women together to form a fellowship where they could talk, share and pray together. She started to invite women to her house for monthly prayer meetings, and the LHSF was born. The first meeting attracted 20 women, the second meeting attracted 40, then 60, and within a year, 200 women were attending the monthly meetings. Within five years the numbers had risen to over a thousand women from a range of different denominations.

The growth in numbers necessitated the need for larger facilities and thus the meetings were moved to the Nairobi Pentecostal Church Valley

Road. Today, meetings are held at the Homecare Retreat Centre in Karen, a comfortable centre recently purchased by the LHSF. While the ministry originally started in Nairobi, they have long since spread to various parts of the country. Thus, from a small, home-based prayer fellowship, LHSF has now grown to become an interdenominational religious organisation with over 20 branches throughout the country and 1 in Zimbabwe.

In 1991 Judy was ordained as a full minister by Bishop Arthur Kitonga of the Redeemed Gospel Churches of Kenya. Like many other women ministers, her church training has predominantly been in leadership and management, rather than theology. She studied at the Haggai Institute for Advanced Leadership Training, an international training centre for Christian leaders which runs courses that are somewhere between an MBA and a course in Theology and which focus on empowering leaders to find their own personalised and culturally appropriate ways of communicating the gospel.

Like many other charismatic churches, LHSF has a focus on 'holistic ministry', meaning that it seeks to combine both spiritual and material transformation. Each branch builds a home, called a prayer tower, consisting of a hall, a prayer room, retreat facilities and a counselling room with telephone help lines operating 24 hours per day. LHSF also runs seminars on leadership and organises development programmes aimed at empowering disadvantaged women. On the material side, LHSF focuses on poor and vulnerable women, especially those living in informal settlements such as the Kibera slum in Nairobi. It runs a shelter for women who have suffered from abuse, including victims of rape, incest and other forms of gender-based violence, and provides emotional support and psychological counselling laced with prayer and devotion. It also has programmes catering for very poor women and children, particularly those orphaned by HIV/AIDS, by providing food, shelter, clothing, counselling and education. LHSF also runs a microfinance facility that partners with local banks to provide loans for needy and vulnerable women members to start small businesses. Many women in this ministry are thus involved in arts and crafts businesses or in small-scale detergent-making enterprises. These ventures have significantly transformed the lives of many such vulnerable women. Mary, for example, was living in a ramshackle hut in the Kibera slum after her husband died of HIV-related complications. Also HIV-positive herself, she was severely ill and malnourished. When she joined LHSF she was given free anti-retroviral drugs and food. Within a couple of months, she felt better and learned how to take care of herself. She also learned new skills such as tailoring and dressmaking. She soon began to make dresses

and earned enough to buy food and rent a small but decent house. She is now able to feed her two children and send them to school. Mary says that LHSF has transformed her life and given her hope and reason to live.

Rev Mbugua is also publicly engaged in women's issues and is an opinion shaper both nationally and internationally. As a well-known televangelist, she regularly reaches large audiences by preaching on Kenyan television. She often speaks on issues of concern to women such as patriarchy, poverty, disease, ignorance, inadequate healthcare and gender-based violence. She has also attempted to interrogate these issues and has challenged governments and other stakeholders to address issues of concern to women in Africa. She is also central to a number of efforts to bring together Christian women's organisations throughout Kenya, and across the African continent. She helped found the National Interdenominational Women's Prayer Network (NIWPN), an organisation consisting of women's networks established to bring together all Kenyan Christian Women's Ministries to pray for the country. This network, which comprises more than 150 women leaders from various Christian denominations, mobilises women leaders and their followers to pray and make intercession for the family unit and the nation at large. NIWPN also maintains a database of all women's ministries in the country, and uses mass media technologies to communicate with them on topical issues affecting the nation.

Rev. Mbugua is also the Director of the Pan African Christian Women's Alliance (PACWA), an organisation linking evangelical women's organisations throughout Africa. PACWA provides information and training for women on social, economic, political and legal issues as diverse as land use, bank loans, gender-based violence and female genital mutilation. PACWA also facilitates development projects among women all over Africa, and their achievements include a tailoring and sewing school in Zambia, training for self-help projects in Madagascar, microbusiness classes and adult literacy classes among Maasai women in Kenya and Tanzania, single mothers' projects in Ghana, chicken projects in Botswana, teenage pregnancy support programmes in Sierra Leone and nutrition centres for street children in South Africa.

Single Ladies Interdenominational Ministry

Another ministry that strives to improve the physical and spiritual needs of women in Kenya is the Single Ladies Interdenominational Ministry (SLIM), founded by Rev. Elizabeth Wahome in June 2004. SLIM began as a prayer and support group for single women who are often ostracised

and shunned in regular Pentecostal churches. Rev. Wahome claims that she received a vision from God to start SLIM to give lonely single women some fellowship after realising that most Christian churches did not address their needs. It has grown rapidly since its founding and now has well over 2000 members. It has branches in Tanzania and Uganda, and plans to develop new branches in Botswana, Malawi, Zimbabwe and the Seychelles. While membership of this organisation was initially restricted to single women, today the church is open to all women, and husbands are welcome as partners and mentors. However, SLIM's focus remains on single women, and it is dedicated to uplifting their lives, particularly those that are poor, marginalised and vulnerable, by empowering them spiritually, socially and economically.

Four different categories of single women are recognised by SLIM – divorcees, single mothers, spinsters and widows – whose conditions are likened to the experiences of female biblical figures such as Mary Magdalene, Ruth, Esther, Hagar and Deborah. Divorced women are represented by Hagar, Sarah's maidservant and second wife to Abraham. When Hagar was rejected and sent away with her son Ishmael, God rescued them and provided them with water. Rev. Wahome draws many parallels between Hagar's story and that of separated and divorced Kenyan women, who are usually left with the sole responsibility for feeding and raising their children. Single mothers are represented by Ruth. These women who have not been married but have children whom they raise alone, are often despised, stigmatised and shunned, and the story of Ruth brings them hope. Spinsters, the third category, are women who have been patiently and hopefully waiting for husbands. Rev. Wahome draws parallels between this group and the Virgin Mary, who was faithful until an angel appeared and announced that she would soon be pregnant with a child. Rev. Wahome was herself single for a very long time, and she can therefore identify with the challenges that affect this category in a culture that frowns on unmarried women. This group is encouraged to stay expectant and hopeful until a suitable husband shows up. Rev. Wahome exhorts women in this category to preoccupy themselves with serving God while waiting for a husband. The last category is that of widows, who, according to Rev. Wahome, have a special place in God's heart. This category is represented by Naomi, who lost her husband and sons in battle, but who nonetheless found a way to carry on. God is here portrayed as the defender of widows and the oppressed. She quotes Psalms 68, where God is said to be a husband to widows and a father to their children. All four categories of single women are encouraged to rise above victimhood and value themselves as children of God.

At home and in the church the women are encouraged to work as the bride of Christ, active in evangelism and ministry (Kalu 2006: 231). They are encouraged to realise that they are not alone because Jesus is their husband, provider, counsellor and helper.

Along with many other women-led churches and ministries in Kenya, SLIM seeks to empower women and change their subjectivities by drawing on positive female heroines and images from the Bible. Nigerian historian and theologian Ogbu Kalu has drawn attention to the important ways in which female imagery can be used as metaphors of power, transformation and encouragement (Kalu 2008). He argues that feminine imagery is found throughout the Bible, with God often portrayed as the mother of Israel. He offers a reading of the Bible in which God's powers of salvation were first activated by women – Elizabeth, Mary, Anna and Mary Magdalene. These women, he argues, had the courage to say yes to the Holy Spirit and became co-workers with God. Their apparent weakness was turned into a powerful, prophetic recovery for both church and community. Women-led Pentecostal churches in Kenya build on Kalu's insights and also seek out exemplary female heroines from the Bible. They place special focus on the use of female biblical characters, such as Deborah, Naomi, Yael, Ruth and Mary, as images and metaphors of empowerment and transformation. These biblical 'women of excellence' serve as role models and many women at SLIM draw strength and inspiration from them and want to be identified with them. The appropriation of feminine biblical imagery and its use as a tool of empowerment is central to SLIM's devotional and motivational practices and aims to build women's self-esteem and confidence and help them to forge links with one another. These metaphors are used to reconstruct Christian womanhood and singlehood and to create a gendered understanding of themselves as single Christian women in a society that frowns upon them. While society brands them as the weaker sex, Pentecostal women in Kenya seek to recast themselves as 'Women of Excellence', 'Daughters of Faith', 'Daughters of Zion', 'Women of Honour' and 'Women without Limits'. SLIM, with its particular focus on often-marginalised single women, encourages its members to change their self-perception from that of victims to that of daughters of God. In this way SLIM and other such churches use these metaphors and feminine biblical imagery, in an attempt, reconstruct their shattered and wounded beings and to reformulate a positive vision of the female self.

Much of SLIM's work thus has a strong therapeutic focus. One of its key programmes is 'Sister Keepers', a ministry that encourages women to

watch over each other as keepers. These are usually networks of prayer support groups in which women listen to each others' problems and pray together. The ministry also has weekly meetings such as Bible study, committee meetings and prayer groups, all of which provide space to talk about problems and challenges. In their annual conferences, cell group meetings and Bible study groups, these women share their stories of suffering and restoration. The meetings allow them to disclose their inner life to other supportive women. The meetings can be powerfully therapeutic, as women narrate their sufferings and pain at the hands of abusive husbands, or the loneliness they felt when deserted by a spouse or their struggles and pain as they fend for their children. The issues that bind them in these fellowships are sadness, loneliness, sorrow, pain, neglect, despair, poverty, domestic violence, sin, suffering and disease (Griffith 1997).

More than many other ministries that I have studied, SLIM has succeeded in empowering women, particularly single women. Scores of women that I interviewed told me how SLIM had changed the way they perceive themselves in relation to God. Several pointed out that their participation in SLIM's meetings had enhanced their self-esteem and confidence, while others insisted that it had led to a total transformation of their lives.

SLIM also aims to help women transform the practical aspects of their lives, particularly their economic situation. For single women having to cope alone, this is of particular importance. In an effort to assist women living in Nairobi's poorest areas, SLIM has opened a bureau that advertises jobs and encourages employers to seek workers through it. Building on the reputation of Pentecostals as honest and hard-working, SLIM's message to employers reads:

> Attention employers, are you looking for honest born-again workers? For secretaries, accountants, housekeepers, and baby sitters, contact the SLIM bureau.

SLIM has also recently opened a skills centre, where it provides a variety of skills training to single women and also to young girls and boys. People learn skills such as information technology, tailoring, baking and confectionery making, catering, detergent and shampoo making and animal husbandry. Women who were not able to finish school due to lack of school fees are given a second chance to go back and complete their studies. Every participant is urged to engage in social and economic pursuits to improve their life, and SLIM secures funding

to assist some of these women get started, in the form of small loans from banks such as The Women's Finance Trust, Equity Bank and Family Bank. An annual exhibition is held to display the wares that have been produced by women who have been trained, and sales from these exhibitions are often significant and help the women to establish business contacts. One of this year's exhibitors, Sabina, a single mother of two and owner of the Sabby Craft and Curio Shop, for example, learned basic business management skills in a programme run by SLIM in collaboration with Family Bank. Sabina joined SLIM in 2003 and received a grant of KSh 1500 to open a small-scale business specialising in African batik and handcrafts. Her business has now grown tremendously and she has achieved a high degree of financial security. Likewise, Anne, a single mother of three, learned to bake cakes in one of the classes at the skills centre and later received a small grant to start a bakery business. This business has totally transformed her life, giving her confidence and security and allowing her to provide for her children.

Rev. Wahome also speaks frequently in the public arena, and has challenged the government to address issues affecting single women and to include women's concerns in the development agenda and in the formulation of policy. She claims that Kenyan women are oppressed and have no one to fight for them. She has drawn attention to the high levels of gender-based violence and insecurity facing women in the country, especially poor and vulnerable women in the country's urban slums and informal settlements. She has called for legal aid to widows whose relatives disinherit them when their husbands die, and for legal aid and education for women in general. Rev. Wahome argues that her ministry serves as a wake-up call to the Christian church and to society as a whole, and challenges them to accept single women and to allow women into leadership positions. She has criticised mainstream Christian churches and called on them to open up opportunities for women as leaders, deacons, preachers and directors of projects. SLIM, then, is clearly politically and socially empowering in that it unquestionably helps build social capital among women and rallies their collective energies to transform their lives and that of their families. SLIM further provides these women with institutional settings for the acquisition of leadership and organisational skills that may be transferred to civic skills. But perhaps most importantly, it is in the area of building self-esteem and confidence that SLIM has brought about a huge transformation in the lives of single women.

SLIM, then, is perhaps more radical than LHSF, with its focus on non-traditional, 'atypical', single women. It is one of the few organisations that give these women a role and a voice. In many other respects, however, the two organisations are very similar and both would agree that it is better for a woman to be married than to be alone. The two organisations are also similar in that, like many other Pentecostal and charismatic churches, they practice 'holistic ministry', combining both spiritual and material matters in their efforts to bring about personal and social transformation.

Conclusion

My observation of Kenya's new women-led Pentecostal organisations suggests that women clergy and laity are using the new faith as a space for struggle, for liberation, for dislocating culture and patriarchy and to contest leadership and public life. They offer a space for healing and personal and communal development. In this space, personal testimonies are cherished as important indicators of how radical personal salvation is expected to be. The messages of these churches are very positive and affirming, and focus on the themes of self-worth and positive engagement with life. In these churches and fellowships the focus is on the transformation of subjectivity, and women are encouraged to rise above stigmatisation and victimhood. Conversion to Pentecostalism is widely considered to bring about a sense of liberation and the opening up of a new moral order in which people can redeem themselves and their situation. For women, this is particularly so in these new women-led churches.

Pentecostal converts seek to shift their mentality from victims to empowered persons who are able to transform their lives using spiritual resources and empowering discourses from biblical sources. They find personal and social integrity in the transformation offered by Pentecostal religiosity, which is both a sort of struggle for gender liberation and a critique of the prevailing patriarchal order. Women Pentecostal leaders challenge gender stereotypes and prejudices in Kenyan society. These movements encourage women to renegotiate some of the cultural practices and expectations of traditional life that restrict them and limit their choices, such as Female Genital Mutilation, early marriage, wife inheritance and polygamy. They exhort women to circumvent restrictions through the power of the gospel, and to use their spiritual gifts to rise to their full potential.

These issues parallel the concerns raised by women-focused NGOs in Kenya, who similarly focus on girls' education and harmful traditional practices. Both consider these issues to be absolutely fundamental for women's empowerment. And likewise, both the churches and the NGOs place a major emphasis on the economic empowerment of women, with skills and enterprise training. Indeed, there are numerous occasions where collaboration has been witnessed between Pentecostal churches and secular NGOs. Both MYWO and FIDA-Kenya, along with many other NGOs, have worked in collaboration with Pentecostal churches to bring about the transformation of women lives. It is not unusual to see lawyers from FIDA giving talks about women's legal rights at meetings organised by women-led Pentecostal churches, or to hear about partnerships between MYWO and various women-led Pentecostal ministries to provide economic empowerment projects to poor women.

Despite the many similarities between the churches and NGOs – in their delineation of the main problems facing women and their desire to work with and empower the most poor and marginalised – there is one major difference in how they work. While the NGOs focus solely on material and economic transformation, the churches combine this with a quest for spiritual transformation, or what we might call a transformation of subjectivities. By coming to see and experience themselves in a whole different way, many members of women-led Pentecostal churches become empowered to change their lives from the inside out.

References

Browning, Melissa and Andrea Hollingsworth. 2010. Your Daughters Shall Prophesy (As Long as They Submit): Pentecostalism and Gender in Global Perspective. In Wilkinson, Michael and Steven Studebaker (Eds), *The Liberating Spirit: Pentecostals and Social Action in North America*. Hamilton: McMaster Divinity College Press.

Gecaga, Margaret. 2001. Women and Political Participation in Kenya. In Amoah, Elizabeth (Ed.), *Divine Empowerment of Women in Africa's Complex Realities*. Accra: Circle of Concerned Women Theologians.

Gifford, Paul. 2009. *Christianity, Politics and Public Life in Kenya*. London: Hurst.

Griffith, Ruth. 1997. *God's Daughters: Evangelical Women and the Power of Submission*. Berkeley: University of California Press.

Hearne, Jane. 2003. The Invisible NGOs: US Evangelical Missions in Kenya. *Journal of Religion in Africa*, 32: 32–60.

Kalu, Ogbu. 2008. *African Pentecostalism: An Introduction*. New York: Oxford University Press.

Kalu, Ogbu. 2006. *Power, Poverty and Prayer: The Challenges of Poverty and Pluralism in African Christianity, 1960–1996*. Frankfurt: Peter Lang.

Kamau, Nyokabi. 2010. *Women and Political Leadership in Kenya: Ten Case Studies.* Berlin: Heinrich Böll Foundation.

Kiragu, Jane. 2006. Is There a Women's Movement? In Muteshi, Jecinta (Ed.), *Mapping Best Practices: Promoting Gender Equality and the Advancement of Kenyan Women.* Berlin: Heinrich Böll Foundation.

Mwaura, Philomena. 2005. Gender and Power in African Christianity: African Instituted Churches and Pentecostal Churches. In Kalu, Ogbu (Ed.), *African Christianity: An African Story.* Pretoria: University of Pretoria.

Nzomo, Maria (Ed.). 1993. *Empowering Kenyan Women: Reports of a Seminar on Post Election Women's Agenda, Forward Looking Strategies to 1991 and Beyond.* Nairobi: National Committee on the Status of Women.

Ochieng, Samuel. 2010. Faith and Figures: Why Christian Numbers Don't Add Up. *The Shepherd*, 32: 6–7.

Olupuna, Jacob. 2002. Africa, West. In Burgess, Stanley and Eduard van der Maas (Eds), *The New International Dictionary of Pentecostal and Charismatic Movements.* Michigan: Zondervan.

Parsitau, Damaris. 2011. Arise oh ye Daughters of Faith: Pentecostalism, Women and Public Culture in Kenya. In Englund, Harri (Ed.), *Christianity and Public Culture in Africa.* Ohio: Ohio University Press.

Parsitau, Damaris. 2009. 'Keep Holy Distance and Abstain Till He Comes': Interrogating a Pentecostal Church Discourses and Engagements with HIV/AIDS and the Youth in Kenya, Africa Today. *Indiana University Press Journals* (Special Issue Christianity and HIV/AIDS in Eastern and Southern Africa), 56(1): 44–64.

Parsitau, Damaris. 2007. From the Periphery to the Centre: The Pentecostalization of Mainline Christianity in Kenya. *Missionalia, Journal of Missiology*, 5(3): 83–111.

Parsitau, Damaris and Philomena Mwaura. 2010. Gospel without Borders: Gender Dynamics of Transnational Religious Movements in Kenya and the Kenyan Diaspora. In Adogame, Afe and Jim Spickard (Eds), *Religions Crossing Boundaries: Transnational Religious Dynamics in Africa and the New African Diaspora.* Leiden: Brill.

Pew Forum on Religion and Public Life. 2006. The Historical Overview of Pentecostalism in Kenya. http://pewforum.org/surveys/pentecostal/countries/print.php?Country.

Walker, Sheila. 1979. Women in the Harris Movement. In Bennetta, Jules-Rosette (Ed.), *The New Religions of Africa.* New York: Ablex.

Index

Abir, M., 166
Abolition of Marital Power Law, 95
abstinence counselling, 28, 93, 94–5
abuse, women, *see* gender-based
    violence
Abyssinian Empire, 162
Action Aid, 147
activism, 54, 55, 63, 204
Adeyemi, Tayo, 74
adultery, prohibition on, 191
'advertising Jesus', 23
affect
    Deleuzian definition of, 58–9, 121
    politics of, 41–63
    and subjectivity, transformations of,
        121–3
Africa
    economic crisis/post-1980 scenario,
        3–4, 10, 24, 112, 125, 127,
        129–30
    growth of capitalism, comparison
        with European context, 17–19
    'New Christian Revolution', 48
    'renewalist' faiths, 45
    rise of NGOs and new religious
        movement, 9–23
    US pastors ordained in, historical
        reversal, 118
    women's organisations, 203–20
    see also specific entries
African Commission, 208
African Commission on Human
    Rights, 208
African Independent Churches, 10,
    18, 27, 48, 70, 78
African Medical Research Foundation
    (AMREF), 181–2
African Reformation, 17
Aga Khan Development Network, 84
Aga Khan Foundation, 84
Agamben, Giorgio, 112

Agricultural Development Led
    Industrialisation (ADLI), 160,
    161, 172
agriculture, commercialisation of, 22,
    159–79, 185–6
AIDS, 28, 49, 93–4, 95, 113, 124, 204,
    205, 213
Akan-speaking churches, 54
Akoko, Robert, 11, 14
alcohol consumption, prohibition
    on, 13, 20, 169–70, 178, 184,
    190, 191
alternative rites, 206–7
Amazing Grace Ministries
    International, 211
American revivalism, 10, 41–2
Amnesty International, 188, 198
AMREF (African Medical Research
    Foundation), 181–2
Anderson, Allan, 10, 11, 71
Andreasson, Stefan, 89, 103
Anglicans, 69–70, 112, 135, 137, 140,
    143, 150, 182, 184, 189, 190–1,
    195, 196, 209
anti-Christ, 119–20
anti-retroviral drugs, free, 213
anti-social wealth accumulation, 15,
    79–83, 84
apartheid, 44, 56, 58
apocalyptic movements, 41, 129
Appadurai, Arjun, 139
Asad, Talal, 45, 50
Asia, 10, 48, 53, 78
Assemblies of God, 11, 50, 70, 71, 111,
    112, 117, 182–5, 189, 190, 191,
    194–7, 199, 200–1
authoritarianism, 58, 112, 119

banks, church-run, 15, 27, 55, 74
Baptism of the Spirit, 11, 12, 19–20,
    45–51, 54, 58, 102, 104, 111, 115,
    116, 117–18, 120, 121–3, 129,

ululations, 12, 23, 154
United Nations, 207
  third United Nations World
      Conference on women (1985),
      207
  United Nations Economic and
      Social Council, 208
Universal Church of the Kingdom of
      God, 42–3
  'Gods and Services', 56
  Mozambique flood relief (2000), 52
  rapid expansion, 44
  spiritual integration with ordinary
      life, 43, 47
  spiritual investment mantra/slogan,
      56
  vs. Weber's model of Protestantism,
      42–3
universities/colleges, church-run, 15,
      55, 73–5, 113
University of Ghana, 111
USA
  church-run prisons/gyms, 43–4
  mega-churches, 43–4, 52–3
  National Association of
      Evangelicals, 47
  revivalism, 41–2
USAID, 161

value chain development, 22, 161–2,
      173
van Dijk, Rijk, 9, 12, 13, 14, 21, 22,
      24, 28, 87–105, 113, 114, 115,
      117, 118, 190,
victimhood, 104, 215–16
videos, gospel, 49, 60
Vincent, Joan, 185, 190
violence
  gender-based, 204, 208, 213, 214,
      217, 218
  in Uganda, 185–90
Vision Terudo, 194, 199

'war against poverty', 2, 6
'war against the demons', *see* 'spiritual
      warfare'
Wataita (Taita people), 135–9, 145–6,
      152, 153, 154, 155, 157
Watchtower movement, 42

water projects, *see* development
      projects
Weber, Max, 3, 15–17, 19, 20, 22, 23,
      26, 30, 41, 42, 43, 48, 51, 56, 58,
      61, 72
  on capitalism, 16, 20, 72
  'disenchantment of the world', 103
  on Protestant ethic, 15–17, 61, 72
wellbeing, human, 1, 6, 27, 115, 167
West Africa, post-Cold War
      Pentecostalism and development
      in Ghana/Togo, 111–12
  affect and subjectivity
      transformations, 121–3;
      Deleuzian definition of affect,
      121; manifestations of, 121–3
  convergences between, 128–30
  NGOs, development of, 123–8;
      BØRNEfonden child
      sponsorship projects, 124–8; PSI
      health awareness projects, 124
  Pentecostal churches, rise of,
      112–14; codes of conduct, 114;
      as development agencies/social
      services, 113; organised
      'neighbourhoods'/networked
      members, 113–14; tithing,
      repatriation scheme (Accra),
      113
  Pentecostal narratives, 114–21;
      'blame tradition',
      underdevelopment as
      sinfulness, 114–15, 128; End
      Times, readiness and everyday
      morality, 119–21;
      God–church–pastor, authority
      figures in regulation of
      everyday life, 119; occult
      phenomena in films, 115–16;
      rejection of traditional culture
      and structures of authority,
      117–19; secret rapture, 119–20;
      village/city, spiritual
      cartography, 116–17
wife inheritance, 204, 219
The Will of God Ministry (Kenya), 211
Winner's Chapel, 11